A LAYMAN'S HEART CONVERSATIONS WITH GOD

CARLOS R. CORREA SR.

Endorsed by Pastor Al Toledo
International author, speaker, and teacher of *DNA of a Leader*

ISBN 978-1-63874-190-9 (paperback)
ISBN 978-1-63874-192-3 (hardcover)
ISBN 978-1-63874-191-6 (digital)

Christian Faith Publishing, Inc.
832 Park Avenue
Meadville, PA 16335
www.christianfaithpublishing.com

Printed in the United States of America

Endorsements

The words on these pages come from a place of daily walking with God. Brother Carlos is someone who has experienced the deep riches of the mercy and grace of Jesus. Ever since surrendering to the Lord, his life has been a living, breathing, and walking testimony to the power and love that can transform the human heart. He has put together a modern collection of psalms that cover a variety of topics that are easily relatable to everyone. They are daily thoughts that will start a conversation between you and the Lord. The reader should come with an open heart and open ears. These are not just poems but prayers that will help you reach the heart of God.

Pastor Al Toledo
International author, speaker, and teacher of *DNA of a Leader*

WHAT OTHERS ARE SAYING

I want to thank you for your continual prayer poems. They have been a highlight for me and a continual tool to help my walk with the Lord...

—Radames DeJesus

Thank you for your godly devotions! May God continue to use you as you light up this world, with words led by the Holy Spirit!

—Nancy Herrera

The reward in reading is to see the truth the Holy Spirit reveals in words that touch my heart and my mind. This has deepened my relationship with the Trinity and in particular with the Holy Spirit! Read them and your soul will be nourished!

—Brian Benakos

"Brother Carlos has found a way, through prose and poetry, to highlight the movement of the HOLY SPIRIT in his own life. An edifying read."

—Wendy Wampler, friend of God

The prayer poems deeply minister to me. Each one carries the heart of one who is seeking Jesus's presence and anchored in biblical truths.

—Kevin Kistner

Amazing! Reading your daily inspirational and devotional texts brings me closer to Christ. And the reading is always what's needed. Always. So, I say thank you.

—Beverly Pinkney

These prayer poems are worthy of reading for spiritual strength. Read them aloud to supplement your praying time. All can appreciate their value!

—Rigoberto Quiles, man of God

Over the years, these writings have brought me comfort in times of heartache, words of edification when I felt uncertain, and they have always guided me to seek direction in the Lord and His word. I pray that your words continue to edify others as it has done for me.

—Amy Ortiz

This Nomad's view.
I liken these spirit-filled writings to an early morning breeze suggesting.
Be planted.
Become as a mighty tree.

—Guillermo Perez

Many times, I've opened the devotions, and I have felt the Holy Spirit speaking directly to me. It's always a powerful moment with the LORD.

—Ana DeLeon

I love the way these poems are always coupled with scripture. These poems are devotions to the Lord that you can read daily and that also take you into a realm of prayer.

—David Carrasco

Thank you, HOLY TRINITY, for equipping me for this work!

To my wife, Maria,

This book is dedicated to you. Your firm loving ways have been my success. I love you!

To Monica, Carlos Junior, Paul and Melissa: may our spiritual accomplishments be your launching pad!

To Pastor Toledo,

Your passion for God and souls are the example of a "DNA of a leader" exemplified!

To Radames DeJesus,

Your loyalty is equal to your relentless faith. You will always be my partner in Christ!

And finally,

Thank you to the many who have encouraged and contributed writing this book. Your interaction has made me bolder!

CONTENTS

PREFACE

A Layman's Heart: Conversations with God is a practical approach to prayer when all else has failed. It will be a guide to encourage and motivate on what and how to pray. It based on getting all apprehensions and fears aside to gain a mastery of prayer for a lifetime. These prayer poems are to be personalized and implemented for best results.

This book was birthed out of need to distract from a worldwide consuming major problem. At this time, I chose to seek God with a reckless abandon.

Please note that I am not a trained theologian or a Bible scholar! The content of this book is a direct practical application of my daily prayer. I encourage to be a Berean in character and see how the Scriptures collaborate what is written (Acts 17:11).

As a layman, I have given myself to studying the Scriptures by going through the Bible five to seven times a year! God in Christ, by the Holy Spirit, is still blessing and granting favor to the fully submitted (Heb. 11:6)!

INTRODUCTION

The content for the book has the following:

1. AM: Thank-you note
   This is a morning acknowledgment of the Trinity in a thank-you form.

2. PM: Thank-you note
   This is an evening acknowledgment of the Trinity...
   The idea was to respect the individuality while giving equal communication. Ultimately, greater appreciation of the Trinity!

3. Closet time are done three times a day:
   M: morning
   A: afternoon
   E: evening
   The idea is to reflect visitation to the private prayer closet for communication with the Trinity.
   Each time, I usually spoke to One of the Three Persons of the Trinity.
   The idea was individual appreciation while understanding their separate functions. Ultimately, a richer relationship within the context of prayer and personal proximity to each.

4. Today: served as a declaration of things to focus for the day. Sometimes highlighting negatives and deficiencies needed to work on. Always cognizant of the Trinity being present and seeking Holy Spirit input.

    Done once a day!

5. Dear ABBA, Father: developing the Heavenly Father relationship while gaining a greater interpersonal communication.

    This process is rewarding (as are the others).

    Done once a day!

The above numbers next to the five topics indicate how long ago I started each one. These numbers are larger as I have continued to date! All others (some with smaller numbers, too) are spontaneous writings that the Holy Spirit would prompt me to write. These often would be the first I would write in the early hours of the morning (2:30–4:00 a.m.).

Part 2

I primarily start these as personal prayers to refocus on God.

The rhymes or "poeticness" was a learning process. I had never done this before!

During this time, while people focused on staying healthy or not dying, my goal was drawing near to God!

Second, I thought of giving my immediate family devotions to help them during this time of uncertainty. The idea was that my prayers would help them to pray along with me.

Third, I questioned the properness of writing my personal prayers to God. I was affirmed one day when God said, "Yes, you can write to me. I wrote you a book!"

Fourth, God later told me that many I knew where afraid to pray for not knowing. He said to me that my prayer poems would help others to pray. (This was confirmed many times!)

Fifth, many really enjoyed the readings and showed appreciation.

Without knowing each, some felt these are book quality.

After getting over my lack of confidence, I sought the Lord on the matter. Doing a GoFundMe was a validation that I felt the Lord was in it!

AM: THANK-YOU NOTE 126

Thank you, ABBA, Father, for helping my day to start.
Thank you, ABBA, Father, that from me You are never far.
Thank you, ABBA, Father, for a life of abundance.
Thank you, ABBA, Father, for help from sinful indulgence!
Thank you, Lord Jesus, for being my Savior.
Thank you, Lord Jesus, for help in changing my behavior.
Thank you, Lord Jesus, for daily grace.
Thank you, Lord Jesus, for help to stay in the faith race!
Thank you, Holy Spirit, for helping me to pray.
Thank you, Holy Spirit, for wisdom with Jesus to stay.
Thank you, Holy Spirit, for vision the Kingdom to see.
Thank you, Holy Spirit, for helping to Jesus to bend my knee!

"Hallelujah! Give thanks to the LORD, for He is good; His loving devotion endures forever" (Ps. 106:1).

"Through Jesus, therefore, let us continually offer to God a sacrifice of praise, the fruit of lips that confess His name" (Heb. 13:15).

Thankfulness permeates every fiber of your mindset.
Jesus by the Spirit helps daily for no regrets!

M: CLOSET TIME 217

ABBA, Father, I come this morning my body to offer.
ABBA, Father, I come to expose inner feelings I suffer.
ABBA, Father, I come to confess and renounce.
ABBA, Father, I come my hidden faults to announce.
ABBA, Father, I come for a heart renovation.
ABBA, Father, I come asking for a childlike restoration.
ABBA, Father, I come to be free from haunting scenes.
ABBA, Father, I come for mercy and healing gleans.
ABBA, Father, I come my spirit to be strengthened.
ABBA, Father, I come my faith and trust to be lengthened.
ABBA, Father, I come by the Spirit Jesus to follow.
ABBA, Father, I come to be kept from the mundane and shallow!

"Test me, O LORD, and try me; examine my heart and mind. For Your loving devotion is before my eyes, and I have walked in Your truth" (Ps. 26:2–3).

Honesty with God is the fastest way to live sin-free.
Jesus by the Spirit will do all that the truth they see.

TODAY...78

Today, I will be vigilant of my heart's needs.
Today, I will look to act upon God-directed deeds.
Today, I will guard my heart diligently.
Today, I will retain the mind of child and do things innocently.
Today, I will present my body a sacrifice that is holy.
Today, I will act to exemplify Jesus only.
Today, I will rejoice my name is in God's book!
Today, I will my heart to heaven hook.
Today, I will treat others with a Christlike respect.
Today, I will by the Holy Spirit my attitude perfect.
Today, I will listen to hear the Holy Spirit speak.
Today, I will to be more like Jesus seek!

"Each morning I will look to You in heaven and lay my requests before You, praying earnestly" (Ps. 5:3).

"Rest in the LORD, and wait patiently for Him: fret not yourself because of him who prospers in his way, because of the man who brings wicked devices to pass" (Ps. 37:7).

Priority praying is the best self-giving gift.
Jesus by the Spirit will reward with grace as a prayer lift!

Dear ABBA, Father 47

I come Thy ways and will to perform.
I come that praising and exalting You becomes the norm.
I come to confess and renounce sins that remain.
I come my heart to expose that from sin I abstain.
I come to seek refuge from the enemy's accusations.
I come to the throne room with great expectations.
I come for forgiveness, mercy, and revival.
I come my spirit and mind to gain an anointing arrival.
I come to be made a whole new creation.
I come to ask for wisdom and revelation.
I come to be strengthened in my faith.
I come to the Trinity better relate!

"My heart is fixed, O God, my heart is fixed: I will sing and give praise" (Ps. 57:7).

"He shall not be afraid of evil tidings: his heart is fixed, trusting in the LORD" (Ps. 112:7).

The throne has an open policy to the humble and needy.
Jesus by the Spirit helps always in simultaneity!

Prayer Benefits

Prayer makes you decisive with resolve.
Prayer allows God to be involved.
Prayer gives humility to humbly submit.
Prayer allows God His wisdom to permit.
Prayer makes for bold decisions.
Prayer lets God to guide steps with precision.
Prayer will get God's attention and favor.
Prayer makes it a joy to labor.
Prayer gives God in Jesus respect.
Prayer enhances the thought of being elect.
Prayer strengthens godliness within.
Prayer will keep from accountable sin!

"Call to Me, and I will answer and show you great and unsearchable things you do not know" (Jer. 33:3).
"Therefore I tell you, whatever you ask for in prayer, believe that you have received it, and it will be yours" (Mark 11:24).

Prayer allows our Father to move unimpeded.
Jesus by the Spirit shows how God's perfect will is repeated!

PM: THANK-YOU NOTE 125

Thank you, ABBA, Father, that You my life bless.
Thank you, ABBA, Father, that I'm a success.
Thank you, ABBA, Father, come be my Defender.
Thank you, ABBA, Father, for a heart that's meek and tender!
Thank you, Lord Jesus, for all You in me have invested.
Thank you, Lord Jesus, that my salvation in I've rested.
Thank you, Lord Jesus, for speaking to angels about me.
Thank you, Lord Jesus, that You inform ABBA as He looks to see!
Thank you, Holy Spirit, for helping me to better Your voice hear.
Thank you, Holy Spirit, for daily drawing near.
Thank you, Holy Spirit, for wisdom and revelation.
Thank you, Holy Spirit, that You're with me for the earthly duration!

"Therefore everyone who confesses Me before men, I will also confess him before My Father in heaven" (Matt. 10:32).

"I tell you, everyone who confesses Me before men, the Son of Man will also confess him before the angels of God" (Luke 12:8).

It is important to know that the Lord speaks of those testifying.
Jesus by the Spirit wants all in the Word to be relying!

E: Closet Time 216

Lord Jesus, my hopes are to make You proud.
Lord Jesus, I testify of You clear and loud!
Lord Jesus, I praise the blood and stripes that heal.
Lord Jesus, daily at the altar my spirit and soul I yield.
Lord Jesus, rebaptize me with the Holy Spirit and fire.
Lord Jesus, help me the lost and backslider inspire.
Lord Jesus, come bring new spiritual wine.
Lord Jesus, help Your light me to shine.
Lord Jesus, search my heart for all the impedes.
Lord Jesus, help me to do ABBA, Father honoring deeds!
Lord Jesus, possess me that You can better guide.
Lord Jesus by the Spirit helps me in to abide!

"If you remain in Me and My words remain in you, ask whatever you wish, and it will be done for you" (John 15:7).
"Do not get drunk with wine, for that is wickedness (corruption, stupidity), but be filled with the [Holy] Spirit *and* constantly guided by Him" (Eph. 5:18).

The Lord has the resources for abundant living.
Jesus by the Spirit will keep us in faith believing!

A: CLOSET TIME 216

ABBA, Father, You are the joy of my sanctification.
ABBA, Father, I look to You for direct confirmation.
ABBA, Father, I come my heart to uncover.
ABBA, Father, by the Spirit help totally recover.
ABBA, Father, in Jesus make me quiet, confident and still.
ABBA, Father, I come for another daily refill.
ABBA, Father, help me with the Spirit to be overflowing.
ABBA, Father, help that Jesus in me is glowing!
ABBA, Father, help me rid all that the Trinity offends.
ABBA, Father, help me release ill ways that I defend.
ABBA, Father, create in me a meek attitude.
ABBA, Father, help me to live with spiritual rectitude.

"But if Christ is in you, though the body is dead because of sin, the spirit is life because of righteousness" (Rom. 8:10).
"But when it pleased God, who set me apart from my mother's womb and called by His grace, to reveal His Son in me" (Gal. 1:15–16).

God has special assignments for all that are sold-out.
Jesus by the Spirit will show us what all is about!

GOD CARES! 2

God has decreed our salvation with much care.
God cares enough to watch us everywhere.
God cares enough to flex His Omnipotent power.
God cares enough to protect us at all hours.
God cares enough to make a way out of sin.
God cares enough to make Jesus the place to begin.
God will rebuke the devourer for our sake.
God cares enough to send the Holy Spirit our sins to shake.
God cares enough to want us free indeed.
God cares enough to oversee all planted seed.
God cares enough to shield us in the mist of strife.
God cares enough in Jesus to assure eternal life!

"For God so loved the world that He gave His one and only Son, that everyone who believes in Him shall not perish but have eternal life" (John 3:16).

"For God did not send His Son into the world to condemn the world, but to save the world through Him" (John 3:17).

God has clearly made His lovingly eternal stance.
Jesus by the Spirit will teach us in the Spirit to sing and dance.

GOD CARES! 1

He created us to be like Him.
He breathed the Holy Spirit within.
He counts the hairs on our head.
When confessing, He forgives instead.
The totally submitted He orders their steps.
He watches over us as we slept.
He protects so that from enemy we are kept.
He gives us Christlike potential.
He provides resources for success essential.
He will stop nature for us to do His will.
In Jesus, He gives a new Holy Spirit refill.
By the Holy Spirit, He gives daily advice.
He intends to make us progressively like Christ!

"I only know that in every city the Holy Spirit warns me that prison and hardships are facing me" (Acts 20:23).

"For God wanted them to know that the riches and glory of Christ are for you…too. And this is the secret: Christ lives in you. This gives you assurance of sharing his glory" (Col. 1:27).

The fact that Christ lives in us is a motivation to enjoy all.
Jesus by the Spirit wants all believers to stand tall!

LIFE IS...2

Life is knowing the Word first hand.
Life is faithfully following the Lord's every command.
Life is retaining a repentant attitude.
Life is living unto Jesus with a childlike gratitude.
Life is looking unto Jesus without guilt.
Life is letting the Holy Spirit your soul rebuilt.
Life is knowing a conscience sin-free.
Life is mimicking Jesus for all to see.
Life is knowing when to turn the other cheek.
Life is responding with grace to those who maliciously speak.
Life is to daily become more like Christ.
Life is letting the Holy Spirit give perfect advice!

"And what do you benefit if you gain the whole world but lose your own soul?" (Mark 8:36).

"For what will a man give in exchange for his soul *and* eternal life [in God's kingdom]?" (Mark 8:37).

Abundant life starts the minute we are in Christ secure.
Jesus by the Spirit will give confidence to be sure!

LIFE IS...1

Life is knowing that God will always be there.
Life is knowing that Jesus for us eternity did prepare.
Life is not how many "friends" we can keep.
Life is knowing the Friend that is faithfully deep.
Life is not how many likes we can get.
Life is honorably serving Jesus without regret.
Life is not fantasying about going viral.
Life is about remembering of our eternal arrival.
Life is about telling others the Gospel story.
Life is about turning the other cheek that gives God glory.
Life is being Holy Spirit led to plant a seed.
Life is a Lord that in trials His peace has decreed!

"Now in fact all who want to live godly lives in Christ Jesus will be persecuted" (2 Tim. 3:12).
"I have told you these things so that in Me you may have peace. In the world you will have tribulation. But take courage; I have overcome the world!" (John 16:33).

Life is knowing eternity is within our grasp.
Jesus by the Spirit will help keep from enemy's trap!

Pretender

The enemy's self-evaluation made him a "Great Pretender."
As pretender, he presents all possibilities with splendor.
In the garden, he pretended that God was restrictive.
All pretenders always retain the right to be vindictive.
Pretenders know how to gift wrap a lie.
Pretenders use reasoning to lure the naive to their side.
Pretenders are experts at setting traps.
Pretenders will spiritual potential saps.
Pretenders distort God with religious jargon on earth.
Pretenders will make "abundant life" of no worth.
Pretenders are mixed with the sheep as goats.
Pretenders learn the Word to put on as "spiritual coats."

"I do not sit with deceitful men, Nor will I go with pretenders" (Ps. 26:4).
"You destroy those who speak falsehood; The Lord abhors the man of bloodshed and deceit" (Ps. 5:6).

Pretenders go through life deceiving.
Jesus by the Spirit encourages by faith believing!

I TRUST YOU!

Lord, there are times that the enemy fear does bring.
Lord, I trust You as faithfully in testings to You I sing.
You are the Sovereign God of all the earth.
In Jesus by the Spirit I am of eternal worth.
Your Word has become my soothing lifeline.
I trust You to be daily strengthen and my spirit refine.
In Your Word, I am secure enough to proclaim…"in God I trust."
Living for You without compromise for me is a must.
Keeping a heart of integrity is a committed task.
I trust You, Holy Spirit, to possess me as daily I ask.
I trust You so that I will not cater to the pressures of the flesh.
I trust You as in Your name I am daily made afresh!

"When I am afraid, I put my trust in you. In God, whose Word I praise, in God I trust; I shall not be afraid. What can flesh do to me?" (Ps. 56:1–3).

The devoted believer knows that God can always be trusted.
Jesus by the Spirit will refocus that that are maladjusted!

God Says, "I Got This"

When He calls, He equips.
From His hands, we can't slip.
He has perfect power and grace.
He will send angels with us to keep pace.
Even in our life He will interrupt.
The devout will see the Lord from heaven irrupt.
It is never about how much we know.
It's all about His power to show.
Moses told Him he couldn't speak.
God just had him daily His to presence to seek.
God flipped him from a self-made man.
Humblest believer obeying God's command.
Jesus by the Spirit has all power and authority.
The submitted lame will enjoy spiritual reality!

"Come to me, all you who are weary and burdened, and I will give you rest. Take my yoke upon you and learn from me, for I am gentle and humble in heart, and you will find rest for your souls" (Matt. 11:28–29).

God in Christ is confident of who can make it.
Jesus by the Spirit will not allow us to fake it!

RANDOM THOUGHTS

Brought back memories of teaching His Word for years.
It also made a picture of how the enemy is deceptively near.
But my faith is on the rebound.
God in Christ, by the Spirit, refurbishing a mind that is sound.
I like being on His easel.
He correctively will the flesh chisel.
Your prayers are making spiritual insulation.
In my last years, I move with godly expectation.
He is always as close as the mention of His name.
Testings are for faith to not stay the same.
Greater test make faith to become deeper.
Truly, by the Holy Spirit, the Lord is our Keeper!

"The LORD is my shepherd, I lack nothing. He makes me lie down in green pastures, He leads me beside quiet waters, He refreshes my soul. He guides me along the right paths for His name's sake" (Ps. 23:1–3).

Universally, the Lord is available to who want Him as Savior.
Jesus by the Spirit teaches spiritual behavior.

ALTAR OF GOD

The altar of God is for an empty vessel.
The altar of God is not a place to wrestle.
The altar of God is for those totally committed.
The altar of God is for offerings permitted.
The altar of God will make a vessel whole.
The altar of God is for those looking to be told.
The altar of God is not for the faint of heart.
The altar of God is where the devout daily start.
The altar of God is for burning the flesh.
The altar of God is for a spiritual refresh.
The altar of God helps with Holy Spirit advice.
The altar of God is for finding Christ!

"Leave your gift there before the altar, and go your way. First be reconciled to your brother, and then come and offer your gift" (Matt. 5:24).

"Brothers, through the compassions of God, present your bodies as a living sacrifice, holy to God, well-pleasing, which is your reasonable service" (Rom. 12:1).

A daily altar visitation will make for prayer commitment.
Jesus by the Spirit gives believers the royal treatment!

M: Closet Time 216

Holy Spirit, I come my heart to surrender.
Holy Spirit, deliver me from being a pretender.
Holy Spirit, there is much that needs purging.
Holy Spirit, I come for renewal with urging.
Holy Spirit, help me gain a heart that is Word devoted.
Holy Spirit, come flush out and let purity be promoted.
Holy Spirit, deliver me from all that growth hinders.
Holy Spirit, I ask for a touch of God's fingers.
Holy Spirit, awaken in me a new hunger and thirst.
Holy Spirit, enhance my quest to seek the Kingdom first.
Holy Spirit, possess me that You may fully control.
Holy Spirit, for God in Christ make me creatively bold!

"And I will give them one heart, and a new spirit I will put within them. I will remove the heart of stone from their flesh and give them a heart of flesh" (Ezek. 11:19).

He saved us, not because of works done by us in righteousness, but according to His own mercy, by the washing of regeneration and renewal of the Holy Spirit" (Titus 3:5).

The Holy Spirit will continue in our lives if daily invited.
Jesus by the Spirit on those who Word meditate is delighted!

AM: Thank-You Note 125

Thank you, Abba, Father, for grace to proceed.
Thank you, Abba, Father, that is Your will for me to succeed.
Thank you, Abba, Father, that I will not be alone.
Thank you, Abba, Father, that You are always in my zone!
Thank you, Lord Jesus, for help in time of need.
Thank you, Lord Jesus, for help to plant every Gospel seed.
Thank you, Lord Jesus, for help in all sins removal.
Thank you, Lord Jesus, for Your consent and approval!
Thank you, Holy Spirit, for waking me this morning.
Thank you, Holy Spirit, for Christlike adorning.
Thank you, Holy Spirit, that today my day is at Your command.
Thank you, Holy Spirit, that You will help with all life's demand!

"He saved us, not because of works done by us in righteousness, but according to His own mercy, by the washing of regeneration and renewal of the Holy Spirit" (Tit. 3:5).

"He will wipe away every tear from their eyes, and death shall be no more, neither shall there be mourning, nor crying, nor pain anymore, for the former things have passed away" (Rev. 21:4).

Salvation has a healing process with a perfecting end.
Jesus by the Spirit reminds of the gift that God did send!

TODAY...77

Today, I will look to ABBA, Father, for healing.
Today, I will seek for renewal of my spirit feelings.
Today, I will seek for my heart to be upgraded.
Today, I will ask for purging of all hint of sin related.
Today, I will ask for a conscience that is heavenly minded.
Today, I will confess and renounce all that is misguided!
Today, I will seek to release all that my progress prevents.
Today, I will from sinful ways sincerely repent.
Today, I will pick up my cross and deny myself.
Today, I will put my feelings on a shelf.
Today, I will look for a Christlike restoration.
Today, I will renew a joy in my salvation!

"Create in me a clean heart, O God, and renew a right spirit within me" (Ps. 51:10).
"And have put on the new self, which is being renewed in knowledge after the image of its Creator" (Col. 3:10).

All confessions based on God's promises and grace succeed.
Jesus by the Spirit looks for all to trustingly proceed!

My Heart Needs Fixing

ABBA, Father, I praise You as I come in trust.
ABBA, Father, coming honestly for me is a must.
ABBA, Father, in Jesus, I come boldly for restoration.
ABBA, Father, by the Spirit, I come without pretension.
ABBA, Father, intercede in my heart's rebuilding.
ABBA, Father, for renewal my heart I am bringing.
ABBA, Father, I repent of a mind that wanders.
ABBA, Father, restore my mind that on the Word ponders.
ABBA, Father, I come in repentance presenting.
ABBA, Father, purge all that is purity preventing.
ABBA, Father, I confess and renounce all within.
ABBA, Father, in Jesus, give a new heart this day to begin!

"The human heart is the most deceitful of all things, and desperately wicked. Who really knows how bad it is?" (Jer. 17:9).

"I will give you a new heart and put a new spirit in you; I will remove from you your heart of stone and give you a heart of flesh" (Ezek. 36:26).

God is a specialist at what we pray for specifically.
Jesus by the Spirit points out what needs spiritual civility!

PM: Thank-You Note 124

Thank you, ABBA, Father, for a day of learning.
Thank you, ABBA, Father, that for You I keep yearning.
Thank you, ABBA, Father, for love that is never withdrawn.
Thank you, ABBA, Father, that from Your sight I'm never gone!
Thank you, Lord Jesus, for never disappointing.
Thank you, Lord Jesus, for a daily new anointing.
Thank you, Lord Jesus, that daily like You I'm becoming.
Thank you, Lord Jesus, that to heaven I am going!
Thank you, Holy Spirit, for helping me this life to navigate.
Thank you, Holy Spirit, for helping me situations to negotiate.
Thank you, Holy Spirit, for helping to overcome temptation.
Thank you, Holy Spirit, for daily Word reflection!

"The angel replied, 'The Holy Spirit will come upon you, and the power of the Most High will overshadow you'" (Luke 1:35a).
"May the grace of the Lord Jesus Christ, and the love of God, and the fellowship of the Holy Spirit be with you all" (2 Cor. 13:14).

The presence and power of God is available to the daily seeker.
Jesus by the Spirit can make the willing lovingly meeker!

M: Closet Time 215

Lord Jesus, I come in humble submission.
Lord Jesus, I come to be better equipped for the great commission!
Lord Jesus, I come to bare my heart and soul.
Lord Jesus, anoint me to prevent getting cold.
Lord Jesus, I come for greater inner strength.
Lord Jesus, renew my resolve to be sent.
Lord Jesus, rebaptize in the Spirit and fire.
Lord Jesus, possess me for Your honor to be inspired.
Lord Jesus, rekindle my quest to be Your clone.
Lord Jesus, help me to have Your empathetic tone.
Lord Jesus, restore my repentant mindset.
Lord Jesus, deliver me from sins that get You upset!

"He must become greater and greater, and I must become less and less" (John 3:30).
"Afterward Jesus found him in the temple and said to him, 'See, you are well! Sin no more, that nothing worse may happen to you'" (John 5:14).

Humble submission is done by understanding and gratitude.
Jesus by the Spirit has power to make Christlike, too!

E: Closet Time 215

ABBA, Father, I praise that You are my Father.
ABBA, Father, I honor and exalt You like no other!
ABBA, Father, it's refreshing that Your eyes are upon me.
ABBA, Father, open my sight that You I better see!
ABBA, Father, strengthen my childlike attitude.
ABBA, Father, deliver me from being insensitive and rude.
ABBA, Father, rekindle in me a Christlike empathy.
ABBA, Father, by the Spirit, may I share with loving clarity!
ABBA, Father, loving You may my life reflect.
ABBA, Father, help me live as one of Your elect.
ABBA, Father, bless my efforts to live a life that is pure.
ABBA, Father, strengthen my faith in You for sure!

"At that time, Jesus said, 'I praise You, Father, Lord of heaven and earth, that You have hidden these things from the wise and intelligent and have revealed them to infants'" (Matt. 11:25).

"Whoever then humbles himself as this child, he is the greatest in the kingdom of heaven" (Matt. 18:24).

Childlikeness is an attribute that merits much of God's attention. Jesus by the Spirit will help us avoid sin through prevention!

Jesus Knows Best 3

Jesus knows best when interrupting Saul on the road.
Becoming as child, it was the beginning of doing what told.
Jesus knows best while we are living against Him.
Jesus knows best as He never judges where we've been.
Jesus knows best sending for tax money from a fish.
Jesus knows best when pointing the two mites on the dish.
Jesus knows best as He lamented Judas's position.
Jesus knows best as He cried over Lazarus's condition.
Jesus knows best staying quiet during His arrest.
Jesus knows best as for the hurting healing He did wrest.
Jesus knows best as He willingly went to the Cross.
Jesus knows best as He rose from the grave for those loss!

"Jesus knew what they were thinking, so He asked them, 'Why do you have such evil thoughts in your hearts!'" (Matt 9:4).

"And Jesus knew their thoughts, and said unto them…" (Matt 12:25a).

"But Jesus perceived their malice, and said, 'Why are you testing Me, you hypocrites?'" (Matt. 22:18).

God knows our thoughts to help us be real.
Jesus by the Spirit wants us to get beyond what we feel!

JESUS KNOWS BEST 2

Jesus knows best as the Spirit guided.
Jesus knows best as ABBA with Him sided.
Jesus knows best as angels were at His disposal.
Jesus knows best as He makes proposals.
Jesus knows best as He sensed what others were thinking.
Jesus knows best as He can save any from sinking.
Jesus knows best while talking to the woman at the well.
Jesus knows best as her heart for Him did swell.
Jesus knows best in eating with a tax collector.
Jesus knows best as He was ABBA, Father's best reflector.
Jesus knows best as He fixated on Calvary.
Jesus knows best as He died for you and me!

"When Jesus woke up, He rebuked the wind and said to the waves, 'Silence! Be still!' Suddenly the wind stopped, and there was a great calm" (Mark 4:39).

"Now we know that You know all things, and have no need for anyone to question You; by this we believe that You came from God" (John 16:30)

Those that daily please God enjoy more resources.
Jesus by the Spirit knows best when to change our life courses!

Jesus Knows Best 1

Jesus just turned him away.
Jesus knew he had something to convey.
Jesus said that Him he could not follow.
Jesus knew that his family in sin did wallow.
Jesus sent him back to reach the spiritually hurting.
Jesus made him born again with salvation burning.
Jesus gave him verbal instructions.
Jesus by the Spirit had healed his tattered emotions.
Jesus told him to tell how God had rendered mercy.
Jesus by the Spirit had delivered from demonic controversy.
Jesus had rearranged his spirit outlook perspective.
Jesus wanted him to talk for the healing to be corrective.
Jesus understood that he would be a "perfect" witness.
Jesus sent him "to be about the ABBA, Father's business."

"But Jesus would not allow him. 'Go home to your own people,' He said, 'and tell them how much the Lord has done for you, and what mercy He has shown you'" (Mark 5:19).

"So the man started off to visit the Ten Towns of that region and began to proclaim the great things Jesus had done for him; and everyone was amazed at what he told them" (Mark 5:20).

We are a creation of God with a daily calling.
Jesus by the Spirit will keep us from falling!

UNIQUELY MADE! 2

ABBA, Father created all with an inner celebration.

ABBA, Father in making us has great expectation.

ABBA, Father purposed in us many a task.

ABBA, Father just waits for us to ask.

ABBA, Father made Abel to show when worship is right.

ABBA, Father created John to point to the Light.

ABBA, Father made Noah to obey while building an Ark.

ABBA, Father made Enoch to show benefits when in fellowship we embark.

ABBA, Father made Elijah for benefits of Holy Spirit proximity.

ABBA, Father made Daniel to show a devout life reality.

ABBA, Father made us all purposely unique.

ABBA, Father in Jesus wants us to Him daily seek!

"I praise You, for I am fearfully and wonderfully made. Marvelous are Your works, and I know this very well" (Ps. 139:14).

"What is man that You are mindful of him, And the son of man that You care for him? Yet You have made him a little lower than God, And You have crowned him with glory and honor" (Ps. 8:4).

As believers discover their godly roots, the easier to worship our Maker.

Jesus by the Spirit opens our mind to know that of His divine nature we are partaker!

UNIQUELY MADE! 1

We are, by ABBA, Father, uniquely made.
ABBA, Father spared no power in to the highest grade.
ABBA, Father invested His image in every human mold.
ABBA, Father created us to be faithful and bold.
ABBA, Father looked to place us strategically.
ABBA, Father created us with potential exceedingly.
ABBA, Father bragged on what He created.
ABBA, Father poured His love is clearly stated.
ABBA, Father put us on earth to prosper and succeed.
ABBA, Father watched as our life would proceed.
ABBA, Father foresaw the problem of sin.
ABBA, Father still breathes the Holy Spirit within.
ABBA, Father knew the outcome of sin's behavior.
ABBA, Father sent a Redeeming Savior!

"So God created man in His own image; in the image of God He created him; male and female He created them" (Gen. 1:27).

"Thank you for making me so wonderfully complex! Your workmanship is marvelous—how well I know it" (Ps. 139:14).

Uniqueness is a cause for daily celebration.
Jesus by the Spirit provides maximum protection!

You Did It

ABBA, Father, You made us to live forever.
ABBA, Father, going to hell was a resounding NEVER!
ABBA, Father, in Jesus, we are predestined and called.
ABBA, Father, by the Spirit, doing good works we are enthralled.
ABBA, Father, Omniscience made us justified.
ABBA, Father, in justifying Your only Begotten was crucified.
ABBA, Father, justified we no longer live in the sin nature.
ABBA, Father, in Jesus by the Spirit, we live for Your pleasure!
ABBA, Father, You made a book where we are identified.
ABBA, Father, seating in heavenly places we are glorified.
ABBA, Father, the only response is gratitude that You are for us.
ABBA, Father, Your protection will repel all sinful fuss!

"And those He predestined, He also called; those He called, He also justified; those He justified, He also glorified. What then shall we say in response to these things? If God is for us, who can be against us?" (Rom. 8:30–31).

Knowing that God is for us helps to best relate.
Jesus by the Spirit will godliness in us create!

SERVING THE LORD 2

Serving the Lord is beyond worship and praise.
Serving is noticing when our voice to others we raise.
Serving is respecting God in Christ.
Serving is when to a rude person we are nice.
Serving the Lord is more than lip service.
Serving the Lord is, by the Spirit, without getting nervous.
Serving is genuinely bringing our body as a living sacrifice.
Serving the Lord with a pure heart which is given as a prize.
Serving at the altar is being sincerely kind.
Serving the Lord is how we treat "the Samaritans" we find.
Serving the Lord has many practical-spiritual ways.
Serving the Lord is beneficial the more we actually pray!

"After bidding them farewell, He left for the mountain to pray" (Mark 6:46).
"For the Son of Man came to seek and save those who are lost" (Luke 19:10).

Daily prayer is one of fastest means of spiritually maturing.
Jesus by the Spirit our standing in heaven is reassuring!

Serving the Lord 1

Serving is a condition of the heart.
Serving will strengthen in prayer closet start.
Serving is a condition of the will.
Serving is best when the flesh we daily kill.
Serving is not just for the Trinity.
Serving is how we treat others in reality.
Serving does have to do with our Savior.
Serving is also honoring a neighbor.
Serving helps those that in sin stumble.
Serving is a fast track to becoming humble.
Serving is Jesus washing others feet.
Serving is acting like Jesus we simply repeat!

"God gave the Holy Spirit and power to Jesus…as He went around doing good and healing everyone who was under the power of the devil" (Acts 10:38).

"Those who say they live like God should live their lives as Jesus did" (1 John 2:6).

Living for God is manifest by how we of Him we are used.
Jesus by the Spirit will never allow believers to be confused!

The Great Provider

ABBA, Father forever has provided.
With humanity, He has always sided.
He provided the trees for many reasons.
He provided weather change with seasons.
He provided trees, fruits, and seeds.
He provided foods for our stomach to feed.
He placed all things for our enjoyment.
Even in at our worse, He gave us employment.
He provided salvation at the fall.
He provided a system on Him to call.
He provided the Spirit to keep us from the shallow.
He provided a Model to save and to follow!

"I bow down toward Your holy temple and give thanks to Your name for Your loving devotion and Your faithfulness; You have exalted Your name and Your word above all else" (Ps. 138:2).

"For God is the One working in you both to will and to work according to His good pleasure" (Phil. 2:13).

As a believer, knowing the Word of God is a life changer.
Jesus by the Spirit will not allow believers to the Word be strangers!

IN HIS NAME 3

In His Name, all that is good has been provided.
In His Name, even life on earth is abundantly excited
In His Name, the winds and seas can be made calm.
In His Name, the diligent believer has no alarm.
In His Name, a fool in the world can be made wise.
In His Name, by the Holy Spirit, there is perfect advice.
In His Name, the truth will always win out.
In His Name, spontaneously, the righteous will shout!
In His Name, there is progressive healing.
In His Name, the prayer closet is a place for kneeling.
In His Name, believers can put demons on the run.
In His Name, for believers on earth, the fun has just begun.
In His Name, there is Holy Spirit inspiration.
In His Name, there will be holy coronation!

"For the Lord Himself will descend from heaven with a loud command, with the voice of an archangel, and with the trumpet of God, and the dead in Christ will be the first to rise" (1 Thess. 4:16).
"Look, I am coming soon! My reward is with Me, and I will give to each person according to what they have done" (Rev. 22:12).

Our Father sees the diligent and will handsomely recompense.
Jesus by the Spirit for the diligent puts a defense!

In His Name 2

In His Name, the galaxies were put in place.
In His Name, the Trinity created the human race.
In His Name, the sun and stars reflect their light.
In His Name, humanity will always know what's right!
In His Name, history was framed.
In His Name, the wrath of sin has been tamed.
In His Name, believers can conquer all fear.
In His Name, we are sure that ABBA, Father is near.
In His Name, we know that evil has been defeated.
In His Name, Satan back to hell will be repeated.
In His Name, the righteous will suffer no more.
In His Name, there is a heavenly place for sure.

"Therefore God also highly exalted Him, and granted to Him the name above every name, that at the name of Jesus every knee should bow, in the heavens and on earth and under the earth, and every tongue should confess that Jesus Christ *is* Lord, to *the* glory of God *the* Father" (Phil. 2:9–11).

The confession and believing in His name will bring salvation. Jesus by the Spirit highlights the name with revelation!

IN HIS NAME 1

In His Name, the worlds were created.
In His Name, humanity for Jesus's glory was slated.
In His Name, Adam from the garden had to leave.
In His Name, the first sinner's mercy did receive.
In His Name, Noah and family weren't destroyed.
In His Name, the world was deluged to counter an evil ploy.
In His Name, righteous Joseph was protected.
In His Name, from the dungeon to stardom, he was projected.
In His Name, the Pharaoh lost even when he didn't budge.
In His Name, Egypt was decimated as well as judged.
In His Name, vile sinners are made saints somehow.
In His Name, the good, the bad, and the ugly will bow!

"For the Scriptures say, 'As surely as I live,' says the LORD, 'every knee will bend to Me, and every tongue will declare allegiance to God'" (Rom. 14:11).

"I Am the Alpha and the Omega, the First and the Last, the Beginning and the End" (Rev. 22:13).

Our Father traded our sins for His only Begotten.
Jesus by the Spirit assures that that of us God hasn't forgotten!

GENTLY ORIGINAL

ABBA, Father looks upon creation gently original.
He listens to hear how to be provisional.
Jesus looks for the gently original elect.
The Holy Spirit will possess those that God respect.
The gently original doesn't put on a prayer show.
The gently original knows how to rightly sow.
The gently original enjoy the Christlike walk.
The gently original wants with the Holy Spirit to talk.
The gently original will relinquish all that hinders.
The gently original daily wants a touch of ABBA's fingers!
The gently original will look to stay at Jesus's feet.
The gently original early mornings with the Trinity meet!

"Have I not commanded you? Be strong and courageous. Do not be afraid; do not be discouraged, for the LORD your God will be with you wherever you go" (Josh. 1:9)
"Those who know Your name trust in You, for you, LORD, have never forsaken those who seek You" (Ps. 9:10).

Following all that God says will lead to stronger believe.
Jesus by the Spirit keeps us from the one who wants to deceive!

DEAR ABBA, FATHER 44

I come my heart and soul to You expose.
I come to learn the enemy's will to appose.
I come to be pleasing in Your sight.
I come to enhance my power as a living light.
I come Your will to advance.
I come against sin to take a stance.
I come to sharpen my spiritual skills.
I come for repeated Holy Spirit refills.
I come to be renewed in my spirit man.
I come to submit and obey all that I can.
I come to increase in being meek to avoid acting haughty.
I come to honor You with mind, spirit, soul, and body!

"So do not fear, for I am with you; do not be dismayed, for I am Your God. I will strengthen you and help you; I will uphold you with My righteous right hand" (Isa. 41:10).

"Do not let your hearts be troubled. You believe in God; believe also in Me" (John 14:1).

A: Closet Time 215

Holy Spirit, please come indwell this temple of mine.
Holy Spirit, lead me to what is spiritually divine.
Holy Spirit, I ask for guidance to places You have designed.
Holy Spirit, possess me that to You I am aligned!
Holy Spirit, take me to a higher spiritual ground.
Holy Spirit, show Jesus in ways more profound.
Holy Spirit, deliver my heart in foolishness to wonder.
Holy Spirit, help anew in the Word to ponder.
Holy Spirit, rekindle a fondness for the straight and narrow.
Holy Spirit, help in Jesus only You to follow.
Holy Spirit, possess me to be a Jesus witness!
Holy Spirit, help me be only about ABBA, Father's business!

"'Why were you looking for Me?' He asked. 'Did you not know that I had to be in My Father's house?'" (Luke 2:49).

"But Mary treasured up all these things and pondered them in her heart" (Luke 2:19).

Believing is enhanced by the Spirit daily leading.
Jesus by the Spirit toward God keeps us proceeding!

AM: THANK-YOU NOTE 124

Thank you, ABBA, Father, for this another day.
Thank you, ABBA, Father, for help in Your presence to stay.
Thank you, ABBA, Father, for help to be faithful.
Thank you, ABBA, Father, for Jesus I am grateful.
Thank you, Lord Jesus, for rest through the night.
Thank you, Lord Jesus, for grace to choose right.
Thank you, Lord Jesus, that You will my life follow.
Thank you, Lord Jesus, that I'll be kept from the shallow.
Thank you, Holy Spirit, for helping me to rightfully think.
Thank you, Holy Spirit, for helping avoid sinful ways to sink.
Thank you, Holy Spirit, that You are my Friend.
Thank you, Holy Spirit, that indeed You are heaven send!

"Give thanks to the Lord, for He is good; His love endures forever" (Ps. 107:1).
"Sacrifice thank offerings to God, fulfill your vows to the Most High, and call on Me in the day of trouble; I will deliver you, and you will honor Me" (Ps. 50:14).

Giving thanks throughout the day will keep the enemy away.
Jesus by the Spirit will help those the Word pray!

TODAY...76

Today, I will discard any type of opinion.
Today, I will avoid my enemy's dominion.
Today, I will walk to please the Holy Spirit, not the flesh.
Today, I will look to ABBA, Father for new anointing afresh.
Today, I will forsake my selfish way.
Today, I will seek to know Jesus when privately I pray.
Today, I will be slow to speak as others I hear.
Today, I will others success gladly cheer.
Today, I will be prepared to be Holy Spirit guided.
Today, I will share the Gospel all Christlike sided!
Today, I will lift my spirit to the throne boldly.
Today, I will praise the Trinity only!

"Surely God is my salvation; I will trust and not be afraid. The LORD, the LORD Himself, is my strength and my defense; He has become my salvation" (Isa. 12:2).

"Trust in the LORD forever, for the LORD, the LORD Himself, is the Rock eternal" (Isa. 26:4).

Confessing what the Word says about God is a great start!
Jesus by the Spirit in spiritual maturity will take us far!

PM: Thank-You Note 123

Thank you, ABBA, Father, for another day to learn.
Thank you, ABBA, Father, that Your presence I yearn.
Thank you, ABBA, Father, for all that You are providing.
Thank you, ABBA, Father, for help in Jesus to continue abiding!
Thank you, Lord Jesus, for help in the storm.
Thank you, Lord Jesus, that to Your image I will conform.
Thank you, Lord Jesus, for help against the deceiver.
Thank you, Lord Jesus, for faith to be a believer.
Thank you, Holy Spirit, for insight and revelation.
Thank you, Holy Spirit, for helping with my sanctification.
Thank you, Holy Spirit, for honoring my request.
Thank you, Holy Spirit, for always giving of Your best!

"The steps of a man are established by the Lord, when He delights in his way; though he fall, he shall not be cast headlong, for the Lord upholds his hand" (Ps. 37:23–24).

The Lord will always come to the rescue of those that call.
Jesus by the Spirit wants all at the prayer closet wall!

E: Closet Time 214

ABBA, Father, help me to diligently obey.
ABBA, Father, touch my ears to hear what You say.
ABBA, Father, renew my quest to the prayer closet.
ABBA, Father, by the Spirit, come make a spiritual deposit.
ABBA, Father, grant me grace to meditate.
ABBA, Father, in Jesus, come new faith in me create.
ABBA, Father, I ask for a new holy revival.
ABBA, Father, I ask for a new anointing and Holy Spirit arrival.
ABBA, Father, give me a spiritual mindset of a child.
ABBA, Father, increase my hope all the while!
ABBA, Father, purge me from all sins that offend.
ABBA, Father, on Your mercy and compassion I depend!

"When he calls to Me, I will answer him; I will be with him in trouble; I will rescue him and honor him" (Ps. 91:15).

"Delight yourself in the Lord, and He will give you the desires of your heart" (Ps. 37:4).

Delighting in the Lord means He is our priority.
Jesus by the Spirit shows that God with us is a majority!

A: Closet Time 214a

Holy Spirit, I come my heart and soul to give.
Holy Spirit, I come a living sacrifice for You to receive.
Holy Spirit, I come to be under Your command.
Holy Spirit, I come to meet all Your spiritual demands.
Holy Spirit, come control my mind by You to be led.
Holy Spirit, come make my body Your homestead.
Holy Spirit, restore my faith to be that of a child.
Holy Spirit, help me with ABBA's will to be reconciled.
Holy Spirit, help me to never rob praise from the Trinity.
Holy Spirit, empower me to think on heaven's infinity!
Holy Spirit, come be my daily Coach.
Holy Spirit, in Jesus, help me live beyond reproach.

"I will instruct you and teach you in the way you should go; I will counsel you with my eye upon you" (Ps. 32:8).

"The steps of a man are established by the Lord, when He delights in his way" (Ps. 37:23).

Pleasing God is not hard if we follow His plan.
Jesus by the Spirit will help in following every command!

DECLARING TRUTH

ABBA, Father, You are Sovereign over all the earth.
ABBA, Father, in Jesus by the Spirit I am of eternal worth.
ABBA, Father, by the Blood, I have an eternal standing.
ABBA, Father, one day the angels, I will be commanding.
ABBA, Father, in Jesus with You, I have a loving relationship.
ABBA, Father, from Your hands, I can never slip.
ABBA, Father, I long to live in humble submission.
ABBA, Father, I look for Your approving permission.
ABBA, Father, I need Your power to flow in my intestines.
ABBA, Father, I ask for the healing for which I'm destined.
ABBA, Father, increase my faith to walk therein.
ABBA, Father, by the Spirit in faith, let my day begin.
ABBA, Father, may Your perfect love on me converge.
ABBA, Father, may this day more Christlike I emerge.

"He sent forth His word and healed them; He rescued them from the Pit" (Ps. 107:20).

"'For I will restore you to health And I will heal you of your wounds,' declares the Lord" (Jer. 30:17).

Healing from the inside out is for those that diligent follow.

Owning Promises

Trinity's pleasure is in promises that any will take hold.
ABBA, Father rejoices when promises are believed as told.
Promises were never to be ornaments on a tree.
Promises are for a diligent sheep who God they want to see.
Owning a promise takes moving only in God's direction.
Owning a promise leads others to criticize your perception.
Owning a promise is a matter of spiritual tenacity.
Owning a promise, the Holy Spirit will make it a reality.
Owning a promise will bring the enemy's distractions.
Owning a promise takes lots of faithful actions.
Owning a promise takes you beyond how you feel.
Owning a promise is rewarded by knowing that God is real!

"Not a single one of all the good promises the LORD had given was left unfulfilled; everything He had spoken came true" (Josh. 21:45).

"'For I know the plans I have for you,' declares the LORD, 'plans to prosper you and not to harm you, plans to give you hope and a future'" (Jer. 29:11).

The greatest promise was to save the lost.
Jesus by the Spirit has detailed salvation's cost!

LOVE GIVES!

Love gives from a heart that deeply cares.
Love gives because it always shares.
God is love, and giving it away is second nature.
Loving through Christ gives profound pleasure.
Loving from Holy Spirit power is gentle and kind.
Love gives to those that on its way finds.
The love that gives is perfectly pure.
Love gives with intent to bring inner cure.
Love gives to avert oncoming disaster.
Love gives assuring of a gentle and merciful Master!
Love gives to secure a place of living forever.
Love gives to keep the promise that forsaking is never!

"The LORD appeared to us in the past, saying: 'I have loved you with an everlasting love; therefore I have drawn you with loving devotion'" (Jer. 31:3).

"For the love of Christ compels us, having concluded this, that One has died for all, therefore all have died" (2 Cor. 5:14).

The love of God is deliberately from a stance of devotion.
Jesus by the Spirit wants all believers in lane of promotion!

LORD OF ALL

You watched as he lost his eternal conviction.
You saw his heavenly eviction.
You watched as from heaven he had a great fall.
You rooted for Adam as he by the enemy was tempted to fall.
You defeated him through the years.
Even now to You he could not come near.
In the wilderness, You had an answer for his lies.
Defeating the enemy, You showed how on the Spirit to rely.
Defeated, he left until an opportune time.
By the Holy Spirit, You defeated him at Your earthly prime.
Through the years, You defeated him at every turn.
You defeated him as on the Word You stood firm.

"Jesus Christ is the same yesterday and today and forever" (Heb. 13:8).

"Behold, I am coming soon, and My reward is with Me, to give to each one according to what he has done" (Rev. 2:12).

A HEAVENLY MIND 5

Knowing our name is in His Book.
Jesus told us that daily to keep an upward look!
Real believers see it as mandatory.
Keeping it real they tell the Gospel story.
They sharpen their mind and skills.
Daily they seek the Holy Spirit refills.
They are humbly bold to ABBA, Father ask.
In Jesus name, they are prepared for the task.
Staying their mind on God is not a fad.
Sincerely lifting Jesus's name they are glad.
Creative they are about pointing up!
It's no wonder they live with a full cup!

"Abundant peace belongs to those who love Your instruction; nothing can make them stumble" (Ps. 119:165).
"You will keep in perfect peace all who trust in you, all whose thoughts are fixed on you!" (Isa. 26:3).

Keeping our minds on God is by daily resolve.
Jesus by the Spirit the righteous from guilt will absolve!

A HEAVENLY MIND 4

A heavenly mind prepares for the fight ahead.
A heavenly mind will not cower; it runs at the problem instead.
A heavenly mind is convinced of God's unique power.
A heavenly mind looks to see God move at all hours.
A heavenly mind makes a prayer closet the war room.
A heavenly mind looking for God to answer is consumed.
A heavenly mind constantly moves in God's direction.
A heavenly mind looks only to the Holy Spirit for correction.
A heavenly mind for the Holy Spirit has high respect.
A heavenly mind knows Jesus sent the Spirit for us to accept.
A heavenly mind the promises on His heart will record.
A heavenly mind is fixated on Jesus Christ as Lord!

"For who has known the mind of the Lord, so as to instruct Him? But we have the mind of Christ" (1 Cor. 2:12).
"Let this mind be in you which was also in Christ Jesus" (Phil. 2:5).

The mind of Christ is a terrible thing to waste.
Jesus by the Spirit warns about doing things in haste!

A HEAVENLY MIND 3

A heavenly mind thinks on things above in all occasions.
A heavenly mind knows how to overcome temptations.
A heavenly mind is aware of the enemy's wiles.
A heavenly mind keeps a Christlike smile.
A heavenly mind is quick to forgive.
A heavenly mind is hard for the enemy to deceive.
A heavenly mind is in perpetual godly training.
A heavenly mind sees with Jesus in eternity reigning.
A heavenly mind trusts God in the storm.
A heavenly mind asks the Spirit in Christ to conform.
A heavenly mind hates sinful behavior.
A heavenly mind is busy pleasing the Savior.

"Jesus told the people who had faith in him, 'If you keep on obeying what I have said, you truly are my disciples'" (John 8:31).

"Set *your* minds on the things above, not the things on the earth" (Col. 3:2).

When our minds are on God, heaven is on the lookout.
Jesus by the Spirit wants us to know showing love is what God is about!

A Heavenly Mind 2

A heavenly mind will validate what God has created.
A heavenly mind amalgamates all that in Christ are related.
A heavenly mind projects positive affirmation.
A heavenly mind will strengthen faith with confirmation.
A heavenly mind knows a person's potential.
A heavenly mind knows mature faith can be exponential.
A heavenly mind overlooks a defeatist attitude.
A heavenly mind points to God as full of perfect rectitude.
A heavenly mind stays focused on God's past deeds.
A heavenly mind assures that God will meet all needs.
A heavenly mind never has doubt.
A heavenly mind knows what God is about!

"Now to Him who is able to do so much more than all we ask or imagine, according to His power that is at work within us" (Eph. 3:20).

"And my God will fill up all your needs according to His riches in glory in Christ Jesus" (Phil. 4:19).

A heavenly mind knows their name is in heaven's book.
Jesus by the Spirit wants believers keeping an upward look!

A Heavenly Mind 1

A heavenly mind sees with the lenses of perfection.
A heavenly mind thinks of others with genuine admiration.
A heavenly mind is not cynical of others.
A heavenly mind desires that all recover.
A heavenly mind doesn't speak behind others back.
A heavenly mind cut sinners much slack.
A heavenly mind avoids judging.
A heavenly mind from being empathetic is never budging.
A heavenly mind is another of God in Christ gift.
A heavenly mind's perspective is to uplift.
A heavenly mind in daily doing good is centralized.
A heavenly mind is Christ by the Spirit in us personified!

"The LORD turned to him and said, 'Go in the strength you have and save Israel from the hand of Midian. Am I not sending you?'" (Judg. 6:14)

"Don't be afraid, for I am with you. Don't be discouraged, for I am your God. I will strengthen you and help you. I will hold you up with my victorious right hand" (Isa. 41:10).

A heavenly mind sees the transformation.
Jesus by the Spirit promises new Word revelation!

AM: Thank-You Note 123

Thank you, ABBA, Father, for love that is second to none.
Thank you, ABBA, Father, that my past sins are gone.
Thank you, ABBA, Father, for Your protective shield.
Thank you, ABBA, Father, that my name in heaven is sealed.
Thank you, Lord Jesus, that my mind in the Word was washed.
Thank you, Lord Jesus, that by grace promises I have cashed.
Thank you, Lord Jesus, for wiping away my tears.
Thank you, Lord Jesus, for making my route clear.
Thank you, Holy Spirit, for wisdom the is perfect and pure.
Thank you, Holy Spirit, that all You show is sure.
Thank you, Holy Spirit, for another day to live holy.
Thank you, Holy Spirit, for the work of making me holy.

"One with many friends may be harmed, but there is a friend who stays closer than a brother" (Prov. 18:24).

"The Lord is my strength and my shield; My heart trusts in Him, and I am helped; Therefore my heart exults, And with my song I shall thank Him" (Ps. 28:7).

The way to God's heart is by what He sees.
Jesus by the Spirit teaches us to plant Gospel seeds!

A: Closet Time 214b

Lord Jesus, my heart is Yours to use.
Lord Jesus, with grace, nothing You want I will refuse.
Lord Jesus, please help me to hate sin's presence.
Lord Jesus, I ask to partake of Your loving Essence.
Lord Jesus, renew my eternal commitment.
Lord Jesus, help me enjoy the abundant life fulfillment.
Lord Jesus, I ask that Your scent in me pervade.
Lord Jesus, of past strongholds, help me form a blockade.
Lord Jesus, come make my heart a permanent playground.
Lord Jesus, help me learn from the Word what is profound.
Lord Jesus, I ask for a demeanor of a spiritual child.
Lord Jesus, daily as I come increase my faith all the while!

"Casting down arguments and every high thing that exalts itself against the knowledge of God, bringing every thought into captivity to the obedience of Christ" (2 Cor. 10:5).

"We do this by keeping our eyes on Jesus, the Champion who initiates and perfects our faith…" (Heb. 12a).

All is by God prepared for His children to enjoy.
Jesus by the Spirit reveals all of the enemy's ploys!

DEAR ABBA, FATHER 43

I come to seek in Your sight to be pleasing.
I come my spirit and soul to You releasing.
I come to gain growth being a vessel of gold.
I come that I become humble and lovingly bold.
I come to enhance my Christlike scent.
I come my priority time with You to have spent.
I come the Word in my mind and spirit accumulate.
I come to gain boldness that testifying I don't hesitate.
I come my heart to Your scrutiny expose.
I come that any hint of sin to declare and appose.
I come presenting my body a living sacrifice.
I come that my ways Your will suffice!

"Therefore…present your bodies *as a* living sacrifice, holy to God, well-pleasing, which is your reasonable service" (Rom. 12:1).

"Let us then approach the throne of grace with confidence, so that we may receive mercy and find grace to help us in our time of need" (Heb. 4:16).

Daily presentations before God will a heart clean.
Jesus by the Spirit shows us how much to God we mean!

TODAY...75A

Today, I will respond to any adversity.
Today, I will treat people loving charity.
Today, I will confess what I know to be sinfully wrong.
Today, I will renounce things I have prolonged.
Today, I will seek a conscience that is clear.
Today, I will do what to ABBA, Father is dear.
Today, I will give the Holy Spirit full control.
Today, I will follow the believers written protocol.
Today, I will draw closer to the throne room.
Today, I will look to Jesus for spiritual bloom.
Today, I will keep away from sins that can be prevented.
Today, I will with the Trinity get better aquatinted.

"But if it is unpleasing in your sight to serve the LORD, then choose for yourselves this day whom you will serve... As for me and my house, we will serve the LORD!" (Josh. 24:15).

"Seek the LORD while He may be found; call on Him while He is near" (Isa. 55:6).

Resolving daily to follow God takes faith labor.
Jesus by the Spirit gives us constant favor.

CONSIDER

Laughing at their problems, their problems will laugh at them.
Changing their ways, they know not where to begin.
Faultfinders are seasoned justifiers.
Accepting a lie are faith deniers.
All complainers fail to confess.
They cannot understand why they are a mess.
These are full of lingering doubt.
They never declare what they are about.
Slowly, they move in the wrong direction.
They settle living life in a misconception.
Unable to receive counsel they know it all.
Their listening is biased as they continually fall!

"My people are destroyed for lack of knowledge. Because you have rejected knowledge, I will also reject you as My priests. Since you have forgotten the law of your God, I will also forget your children" (Hosea 4:6).

"Elijah stood in front of them and said, 'How much longer will you try to have things both ways? If the LORD is God, worship Him! The people did not say a word'" (1 Kings 18:21).

A double mind has taken many toward not living well.
Jesus by the Spirit of abundant life will tell!

BLAMELESS FAITH 1

Faith is the substance of things not seen.
Faith in heaven is mutually done on a daily scene.
Faith is the evidence of things hoped.
Blameless faith with dire needs in God has sincerely coped!
Blameless faith doesn't know any excuses.
Blameless faith accusing in the heart refuses.
Blameless faith is strong in God and His might.
Blameless faith never questions if God is right.
Blameless faith is prepared to trustingly die.
Blameless faith in the promises of God rely!
Blameless faith knows the Name above every name.
Blameless faith trust that Jesus by the Spirit is still the same!

"Behold the proud, his soul is not upright in him; but the just shall live by faith" (Hab. 2:4).

"And without faith it is impossible to please God, because anyone who approaches Him must believe that He exists and that He rewards those who earnestly seek Him" (Heb. 11:6).

God knows those that are sincerely seeking Him.
Jesus by the Spirit wants to be first in the heart within!

E: Closet Time 213

Holy Spirit, I ask that You come my temple to possess.
Holy Spirit, empower my words that others I bless.
Holy Spirit, renew my sense of devotion.
Holy Spirit, deliver me from going through the motions.
Holy Spirit, come make me more meek and humble.
Holy Spirit, anoint me to help those that stumble.
Holy Spirit, give me a mindset to easily others forgive.
Holy Spirit, help me from You my orders receive.
Holy Spirit, come fill me to overflowing.
Holy Spirit, help me in perfect love to be growing.
Holy Spirit, control my spirit and make me like Christ.
Holy Spirit, help me heed ABBA, Father's advice!

"I will be glad and rejoice in Your loving devotion, for You have seen my affliction; You have known the anguish of my soul" (Ps. 31:7).

God in heaven has commanded blessings upon blessings.
Jesus by the Spirit wants our doubts to be addressing!

PM: Thank-You Note 122

Thank you, ABBA, Father, for another day of growing.
Thank you, ABBA, Father, for the things You keep showing.
Thank you, ABBA, Father, that You never disappoint.
Thank you, ABBA, Father, that daily my spirit You anoint!
Thank you, Lord Jesus, my heart to You belongs.
Thank you, Lord Jesus, as You help me gain new songs.
Thank you, Lord Jesus, for help to always caring.
Thank you, Lord Jesus, for help when the Gospel I'm sharing!
Thank you, Holy Spirit, for being my Guide.
Thank you, Holy Spirit, for helping me in Jesus to abide.
Thank you, Holy Spirit, that You my heart bless.
Thank you, Holy Spirit, for helping me from carnal stress!

"Devote yourselves to prayer, being watchful and thankful" (Col. 4:2).

"Therefore, since we are receiving a kingdom that cannot be shaken, let us be thankful, and so worship God acceptably with reverence and awe" (Heb. 12:28).

God has invited us to His eternal best.
Jesus by the Spirit can give us daily peace and rest!

A: Closet Time 213

ABBA, Father, I want to serve You with integrity.
ABBA, Father, help me live in Holy Spirit solidarity.
ABBA, Father, grant me to be fixated on honoring You.
ABBA, Father, give me a spirit that loves Jesus too.
ABBA, Father, help my heart and mind to be done with sin.
ABBA, Father, control my mind as each begin.
ABBA, Father, give me a heart that is tender and kind.
ABBA, Father, help me a humble childlike faith to find.
ABBA, Father, secure in me to be Holy Spirit filled.
ABBA, Father, in Jesus, help me to be done with self-willed.
ABBA, Father, curb my straying thinking ways.
ABBA, Father, empower me to do what You say!

"Do you not know that your bodies are temples of the Holy Spirit, who is in you, whom you have received from God? You are not your own; you were bought at a price. Therefore honor God with your bodies" (1 Cor. 6:19–20).

All of heaven is prepared to help believers be elevated.
Jesus by the Spirit is all about how to heaven we are related!

A: CLOSET TIME 179

Lord Jesus, I will always worship You as Lord.
Lord Jesus, by the Spirit, to the Trinity may I be in accord.
Lord Jesus, thank you for being my Savior.
Lord Jesus, empower me to change my behavior.
Lord Jesus, renovate my thought process.
Lord Jesus, deliver me from spirit and soul regress.
Lord Jesus, search the crevices of my heart.
Lord Jesus, honoring the Word, grant me a new start.
Lord Jesus, by the Spirit from the world, I commit to separate.
Lord Jesus, by the Spirit, new holiness in me create.
Lord Jesus, renew my prayer closet desire.
Lord Jesus, help my love for You not expire.

"I am the gate. If anyone enters through Me, he will be saved. He will come in and go out and find pasture" (John 10:9).
"Jesus answered, 'I am the way and the truth and the life. No one comes to the Father except through Me'" (John 14:6).

The way to salvation for humanity is clear.
Jesus by the Spirit wants all to Him to draw near!

PM: THANK-YOU NOTE 89

Thank you, Holy Spirit, for never leaving.
Thank you, Holy Spirit, for helping me in faith believing.
Thank you, Holy Spirit, for wisdom to serve.
Thank you, Holy Spirit, that God's love in me You preserve.
Thank you, ABBA, Father, for daily blessings.
Thank you, ABBA, Father, for my deficiencies addressing.
Thank you, ABBA, Father, that beneath are Your strong arms.
Thank you, ABBA, Father, by the Spirit I am kept from harm.
Thank you, Lord Jesus, that You never fail.
Thank you, Lord Jesus, that Your insights are my priority mail.
Thank you, Lord Jesus, for my name in Your Book.
Thank you, Lord Jesus, that doing Your will I am on the hook!

"Enter His gates with thanksgiving and His courts with praise; give thanks to Him and praise His name. For the Lord is good and His love endures forever; His faithfulness continues through all generations" (Ps. 100:4–5).

The faithfulness of God has been well documented.
Jesus by the Spirit makes sure that all in the fold are protected!

E: Closet Time 179

Holy Spirit, my spirit belongs in Your possession.
Holy Spirit, I come to make my confession.
Holy Spirit, I confess my faults and failures as sins.
Holy Spirit, search my heart for un-Christlike things.
Holy Spirit, help me develop the mind of Christ.
Holy Spirit, anoint my ears to hear Your advice.
Holy Spirit, guide me to be guilt-free.
Holy Spirit, help me have a clear conscience unto Thee.
Holy Spirit, rekindle in me a mind easy to repent.
Holy Spirit, strengthen me that lukewarmness I prevent.
Holy Spirit, help me to hear and know You better.
Holy Spirit, please come in me to be my Pacesetter!

"If you then, being evil, know how to give good gifts to your children, how much more will your heavenly Father give the Holy Spirit to those who ask Him?" (Luke 11:13).

"Then Peter replied, 'I see very clearly that God shows no favoritism'" (Acts 10:34).

God sees all creation in a very unique way.
Jesus by the Spirit assures all that God will never betray!

REFUSING TO DOUBT

ABBA, Father has done too much for anyone doubting.
Remaking the earth had all of heaven shouting.
Watching the stars being put in position.
Enjoying how God in Jesus made every decision.
Seeing humans made was a marvelous wonder.
Looking upon Adam, all angels did ponder.
Out of dirt came the human race.
With everyone, the Holy Spirit would keep pace.
About God caring has never been any doubt.
Many received answers as to God they called out.
Doubting is a seed planted by the deceiver.
Doubting is "real" as the duped becomes a believer.
There is no doubt that Jesus had a resurrection.
Rather than doubt, believe to see a Holy Spirit revelation!

"Sustain me according to Your word, that I may live; And do not let me be ashamed of my hope" (Ps. 119:116).

"The teaching of Your word gives light, so even the simple can understand" (Ps. 119:130).

Abundant life is vibrant because every day, God will show something new.

Jesus by the Spirit will expose the secrets to not just a few!

DOUBT: SELF-INFLICTED

That doubt is self-inflicted one can't deny.
Doubting is harder to do then in faith to rely.
All creation points toward a Maker.
A believer by faith becomes a blessing partaker.
The woks of God through the ages leave no doubt.
Studying His Word will make the simpleton find out.
Doubt is self-inflicted as we give it voice.
Doubt versus faith is a matter of choice.
Faith is a gift to everyone in the human race.
Doubting is flipping faith in a reverse place.
Doubt is self-inflicted as fueled by the enemy.
Accept Jesus as Savior and doubt you won't have any!

"How long will you waver between two opinions? If the LORD is God, follow Him… But the people did not answer a word" (1 Kings 18:21)
"Jesus…took hold of him, saying to him, 'O you of little faith, why did you doubt?'" (Matt. 14:31).

Faith has been given to every person capable of making a God decision.
Jesus by the Spirit wants to enhance faith with a spiritual vision!

DEAR ABBA, FATHER 10

I come to You in need of safety and assurance.
I come because, in Jesus, I have protection insurance.
I come, ABBA, for Your prompt intervention in daily affairs.
I come to ask that the situation moves nowhere.
I come for favors in this most delicate matter.
I come to prevent anyone heart feeling of shatter.
I come for grace to interact in the discussion.
I come for help to keep in check my emotions.
I come to ask for healing of all past ways.
I come for new ears to hear what You have to say.
I come to listen and put the Word into action.
I come to refocus my heart on heavenly attraction.
I come to retrain my mind to meditate.
I come for a Word mind thinking to activate.
I come presenting my body as a living sacrifice.
I come to relinquish behaviors that to You don't suffice.
I come to live on progressive learning and insight.
I come to make brighter in me the Christlike Light!

"Seek the Lord and His strength; Seek His face continually" (1 Chron. 16:11).
"I love those who love Me; And those who diligently seek Me will find Me" (Prov. 8:17).

The Lord has paved for all to enjoy eternal living.
Jesus by the Spirit has given all a measure of believing!

M: Closet Time 213

Lord Jesus, I come my heart to You open.
Lord Jesus, by the Spirit, on You alone I depend.
Lord Jesus, forgive me for any hint of sin hidden.
Lord Jesus, by the Spirit, deliver me from the forbidden.
Lord Jesus, make my heart to be spiritually healthy.
Lord Jesus, enrich my soul to be emotionally wealthy.
Lord Jesus, deliver me from going through the motions.
Lord Jesus, rekindle genuine repentant devotions.
Lord Jesus, search me where my commitment is lacking.
Lord Jesus, empower me to do all that You are asking!
Lord Jesus, to You I commit this day!
Lord Jesus, in the Spirit, help me to pray!

"And you shall seek Me, and find Me, when you shall search for Me with all your heart" (Jer. 29:13).

"My little children, I am writing these things to you so that you might not sin. And if anyone should sin, we have an advocate with the Father, Jesus Christ *the* Righteous *One*" (1 John 2:1).

God has prepared all for sin prevention.
Jesus by the Spirit will train to avoid sinful deception!

TODAY...75B

Today, I will seek the Lord with expectation.
Today, I will honor God with loving appreciation.
Today, I will wash my mind by Word pondering.
Today, I will ask, seek, and knock rather than wondering.
Today, I will speak Truth to my weakness.
Today, I will be about my Father's business.
Today, I will seek Holy Spirit control.
Today, I will be a sheep within the fold.
Today, I will frequent the prayer closet.
Today, I will look for God sent deposits!
Today, I will the Trinity celebrate and hallow.
Today, I will in Jesus's footsteps follow!

"'Come, follow Me,' Jesus said, 'and I will send you out to fish for people'" (Matt. 4:19).
"Be imitators of me, as I also *am* of Christ" (1 Cor. 11:1).

Living like Jesus is gets stronger and easier every day.
Jesus by the Spirit going to the prayer closet to pray!

GROWTH ACTING

God knows a thought before it is formed.
It is clear to God when to the world we have conformed.
Adam could have conquered sin by obeying.
He kept listening to what the deceiver was saying.
His soul was embracing what was being projected.
"Bad company corrupts good character," once idly accepted.
Growth acting will bring wrong sacrifice to the altar.
Just "any" sacrifice is a growth falter.
Growth acting will God's correction reject.
Growth acting the Truth directly from God will not accept.
Growth acting will disregard God's direct plea.
Growth acting is blinded to what they clearly see!

"If you do what is right, will you not be accepted? But if you refuse to do what is right, sin is crouching at your door; it desires you, but you must master it" (Gen. 4:7).

"This is what the LORD Almighty says: 'Give careful thought to your ways'" (Haggai 1:7).

Knowing the Word is prerequisite to avoid growth acting.
Jesus by the Spirit wants to show when to God's will we are reacting!

97

Pursue: Projection

Moses thought that he was a self-proclaimed liberator.
Moses soon was running in need of a Savior.
Moses, in his heart, wanted to know God firsthand.
Moses would learn to pursue all of God's command.
Moses pursued the bush inflamed.
Moses realized that he was spiritually lame.
Moses obeyed as he took off his sandals.
Moses learned the spiritual was best for God to handle.
Moses daily by his deeds became godlier.
Moses's countenance got brighter as he became holier.
God projects His Essence upon those that pursue.
Pursue with projection can happen to me and you!

"My son, do not forget my teaching, But let your heart keep my commandments" (Prov. 3:1).

"But God commends His own love toward us, in that while we were yet sinners, Christ died for us" (Rom. 5:8).

Those that genuinely learn to meditate His Word have best godly results.

Jesus by the Spirit is never looking to mock faults!

E: CLOSET TIME 212

ABBA, Father, I worship You in my day.
ABBA, Father, help me live only on what You say.
ABBA, Father, refresh my mind to the things above.
ABBA, Father, help me be filled with Your mercy and love.
ABBA, Father, renew my quest to be perfectly holy.
ABBA, Father, by the Spirit grant me a heart that is lowly.
ABBA, Father, create a mind that seeks You to please.
ABBA, Father, flush my heart of all that needs release.
ABBA, Father, heal me from hints of sin within.
ABBA, Father, I ask by the Spirit to be free from sin!
ABBA, Father, help me to retain a mindset of Your child.
ABBA, Father, help me look to You all my earthly while!

"For God did not send His Son into the world to condemn the world, but to save the world through Him" (John 3:17).

"Let us fix our eyes on Jesus, the author and perfecter of our faith, who for the joy set before Him endured the cross, scorning its shame, and sat down at the right hand of the throne of God" (Heb. 12:2).

Looking at the author and perfecter of our faith we are growth bound.

Jesus by the Spirit is the best Friend found!

SEEK AND GROW

ABBA, Father enjoys by His creation being pursued.
ABBA, Father specially rewards those His Word have accrued.
The Holy Spirit appeals to be allowed to possess.
Jesus our Shepherd daily wants the elect to bless.
ABBA, Father keeps His eyes on the diligent to motivate.
Jesus tells us the Helper with us will relate.
The Holy Spirit clearly knows the fruitful route.
ABBA, Father says in heaven, "I know what it is all about."
Growing is a choice but God has "willed for us to will."
Jesus told us we would by the Spirit get a refill.
Ask, seek, and knock is to be a continuum.
Seeking to grow is nurtured by the Trinity with a premium!

"But Jesus told him, 'No!' The Scriptures say, 'People do not live by bread alone, but by every word that comes from the mouth of God'" (Matt. 4:4).

"For it is God who works in you to will and to act on behalf of His good purpose" (Phil. 2:13).

Growing is a constant that God will daily supplement.
Jesus by the Spirit wants all believers to carry His scent!

PM: THANK-YOU NOTE 118

Thank you, ABBA, Father, that You are protective.
Thank you, ABBA, Father, that You are corrective.
Thank you, ABBA, Father, for providing all needs.
Thank you, ABBA, Father, for affirming my spiritual deeds.
Thank you, Lord Jesus, that in heaven You speak of me.
Thank you, Lord Jesus, for help like You to be.
Thank you, Lord Jesus, for a place in heaven's Book.
Thank you, Lord Jesus, for a daily heavenly outlook.
Thank you, Holy Spirit, for helping to see the Kingdom best.
Thank you, Holy Spirit, for power, peace and rest.
Thank you, Holy Spirit, for a closer walk.
Thank you, Holy Spirit, for ears to hear You talk!

"The LORD is my strength and my shield; my heart trusted in Him, and I am helped: therefore my heart greatly rejoiceth; and with my song will I praise Him" (Ps. 28:7).

"Giving thanks always for all things unto God and the Father in the name of our Lord Jesus Christ" (Eph. 5:20).

Thanking the Holy Trinity daily breeds familiarity.
Jesus by the Spirit will keep us spiritual reality!

A: Closet Time 212

Holy Spirit, I come to learn Your ways.
Holy Spirit, I come for power to set the world for Jesus ablaze.
Holy Spirit, I come to gain more tenderness and empathy.
Holy Spirit, help me disseminate the Word with clarity.
Holy Spirit, create a new desire for growing.
Holy Spirit, possess me that Jesus in me would be glowing.
Holy Spirit, search the crevices of my heart to purge.
Holy Spirit, take from me any hint of sinful and its urge.
Holy Spirit, take my heart and make it holy.
Holy Spirit, possess me for I seek You direction only.
Holy Spirit, come I confess and renounce how You I grieve.
Holy Spirit, help me be redirected from what deceives!

"The Spirit of God has made me, And the breath of the Almighty gives me life" (Job 33:4).
"I will ask the Father, and He will give you another Helper, that He may be with you forever" (John 14:16).

Intimacy with the Holy Spirit will expedite maturity.
Jesus by the Spirit will keep us for sinful impurity!

PM: THANK-YOU NOTE 119

Thank you, ABBA, Father, for eternal security.
Thank you, ABBA, Father, for a life of grace and purity.
Thank you, ABBA, Father, that You love me to perfection.
Thank you, ABBA, Father, for meeting all expectations.
Thank you, Lord Jesus, that You are my Friend.
Thank you, Lord Jesus, for the Holy Spirit that You did send!
Thank you, Lord Jesus, forgiving me when I repent.
Thank you, Lord Jesus, for correction for sin to prevent.
Thank you, Holy Spirit, for never leaving.
Thank you, Holy Spirit, for helping me in believing.
Thank you, Holy Spirit, for showing things to come.
Thank you, Holy Spirit, for the spiritual man I've become!

"May the words of my mouth and the meditation of my heart be pleasing to You, O LORD, my Rock and my Redeemer" (Ps. 19:14).

"When the Advocate comes, whom I will send to you from the Father—the Spirit of truth who goes out from the Father—He will testify about Me" (John 15:26).

Words we speak and our heart meditation has to be God pleasing.

Jesus by the Spirit makes God's will very appealing!

AM: THANK-YOU NOTE 120

Thank you, ABBA, Father, for a day in Your jurisdiction.
Thank you, ABBA, Father, for holy conviction.
Thank you, ABBA, Father, for a life of peace.
Thank you, ABBA, Father, that Your love to others I can release!
Thank you, Lord Jesus, that You are my Friend.
Thank you, Lord Jesus, that me to the world You did send.
Thank you, Lord Jesus, that You forgave my past.
Thank you, Lord Jesus, that in heaven I will see You at last.
Thank you, Holy Spirit, for being my Guide today.
Thank you, Holy Spirit, for ears to hear what You say.
Thank you, Holy Spirit, for wisdom to have success.
Thank you, Holy Spirit, that daily You my spirit bless!

I will give You thanks forever, because You have done it, And I will wait on Your name, for it is good, in the presence of Your godly ones" (Ps. 52:9).

"You gave Your good Spirit to instruct them, Your manna You did not withhold from their mouth, And You gave them water for their thirst" (Neh. 9:20).

God never tires of our praying.
Jesus by the Spirit shows if our prayers are delaying!

M: Closet Time 211a

Holy Spirit, I come to secure our day's relationship.
Holy Spirit, help me from Your influence not to slip.
Holy Spirit, let me know I grieve or quench.
Holy Spirit, come in power and my spirit drench.
Holy Spirit, advance in me a hatred for sin.
Holy Spirit, come control me as the day begin.
Holy Spirit, create in me a new gentle and kind soul.
Holy Spirit, possess me and take control.
Holy Spirit, bless me with obeying.
Holy Spirit, guard my tongue in what I am saying.
Holy Spirit, help me be cognizant of Your will.
Holy Spirit, change me to be quiet, confident, and still.

"You send forth Your Spirit, they are created; And You renew the face of the ground" (Ps. 104:30).

"If you then, being evil, know how to give good gifts to your children, how much more will your heavenly Father give the Holy Spirit to those who ask Him?" (Luke 11:13).

Sincerely asking for salvation opens the door for the rest.
Jesus by the Spirit wants us to know that the enemy is a pest!

TODAY...71

Today, I will be joyous of my heavenly standing.
Today, I will live on what Jesus is commanding.
Today, I will talk less.
Today, I will with the Gospel others bless.
Today, I will esteem others more that myself.
Today, I will put my personal feelings on a shelf.
Today, I will bury opinions so as to have none.
Today, I will make sure my selfie ways are gone.
Today, I will think on things above.
Today, I will let ABBA, Father refill me with perfect love.
Today, I will deny self and pick up my cross.
Today, I will in the love of Jesus warn the loss!

"I will give thanks to You, O Lord my God, with all my heart,
And will glorify Your name forever" (Ps. 86:12).
"Seven times a day I praise You, Because of Your righteous ordinances" (Ps. 119:164).

Resolutions made with God's grace will have success.
Jesus by the Spirit, if trusted, will not allow us to regress!

A: Closet Time 211a

ABBA, Father, my hopes are based on Your power.
ABBA, Father, I lift my soul to You this hour.
ABBA, Father, I come for a heart to be purged and renewed.
ABBA, Father, help me the Word to meditate and accrued.
ABBA, Father, increase in me the desire to teach.
ABBA, Father, open avenues for many to reach.
ABBA, Father, revive my will to quickly obey.
ABBA, Father, anoint my tongue to speak what You say.
ABBA, Father, bless me to love the sinfully vile.
ABBA, Father, by the Spirit, help the Word in me compile.
ABBA, Father, in Jesus, help me to transform.
ABBA, Father, by the Spirit, help me Your will to conform!

"O God… I give thanks and praise, For You have given me wisdom and power; Even now You have made known to me what we requested of You…" (Dan. 2:23).

"Whatever you do in word or deed, do all in the name of the Lord Jesus, giving thanks through Him to God the Father" (Col. 3:17).

Our Father enjoys being recognized my His creation.
Jesus by the Spirit helps us employ the gifts of salvation!

PM: THANK-YOU NOTE 120

Thank you, ABBA, Father, for being my eternal Maker.
Thank you, ABBA, Father, for the Holy Spirit as my Caretaker.
Thank you, ABBA, Father, for help with the deceiver.
Thank you, ABBA, Father, that my faith is stronger as a believer.
Thank you, Lord Jesus, for daily grace and insight.
Thank you, Lord Jesus, for daily leading me right.
Thank you, Lord Jesus, for daily guiding.
Thank you, Lord Jesus, that in You, by the Spirit, I'm abiding!
Thank you, Holy Spirit, for power filled words to speak.
Thank you, Holy Spirit, that You help when in spirit I'm weak.
Thank you, Holy Spirit, for help to live for Christ.
Thank you, Holy Spirit, for daily wisdom and advice!

"I will praise You forever, because You have done it. I will wait on Your name—for it is good—in the presence of Your saints" (Ps. 52:9).

"I shall give thanks to You, for You have answered me, And You have become my salvation" (Ps. 18:21).

Giving thanks after salvation makes the relationship better.
Jesus by the Spirit will always be our Pacesetter!

DEAR ABBA, FATHER 41A

I come with You to reconnect.
I come by the Spirit of the Trinity gain greater respect.
I come this day Your perfect will to do.
I come by the Holy Spirit to serve and honor You.
I come to be in Jesus more perfected.
I come to be a willing vessel of the elected.
I come to learn greater ways of self-denial.
I come by the Spirit to overcome testings and trials.
I come my tongue to be touched by the coals of Your fire.
I come that in Your perfect will I may retire.
I come to be made more like Jesus Christ.
I come to be led by Holy Spirit advice.

"Death and life are in the power of the tongue, And those who love it will eat its fruit" (Prov. 18:21).

"He who conceals his transgressions will not prosper, But he who confesses and forsakes them will find compassion" (Prov. 28:13).

Confessing daily to God makes our soul less controlling.
Jesus by the Spirit our hearts from evil is patrolling!

TODAY...74

Today, I will pick up my cross and do self-denial.
Today, I will lift up Jesus all the while.
Today, I will refuse to partake in sinful behavior.
Today, I will point people to my Savior.
Today, I will return good for evil.
Today, I will help others in their restoration retrieval.
Today, I will seek to be rebaptized with fire.
Today, I will by the Spirit look to be inspired.
Today, I will walk with a humble attitude.
Today, I will look by the Holy Spirit for a life of servitude.
Today, I will be quiet, confident and still.
Today, I will seek a revival of Jesus in me refill.

"Therefore you will joyously draw water From the springs of salvation" (Isa. 12:3).

"The Spirit and the bride say, 'Come!' Let the one who hears say, 'Come!' And let the one who is thirsty come, and the one who desires the water of life drink freely" (Rev. 22:17).

All heaven's benefits are beyond salvation free.
Jesus by the Spirit wants all to come to God and see!

AM: THANK-YOU NOTE 118

Thank you, Holy Spirit, for wisdom in the prayer closet.
Thank you, Holy Spirit, for all insights in my spirit You deposit.
Thank you, Holy Spirit, for helping me to stay above carnality.
Thank you, Holy Spirit, for keeping me in spiritual reality!
Thank you, Lord Jesus, for love that daily is new.
Thank you, Lord Jesus, for the ability to love You!
Thank you, Lord Jesus, that my life is in Your hands.
Thank you, Lord Jesus, that I can will myself to follow commands!
Thank you, ABBA, Father, for a life that is fruitful.
Thank you, ABBA, Father, for willing me to be grateful!
Thank you, ABBA, Father, for help to be about Your business!
Thank you, ABBA, Father, for grace to witness!

"The Lord is my Shepherd; I have all I need" (Ps. 23:1).
"The Lord is compassionate and merciful, slow to get angry and filled with unfailing love" (Ps. 103:8).

Loving God is easy knowing that His love is unfailing.
Jesus by the Spirit teaches how in the godly we can be prevailing!

M: Closet Time 212

Lord Jesus, my love for You is wrapped in appreciation.
Lord Jesus, I am eternally grateful for salvation.
Lord Jesus, I love that You sent the Spirit the work to complete.
Lord Jesus, by the Spirit, my needs You will meet.
Lord Jesus, I love that my ways are being perfected.
Lord Jesus, I love that daily there is more to be expected.
Lord Jesus, I praise You now and forever.
Lord Jesus, by the Spirit, leaving You is a resounding never!
Lord Jesus, help me ABBA, Father to please.
Lord Jesus, my will to You I gladly release!
Lord Jesus, help me to retain a repentant mindset.
Lord Jesus, by the Spirit, keep me from regret.
Lord Jesus, whatever You want I'm willing!
Lord Jesus, I ask for a Holy Spirit refilling!

"But even now I know that God will give You whatever You ask of Him" (John 11:22).

"And I will do whatever you ask in My name, so that the Father may be glorified in the Son" (John 14:13).

God will always answer all prayers in Jesus's name.
Jesus by the Spirit teaches all to know when the answer came!

LOVE YOU!

Holy Trinity, I love what You have daily for eternity provided.
I love You for making it all one sided.
ABBA, Father, I love the thought that by You I am originated.
Holy Spirit, I love knowing that You took part as I was created.
Lord Jesus, I love the intense interest You showed.
Even while in sin Your love for me did not slowed.
ABBA, Father, You sent heaven's Best!
Holy Spirit, You worked feverishly to get me eternal rest.
Holy Spirit, You saw me broken to pieces.
You worked overtime to get me to Jesus.
ABBA, Father, in Jesus by the Spirit I'm lovingly secured.
Holy Trinity, when I say I LOVE YOU…that's for sure!

"And you must love the LORD your God with all your heart, all your soul, and all your strength" (Deut. 6:5).

Jesus replied: "'Love the Lord your God with all your heart and with all your soul and with all your mind" (Matt. 22:37).

Loving God is truly possible if He is first.
Jesus by the Spirit helps us for God to hunger and thirst!

PM: Thank-You Note 73

Thank you, ABBA, Father, for providing all my needs.
Thank you, ABBA, Father, as the Holy Spirit leads.
Thank you, ABBA, Father, for all of heaven's perks.
Thank you, ABBA, Father, that You affirm my works!
Thank you, Lord Jesus, for changing my life.
Thank you, Lord Jesus, for calming my sinful strife.
Thank you, Lord Jesus, that for me You intercede.
Thank you, Lord Jesus, for the Holy Spirit to proceed!
Thank you, Holy Spirit, that of me You are never weary.
Thank you, Holy Spirit, for helping me in Jesus to stay cheery.
Thank you, Holy Spirit, for holy conviction.
Thank you, Holy Spirit, for helping me in my sanctification!

"How kind the Lord is! How good He is! So merciful, this God of ours!" (Ps. 116:5).

"Give your burdens to the Lord, and He will take care of you. He will not permit the godly to slip and fall" (Ps. 55:22).

The people of salvation know to honor God best.
Jesus by the Spirit daily can give peace and rest!

A: Closet Time 211b

ABBA, Father, I worship and praise You for who You are.
ABBA, Father, I exalt Your power near and far.
ABBA, Father, where sin abounds Your grace is greater.
ABBA, Father, I honor You as my Vindicator.
ABBA, Father, I ask forgiveness for my sins of commission.
ABBA, Father, strengthen my spiritual vision.
ABBA, Father, renew my joy of heaven's citizenship.
ABBA, Father, in Jesus from Your hands I will never slip!
ABBA, Father, I ask for a deeper walk.
ABBA, Father, by the Spirit help me of Your Word to talk.
ABBA, Father, help me from serving to not stray.
ABBA, Father, fill me with deeper desire to pray!

"Then they cried to the Lord in their trouble…brought them out of their distresses. He caused the storm to be still…the sea were hushed. Then they were glad because they were quiet, So He guided them to their desired haven" (Ps. 107:28–30).

Our Father wants to guide the willing on earth.
Jesus by the Spirit wants to show how much to God we are worth!

E: Closet Time 211

Holy Spirit, I long to know You in spirit and truth.
Holy Spirit, I ask that my obeying would lead me to You.
Holy Spirit, I call upon You to manifest.
Holy Spirit, in Your power and will I want to rest.
Holy Spirit, sharpen my hearing to know Your speaking.
Holy Spirit, anoint my mind that daily You I am seeking.
Holy Spirit, help me keep a meek and lowly in heart attitude.
Holy Spirit, help me live with spiritual rectitude.
Holy Spirit, help not conform to less than diligent.
Holy Spirit, deliver me from being Word meditation negligent.
Holy Spirit, renew in me to be empathetic and tender.
Holy Spirit, possess me that I may easier surrender!

"For to us God revealed them through the Spirit; for the Spirit searches all things, even the depths of God" (1 Cor. 2:10).
"Now may the God of hope fill you with all joy and peace as you believe in Him, so that you may overflow with hope by the power of the Holy Spirit" (Rom. 15:13).

Our Father has put benefits in place beyond salvation.
Jesus by the Spirit will fulfill all heavenly expectation!

DEAR ABBA, FATHER 40

I come to gain greater empathy for others.
I come to be equipped to help the many recover.
I come to die to self while being more like Jesus.
I come to be healed in my remaining broken pieces.
I come to forget the past as I look to Your will.
I come Your ways and commands to fulfill.
I come to speak truth to those willing to hear.
I come to the Holy Spirit be close and near.
I come to be Your vessel of gold.
I come to all commands in the word I've been told.
I come to retain a spiritual repentant mindset.
I come to help heal the broken and mentally upset.
I come to a brighter shining light on the hill.
I come for strength and a Holy Spirit refill.

Set your mind on the things above, not on the things that are on earth" (Col. 3:2).

"Therefore, prepare your minds for action, keep sober in spirit, fix your hope completely on the grace to be brought to you at the revelation of Jesus Christ" (1 Pet. 1:13).

The mind of a believer has to be made new.
Jesus by the Spirit wants to help you!

Our Father

Our Father, I purposely trust Your eternal intent.
Our Father, I worship at Your feet without relent.
Our Father, as time moves on Your Word stands real.
Our Father, thank you for faith to live which negates how I feel.
Our Father, my heart is devoted You to follow.
Our Father, I am fixed avoiding the mundanely shallow.
Our Father, grant me wisdom and grace to be faithful.
Our Father, make me diligently grateful.
Our Father, forgive and deliver me from sinful ways.
Our Father, renew my ears to obey all that You say.
Our Father, strengthen hope in my eternal destination.
Our Father, bless me in sharing of Jesus' salvation!

"So then, this is how you should pray: 'Our Father in heaven, hallowed be Your name" (Matt. 6:9).

"For whoever does the will of My Father who is in heaven, he is My brother and sister and mother" (Matt. 12:50).

Our Father tenderly looks at His creation with longing.
Jesus by the Spirit discourages non-prayer prolonging!

DEAR ABBA, FATHER 42

I come to trust You with all my heart.
I come to bear my soul for temptation to depart.
I come to walk in the Spirit not fulfill carnality.
I come to live cognizant of Your present reality.
I come to free from any hint of sins.
I come to gain the joy of the Lord as my day begins.
I come to strengthen forgiving.
I come to enhance my ability of grace receiving.
I come to genuinely be available for others to care.
I come to be anointed the Gospel to share.
I come by Your power to be reaffirmed.
I come for a new infilling in me to be confirmed.

"Praise His glorious name forever! Let the whole earth be filled with His glory. Amen and amen!" (Ps. 72:19).

"But as for me, I am poor and needy; please hurry to my aid, O God. You are my helper and my savior; O Lord, do not delay" (Ps. 70:5).

God has always intended to provide and protect.
Jesus by the Spirit always wants us to prayerfully connect!

Dear Abba, Father 41b

I come my heart and soul to bare.
I come of Your greatness to partake and share.
I come that, by the Spirit, I may know You more.
I come in Jesus to get closer and to Your presence soar.
I come to be a vessel of Your power.
I come to live out walking in the Spirit all hours.
I come to expose my hidden sins and faults.
I come to gain deeper spiritual results.
I come to seek help with being meek and low of heart.
I come that, by the Spirit, I can gain a new start!
I come to regain a life to the commands I'm submissive.
I come to be strengthened in witnessing aggressive.

"O Lord, I have come to You for protection; don't let me be disgraced. Save me and rescue me, for You do what is right. Turn Your ear to listen to me, and set me free" (Ps. 71:1–2).

Coming to prayer is the best time spent for the new day.
Jesus by the Spirit will always guide the best way!

TODAY...73

Today, I will trust in the Lord regardless.
Today, I will look to the Lord to bless.
Today, I will confess my failures and faults.
Today, I will look to gain deeper spiritual results.
Today, I will have the Holy Spirit give me a heart check.
Today, I will not allow sin in my sight not even a speck.
Today, I will avoid all that is sinfully evil.
Today, I will act childlike lovingly civil.
Today, I will learn to further hate sin.
Today, I will seek the Holy Spirit as my day begins.
Today, I will seek with the Trinity to be in accord.
Today, I will look to honor and please my Lord!

"Seek out the LORD and His strength; seek His face always" (Ps. 105:4).

"As for me, I look to the LORD for help. I wait confidently for God to save me, and my God will certainly hear me" (Mic. 7:7)

Resolving to do right allows God to help us along.
Jesus by the Spirit hopes to put in our heart a genuine song!

TODAY...72

Today, I will forgive others easily.
Today, I will turn the other cheek readily.
Today, I will look to helping the outcast.
Today, I will plant and water seeds that last.
Today, I will be humble and meek.
Today, I will continue to diligently seek.
Today, I will allow the Holy Spirit to be my Coach.
Today, I will in witnessing look for a new approach.
Today, I will rejoice that my name is in God's Book!
Today, I will keep an upward look! Today I will seek to be Holy Spirit guided.
Today, I will by day's end in Jesus have abided!

"Oh give thanks to the Lord, call upon His name; Make known His deeds among the peoples" (Ps. 105:1).
"You will also declare a thing, And it will be established for you; So light will shine on your ways" (Job 22:28).

Declarations that are Word based often help the diligent seeker. Jesus by the Spirit advances resources to the meeker!

AM: Thank-You Note 121

Thank you, Holy Spirit, for being so faithful.
Thank you, Holy Spirit, for helping me to stay grateful.
Thank you, Holy Spirit, for showing me when I sin.
Thank you, Holy Spirit, for daily coming fully within!
Thank you, Lord Jesus, for Your blood that recovers.
Thank you, Lord Jesus, that living in sin is over.
Thank you, Lord Jesus, for help to do things right.
Thank you, Lord Jesus, for a love to honor God with all my might.
Thank you, ABBA, Father, for always caring.
Thank you, ABBA, Father, for love of Jesus to be sharing.
Thank you, ABBA, Father, that I am in Your sight.
Thank you, ABBA, Father, for making me a Christlike light!

"Be glad in the Lord, you righteous ones, And give thanks to His holy name" (Ps. 97:12).
"Enter His gates with thanksgiving And His courts with praise. Give thanks to Him, bless His name" (Ps. 100:4).

Thankfulness advances our total healing.
Jesus by the Spirit to our heart is constantly appealing!

M: Closet Time 211b

Lord Jesus, I need Your touch.
Lord Jesus, today I will think upon You much.
Lord Jesus, come calm my storms.
Lord Jesus, possess me to not deviate from Spirit norms.
Lord Jesus, make my heart tender to listen.
Lord Jesus, help me do what in the Word is written.
Lord Jesus, restore a heart that is forgiving.
Lord Jesus, help me perceive what is deceiving.
Lord Jesus, renew a commitment to meditation.
Lord Jesus, strengthen my Word retention.
Lord Jesus, help me to keep my mind on things above.
Lord Jesus, purify me with a new measure of Your love!

"I sought the LORD, and he answered me; He delivered me from all my fears" (Ps. 34:4).

"The righteous cry out, and the LORD hears them; He delivers them from all their troubles" (Ps. 34:17).

Deliverance is always only one call away.
Jesus by the Spirit puts a premium on who's name to pray!

DELIVER ME

ABBA, Father, deliver me from dichotomous thinking.
ABBA, Father, deliver me from sinful ways winking.
ABBA, Father, deliver me from glorifying the past.
ABBA, Father, deliver me from making decisions fast.
ABBA, Father, deliver me from judging.
ABBA, Father, deliver me from grudging.
ABBA, Father, deliver me from all to You is vile.
ABBA, Father, deliver me from others sin compile.
ABBA, Father, deliver me from interrupting.
ABBA, Father, deliver me from doing what is disgusting.
ABBA, Father, deliver me from a heart that's deceptive.
ABBA, Father, deliver me not being correction receptive.

"Submit yourselves, then, to God. Resist the devil, and he will flee from you" (James 4:7)

"You, dear children, are from God and have overcome them, because the one who is in you is greater than the one who is in the world" (1 John 4:4).

The Lord wants deliver from past behavior.
Jesus by the Spirit highlights the benefits of our Savior!

E: Closet Time 210

ABBA, Father, You are my Sovereign Creator.
ABBA, Father, You are my eternal Curator.
ABBA, Father, You to from hell's grip.
ABBA, Father, in Jesus, from Your hands I will not slip.
ABBA, Father, You made me a citizen of the heavenly city.
ABBA, Father, thank you for merciful pity.
ABBA, Father, I want to be guided by Your eyes.
ABBA, Father, help me walk with You faithfully wise.
ABBA, Father, in Jesus bless the seeds that I am casting.
ABBA, Father, help me bring many to life everlasting!
ABBA, Father, help me hate sin as You do.
ABBA, Father, by the Spirit, help me live to please You!

"The steps of a man are ordered by the LORD who takes delight in his journey" (Ps. 37:33).

"But without faith no one can please God. We must believe that God is real and rewards everyone who searches for Him" (Heb. 11:6).

Everything in the Word we want to excel in God will provide.
Jesus by the Spirit from never wants us to hide!

A: Closet Time 210

Holy Spirit, I honor You as a Person worthy of praise.
Holy Spirit, to You my worship I raise.
Holy Spirit, take me closer and deeper.
Holy Spirit, reveal anew my Keeper.
Holy Spirit, bless me with greater humility.
Holy Spirit, grant me more empathy for fallen humanity.
Holy Spirit, heal my brokenness to better serve.
Holy Spirit, help me daily the will of ABBA, Father to observe.
Holy Spirit, create a new joy of my name in heaven's Book.
Holy Spirit, strengthen in me a heavenly outlook.
Holy Spirit, help me to be holy as You are Holy.
Holy Spirit, in Jesus, help me serve ABBA, Father only!

"Therefore you shall be perfect, just as your Father in heaven is perfect" (Matt. 5:48).

"But as He who called you *is* holy, you also be holy in all *your* conduct" (1 Pet. 1:15).

Becoming holy is part of God's graceful package.
Jesus by the Spirit wants all to get rid of sinful baggage!

SEEING PERFECT 4

ABBA, Father prepares to send heaven's Perfect gift.
ABBA, Father sends the beginning of the perfect lift.
The Holy Spirit in the process is all involved.
The Holy Spirit who hates sin wants it perfectly resolved.
The Holy Spirit works at ABBA's direction.
The angels are ready for action without exception.
The seasons are prepared for any heavenly task.
The stars are ready to do their part when asked.
The birds sing with perfect delight.
The King of Glory is ready to do the ultimate right.
The Holy Spirit has been prepping the devout faithful.
The Perfect Gift coming will make many grateful!

"Behold, God is exalted, and we do not know Him; The number of His years is unsearchable" (Job 36:26).

"How precious also are Your thoughts to me, O God! How vast is the sum of them!" (Ps. 139:17).

There is nothing that cannot do for those Him they please.
Jesus by the Spirit wants from sin to be released!

Seeing Perfect 3

A citizen of heaven has one way thinking.
Their brains are wired toward perfection linking.
Everyone in heaven is perfect beyond compare.
Each other's perfection is affirmed everywhere.
It is a world of sincere perfect complementing.
All citizens are graceful while assenting.
Heavenly environment allows for all to be in what they say.
Complimenting each other is just a "normal" way.
In heaven, esteeming others more than self is the norm!
Perfect thinking leads to perfect acting as all conform.
Perfecting is what the Holy Spirit does in a fallen nature.
Perfecting brings ABBA, Father in Jesus much pleasure!

"The plans of the heart belong to man, But the answer of the tongue is from the Lord" (Prov. 16:1).
"For My thoughts are not your thoughts, Nor are your ways My ways," declares the Lord" (Isa. 55:8).

Allowing God to fully direct our life brings blissful fulfillment.
Jesus by the Spirit is looking for genuine commitment!

SEEING PERFECT 2

The Trinity understands the power of perfecting.
In heaven, all there are naive to evil and rejecting.
Perfect love does cast out all fear.
Perfect love in heaven makes for the masses to be near.
In heaven, all are used to seeing things perfect.
In such mindsets, there is nothing to reject.
When they enter the natural, they still perceive the same.
As they interact, they speak and act from where they came.
They could look at a person that was being a coward.
In thinking, they project "You mighty man of power."
Training unto godliness has great potential.
Speaking heavenly perfect is essential!

"I know that You can do all things, And that no purpose of Yours can be thwarted" (Job 42:2).

"Many, O Lord my God, are the wonders which You have done, And Your thoughts toward us; There is none to compare with You. If I would declare and speak of them, They would be too numerous to count" (Ps. 40:5).

Living daily for God allows for experiencing His wonders.
Jesus by the Spirit wants us all on the Word to ponder!

SEEING PERFECT 1

ABBA, Father sees all from the lenses of perfection.
ABBA, Father, in Jesus, restores what was sinful frustration.
ABBA, Father cannot look upon sinful behavior.
ABBA, Father to replenish the original sent a Savior.
ABBA, Father doesn't deny the evil, instead, He sees the good!
ABBA, Father, by the Spirit, sees what all could.
ABBA, Father understands the power of projection.
ABBA, Father, in Jesus, projects total restoration.
ABBA, Father says all in Jesus by the Spirit are new.
ABBA, Father was speaking of sinners like me and you.
ABBA, Father sent His Word to bring healing.
ABBA, Father stands amazed on the many who live on a feeling.

"Many plans are in a man's heart, But the counsel of the Lord will stand" (Prov. 19:21).

For I know the plans that I have for you,' declares the Lord, 'plans for welfare and not for calamity to give you a future and a hope" (Jer. 29:11).

When God restores it is done to the original intent.
Jesus by the Spirit looks for sincere daily repent!

TRUST REGARDLESS

I will be trusting regardless what I may see.
I will trust regardless as my faith is unto Thee.
I will trust regardless because with You I have surety.
Trusting regardless is a spiritual reality.
The arm of the flesh at best is deceptive.
Trusting regardless helps my prayers in heaven be receptive.
Trusting in man has unexpected limitations.
Trust regardless strengthens heavenly relations.
Trusting regardless is what the faithful do.
Trusting regardless says "God I am looking to only You."
Trusting regardless takes you to one step beyond.
Trusting regardless hopes only on God to respond.

"Trust in the LORD forever, for the LORD, the LORD himself, is the Rock eternal" (Isa. 26:4).
"Let us then with confidence draw near to the throne of grace, that we may receive mercy and find grace to help in time of need" (Heb. 4:16).

Trusting regardless takes us to deeper walk of obeying.
Jesus by the Spirit wants us to hear what He is saying!

DICHOTOMY 1

Dichotomous thinking makes the person center of the universe.
Dichotomous thinking actually works in reverse.
You can choose either world as it is beneficial.
Dichotomous thinking makes a person superficial.
Dichotomous thinking doesn't allow spiritual traction.
Dichotomous living makes for constant reaction.
Dichotomous thinking doesn't allow for a right choice.
Dichotomy often speaks words in wrong voice.
Dichotomy learns to master the double mind.
Dichotomous learning cannot in the Word power find.
Dichotomous believers stay in the wilderness experience.
Dichotomous thinkers carry their own spiritual criteria.

"Do not call to mind the former things; pay no attention to the things of old" (Isa. 43:18).
"This means that anyone who belongs to Christ has become a new person. The old life is gone; a new life has begun!" (2 Cor. 5:17).

Holding on to wrong thinking leads to selfish living.
Jesus by the Spirit want us the Word to continue receiving!

AM: THANK-YOU NOTE 119

Thank you, ABBA, Father, for waking me today.
Thank you, ABBA, Father, for grace along the way.
Thank you, ABBA, Father, that I am Your child.
Thank you, ABBA, Father, for loving me all the while.
Thank you, Lord Jesus, for a day under Your protection.
Thank you, Lord Jesus, for my heavenly occupation.
Thank you, Lord Jesus, for victory in Your name.
Thank you, Lord Jesus, that You are always the same!
Thank you, Holy Spirit, that the way to Jesus You did pave.
Thank you, Holy Spirit, for when I did get save.
Thank you, Holy Spirit, for helping me in my success.
Thank you, Holy Spirit, daily my spirit You do bless!

"Great is the Lord, and highly to be praised, And His greatness is unsearchable" (Ps. 145:3).

"Exalt the Lord our God And worship at His footstool; Holy is He" (Ps. 99:5).

Our life is much more peaceful when to God connected.
Jesus by the Spirit looks for past habits that need to be perfected!

M: Closet Time 210

ABBA, Father, I call to You on my inner distress.
ABBA, Father, to You my needs I do address.
ABBA, Father, in Jesus restore my childlike joy.
ABBA, Father, come in power and sins of the destroy.
ABBA, Father, help me worship in spirit and truth again.
ABBA, Father, help me in Your presence to remain.
ABBA, Father, release my heart from the day's cares.
ABBA, Father, revive my within everywhere.
ABBA, Father, grant me revival.
ABBA, Father, help me forgive my rivals.
ABBA, Father, renew in me a mindset to forgive.
ABBA, Father, give me insight for those wanting to deceive.

"Help me, O Lord my God; Save me according to Your loving-kindness" (Ps. 109:26).
"Be pleased, O Lord, to deliver me; Make haste, O Lord, to help me" (Ps. 40:13).

Prayer honesty gets the greater attention.
Jesus by the Spirit show us how prayer can help sin prevention!

GOD'S ATTENTION 4

Throughout the day, You never cease of me to be distracted.
In my morning rise, in me, You are joyously attracted.
It's hard for me to conceive how anyone can wickedly stray.
As You do, too, I hate every wicked way.
Lord, is it right for me to hate those that hate You?
Yes, Lord, I've concluded that I should hate the wicked, too!
Lord, search every crevice within my wondering heart.
Each morning grant me a faithful start.
Feel free to test my thoughts to show me godly thinking.
ABBA, Father let not my ways in sin be sinking.
Deliver me from making You sad.
May each day I live make Your Spirit ever so glad!

"How precious are your thoughts about me, O God... And
when I wake up, you are still with me! O Lord, shouldn't I hate those
who hate you?... Search me, O God, and know my heart... Point
out anything in me that offends you..." (Ps. 139:17–24).

The tender love that God has for all is without measure.
Jesus by the Spirit teaches us how to bring God pleasure!

God's Attention 3

While in the womb, Your loving hands knitted my inner parts.
In completion, Your handiwork was perfect art.
When I think upon all this, my spirit exudes Your praises.
Hallelujahs in exaltation, my lips spontaneously raises!
Your attentive love is upon the unborn.
While in the womb, entry into Your Book is formally a norm.
My life was scheduled for every moment of living.
In my success and prosperity, You kept believing.
Every day of my earthly life was written in Your Book.
Even angels of such works take a closer look.
How touching to think that I am constantly on Your mind.
You made me so unique that I am one of a kind!

"You formed my inward parts; You covered me in my mother's womb… My frame was not hidden from You… Your eyes saw my substance, being yet unformed…" (Ps. 136:13–16).

Our Father has the greatest interest in our well-being.
Jesus by the Spirit want us with Him to be agreeing!

GOD'S ATTENTION 2

ABBA, Father from the Holy Spirit there is no hiding.
Fleeing from Your presence is like openly abiding.
Upon entering the Heavens, You are everywhere.
Even attempting to hide in hell, I will find You there.
Riding the wind to its furthest will not keep me from You.
No matter where, You will guide as Your hand is upon me too.
In the darkest place in hiding is to You noticeably light.
In Your presence, the greatest darkness becomes bright.
Riding the wind to its furthest will not keep me from You.
No matter where, You will guide as Your hand is upon me too.
In the darkest place in hiding is to You noticeably light.
In Your presence, the greatest darkness becomes bright.

"Where can I go from Your Spirit?… If I ascend into heaven, You are there… Your hand shall lead me…darkness and light are the same to You" (Ps. 139:7–12).

Every intimacy about is God knows.
Jesus by the Spirit only wants His unconditional love to show!

GOD'S ATTENTION 1

Before I was in the womb, You knew my features.
Even the Holy Spirit was prepared to be my Teacher.
Upon birth, You where laser focused of my welfare.
As I am sitting or rising, You know me there.
My every thought You know quite well.
You comprehend all about me, that I can tell.
Before I utter a word, You know it first.
Such omniscient knowledge for You makes me thirst.
I feel so protected as You hem me in behind and before.
As You lay Your hand upon me, my spirit and soul wants more!
The depth of Your knowledge is beyond my comprehension.
Such unique knowledge within my mind there is no retention!

"O LORD, You have searched me and known me… Such knowledge is to wonderful…it is high, I cannot attain it" (Ps. 139:1–6).

God has made us fearfully and wonderfully made.
Jesus by the Spirit wants all believers to meet the spiritual grade!

E: CLOSET TIME 209

ABBA, Father, I will forever sing Your praises.
ABBA, Father, my spirit and soul from within me raises.
ABBA, Father, I am grateful for daily provisions.
ABBA, Father, daily I will seek Your permission.
ABBA, Father, help me to be faithfully diligent.
ABBA, Father, strengthen my spirit to be gracefully vigilant.
ABBA, Father, in Jesus help me His mannerisms duplicate.
ABBA, Father, restore a childlike faith that to You I better relate.
ABBA, Father, help me not be weary in well doing.
ABBA, Father, by the Spirit help me in the Way to keep going.
ABBA, Father, help me to be a diligent witness.
ABBA, Father, help me to be about heaven's business!

"I will praise You with my whole heart; Before the gods I will sing praises to You" (Ps. 138:1).

"Without faith it is impossible to be well pleasing to Him, for he who comes to God must believe that He exists, and that He is a rewarder of those who seek Him" (Heb. 11:6).

Faith in God is tested by our daily lifestyle.

Jesus by the Spirit wants us to frequent the prayer closet long whiles!

PM: THANK-YOU NOTE 117

Thank you, ABBA, Father, for celebrating my birth.
Thank you, ABBA, Father, for giving me eternal worth.
Thank you, ABBA, Father, that angels watch as I labor.
Thank you, ABBA, Father, that I have constant favor.
Thank you, Lord Jesus, for being my Substitute.
Thank you, Lord Jesus, for help in Your will to pursue.
Thank you, Lord Jesus, for a life of abundant living.
Thank you, Lord Jesus, that godly faith I keep receiving.
Thank you, Holy Spirit, for healing my heart's broken pieces.
Thank you, Holy Spirit, that daily You expose Jesus!
Thank you, Holy Spirit, for conviction when I am wrong.
Thank you, Holy Spirit, for being with me for so long!

"Exalt the Lord our God And worship at His footstool; Holy is He" (Ps. 99:5).
"O magnify the Lord with me, And let us exalt His name together" (Ps. 34:3).

Everyday making time to thank our Maker makes us more like Him.
Jesus by the Spirit wants to teach us how to spiritually swim!

Follow Jesus 10

Follow Jesus as the paralytic He makes walk.
Follow Jesus as the mute begins to talk.
Follow Jesus when He meets with the adulterous sinner.
Follow Jesus as He makes her a godly beginner.
Follow Jesus in the market with a whip.
Follow Jesus as from the cliff He slips.
Follow Jesus as He explains insight and revelation.
Follow Jesus as He imparts truth and motivation.
Follow Jesus as He stops the issue of blood.
Follow Jesus as to Him the sick and needy flood.
Follow Jesus as He habitually points to ABBA, Father above.
Follow Jesus on how for His disciples He spreads love!

"Jesus replied, 'Blessed are you, Simon son of Jonah! For this was not revealed to you by flesh and blood, but by My Father in heaven'" (Matt. 16:17).

"No longer do I call you servants, for a servant does not understand what his master is doing. But I have called you friends, because everything I have learned from My Father I have made known to you" (John 15:15).

Intimacy is what God wants to develop in all.
Jesus by the Spirit knows that it begins answering His call!

A: Closet Time 209

Holy Spirit, come upon me in power make me vessel.
Holy Spirit, possess me that I may best with sin wrestle.
Holy Spirit, come fill me to overflowing.
Holy Spirit, cleanse me that Jesus in me is glowing.
Holy Spirit, help me from hints of sin to recover.
Holy Spirit, possess me and do a complete makeover.
Holy Spirit, create in me a humble attitude.
Holy Spirit, help in meditation that the Word I accrued.
Holy Spirit, make me to regain a mind of child.
Holy Spirit, increase obedience in my will with You to be reconciled!
Holy Spirit, tenderize my heart to be gentle and kind.
Holy Spirit, help me humbleness in Jesus to find!

"Do you not know that your bodies are temples of the Holy Spirit, who is in you, whom you have received from God? You are not your own" (1 Cor. 6:19).

"But the fruit of the Spirit is love, joy, peace, forbearance, kindness, goodness, faithfulness, gentleness and self-control..." (Gal. 5:22–23a).

The Holy Spirit is a Person that longs for intimate respect.
Jesus by the Spirit will guide to a place of no regret!

JAILERS, BAILERS, AND SAILORS 3

Sailors are always preparing for the journey.
Sailors learn early that they have a Heavenly Attorney!
Sailors knows to prepare for what lies ahead.
Sailors are not rebellious; they turn the other cheek instead.
Sailors will avoid known pitfalls.
Sailors when told to change directions will heed the calls.
Sailors never stop their training.
Sailors look for what self-adjustment is remaining.
Sailors keep their mind on their destination.
Sailors trust in divide inspiration.
Sailors are command listeners and takers.
Sailors know how to habitually thank their Maker!

"Instruct a wise man, and he will be wiser still; teach a righteous man, and he will increase his learning" (Prov. 9:9).

"Let the wise hear and increase in learning, and the one who understands obtain guidance" (Prov. 1:5).

The saved are sailing on to their eternal destination.
Jesus by the Spirit wants all to prepare with salvation!

JAILERS, BAILERS, AND SAILORS 2

Bailers are full of misguided intent.
Bailers for others will even repent!
Bailers are okay with being used.
Bailers in the long run will be abused.
Bailers have a deep desire to rescue.
Bailers are so focus that if corrected will turn on you!
Bailers retain a one-track mind.
Bailers when corrected faults in them find.
Bailers will work their finger to the bone.
Bailers are fearful of being alone.
Bailers love to live in the past.
Bailers are enablers and justifiers till the last!

"Now the sons of Eli were scoundrels who had no respect for the LORD" (1 Sam. 2:12).

"A slack hand causes poverty, but the hand of the diligent makes rich" (Prov. 10:4).

"For each will have to bear his own load" (Gal. 6:5).

Bailers and enablers stunt growth two ways.
Jesus by the Spirit wants us to hear what the Word says!

JAILERS, BAILERS, AND SAILORS 1

Jailers are the ones to do the least.
Jailers changing their ways always resist.
Jailers have conformity on their mind.
Jailers will go along with everyone they find.
Jailers enjoy the status quo.
Jailers to changing seminars will not go.
Jailers are great about on others depending.
Jailers their habitual ways are always defending.
Jailers are experts at passing blame.
Jailers, day after day, stay the same.
Jailers are top notch creative manipulators.
Jailers will always be "involved" spectators!

"As a dog returns to its vomit, so a fool repeats his foolishness" (Prov. 26:11).

"Don't waste your breath on fools, for they will despise the wisest advice" (Prov. 23:9).

Even God cannot teach the unwilling.
Jesus by the Spirit wants to give us all a daily refilling!

RESTORING JOY

Lord, I come for a joy and peace restoration.
Lord, I come for a new joy about my salvation.
Lord, I come to regain my joy for Your perfect will.
Lord, I come for the joy of a Holy Spirit refill!
Lord, I come to ask for a new anointing of joy.
Lord, I come for new insights and ways to employ.
Lord, I come for a renew joy today.
Lord, I come because You hear and answer what I pray.
Lord, I come because the joy of You is my strength.
Lord, I come so that my day in joy I will have spent.
Lord, I come for a new joyous citizenship celebration.
Lord, I come for strengthen joy of my eternal expectation!

Restore to me the joy of Your salvation, And sustain me with a willing spirit" (Ps. 52:12).

"Make me to hear joy and gladness, Let the bones which You have broken rejoice" (Ps. 51:8).

The joy of God is available daily as we live for Christ.
Jesus by the Spirit wants to give us perfect advice!

TODAY...70

Today, I will look to God in Jesus to be renewed.
Today, I will offer my heart so that by Spirit in can be viewed.
Today, I will seek for a new joy of the Lord.
Today, I will look to the Trinity to be in accord.
Today, I will ask, seek and knock for revival.
Today, I will anticipate the Holy Spirit new arrival.
Today, I will remember that my fight is not with others.
Today, I will focus on the enemy not wanting me to recover.
Today, I will praise and worship with appreciation.
Today, I will rejoice in my lasting salvation!
Today, I will pay attention to use my sharpened sword.
Today, I will maintain the love and joy of the Lord!

"Hear, O Lord, and be gracious to me; O Lord, be my helper" (Ps. 30:10).
Make haste to help me, O Lord, my salvation!" (Ps. 38:22).

Every day is always filled with the unexpected.
Jesus by the Spirit will our days be there to show we're accepted!

LORD, HELP ME SEE

Lord, how is it that in many circles I am thought to be godly?
Lord, why is it that to others I am oddly?
Lord, many say that I am elder leader.
Lord, there are those questioning me who are repeaters.
Lord, for years, You gave me places to teach.
Lord, with grace, I did all I could the Word to preach.
Lord, then there were those that my talents rejected.
Lord, many where the "reasons" for not being accepted.
Lord, I forgive give those that painted me wrong.
Lord, help me see what sin in my heart progress prolongs.
Lord, it hurts when constantly giving a double message.
Lord, in my older days, use me and show a sign as presage.
Lord, many gave testimony of Your anointing upon me.
Lord, help me rightly discern what I need to see.

"Help, Lord, for the godly man ceases to be, For the faithful disappear from among the sons of me" (Ps. 12:1).

"Help me, O Lord my God; Save me according to Your loving-kindness" (Ps. 109:26).

The Lord will speak directly to those that ask.
Jesus by the Spirit renewing our mind is a primary task!

Not Good Enough

Lord, I can imagine as Jabez for years was ridiculed.
Lord, it was awful to be treated as unschooled.
Lord, but he took time to make a life inventory.
Lord, to You in prayer he detailed his miserable story.
Lord, You heard in heaven his sincere appeal.
Lord, You could tell in his voice and soul he was for real.
Lord, without a moment to spare, You took the prayer at hand.
Lord, with lighting speed, You decreed a command.
Lord, You made it clear that the prayer was done.
Lord, the angels on assignment were suddenly gone.
Lord, overnight, Jabez's life would begin to change.
Lord, constant grace would his life now rearrange.
Lord, You will always respond to the prayer of the destitute.
Lord, that You are responsively good is beyond dispute!

"Jabez was more honorable than his brothers. His mother had named him Jabez, saying, 'I gave birth to him in pain.' Jabez cried out to the God of Israel, 'Oh, that you would bless me and enlarge my territory! Let your hand be with me, and keep me from harm so that I will be free from pain.' And God granted his request" (1 Chron. 4:9–10).

God thrives on showing might the deeper the pain.
Jesus by the Spirit teach us to call out for much gain!

Dear Abba, Father 39

I come my heart and soul to offer as a living sacrifice.
I come my spirit by Your wisdom to receive advice.
I come to be settled that nothing misses Your attention.
I come to gain spiritual traction and intention.
I come for a touch of Your finger.
I come that my walk of faith by distractions be not hinder.
I come to be upgraded on a real repentant mindset.
I come that if I sin, I have genuine holy regret!
I come to the throne my heart to expose.
I come to restart on the will for me that You chose!
I come to be a vessel for Your best use.
I come to upgrade humility and obeying not refuse!

"He heals the brokenhearted, And binds up their wounds [healing their pain and comforting their sorrow]" (Ps. 147:3).
"Repent, then, and turn to God, so that your sins may be wiped out, that times of refreshing may come from the Lord" (Acts 3:19).

Asking for forgiveness cleanses the soul.
Jesus by the Spirit guides toward being made whole!

M: Closet Time 209

Lord Jesus, my heart is heavy with thoughts that are troubling.
Lord Jesus, the enemy is attempting thoughtful rumbling.
Lord Jesus, I come for Your protective grace.
Lord Jesus, come in my spirit and fill the space.
Lord Jesus, purge me from all that freedom obstructs.
Lord Jesus, possess me as a kind heart You reconstruct.
Lord Jesus, help me live in peace and daily joy.
Lord Jesus, by the Spirit help me better detect Satan's ploy.
Lord Jesus, my will to You I submit.
Lord Jesus, Your Lordship over my life I re-permit.
Lord Jesus, help me see the spiritual realm clearer.
Lord Jesus, by the Spirit help me to You draw nearer!

"This poor man cried, and the Lord heard him, And saved him out of all his troubles" (Ps. 34:6).
"From the end of the earth I call to You when my heart is faint; Lead me to the rock that is higher than I" (Ps. 61:2).

Prayers sincerely directed at God have special attention.
Jesus by the Spirit wants us to give praying appreciation!

AM: Thank-You Note 117

Thank you, ABBA, Father, for always being there for me.
Thank you, ABBA, Father, that daily Your blessings I see.
Thank you, ABBA, Father, for help to speak without rancor.
Thank you, ABBA, Father, that You are my eternal Anchor.
Thank you, Lord Jesus, for being my eternal Friend.
Thank you, Lord Jesus, that my living You defend.
Thank you, Lord Jesus, for help in the faith race to proceed.
Thank you, Lord Jesus, for help and motivation to plant seeds.
Thank you, Holy Spirit, that You are my Comforter.
Thank you, Holy Spirit, that over my feelings You're Governor.
Thank you, Holy Spirit, that to the diligent You speak.
Thank you, Holy Spirit, for the desire and initiative to seek!

"I will give thanks to You, O Lord my God, with all my heart,
And will glorify Your name forever" (Ps. 86:12).
"So I will bless You as long as I live; I will lift up my hands in
Your name" (Ps. 63:4).

Our feelings can be deceptive, but God hear our weary heart.
Jesus by the Spirit wants us to shine brighter than stars!

A: Closet Time 205

Holy Spirit, come fix my heart to be devoted.
Holy Spirit, take me deeper to be spiritually promoted.
Holy Spirit, show what in my heart is deficient.
Holy Spirit, come in power and make me spiritually proficient.
Holy Spirit, help me to hate sin like the Trinity.
Holy Spirit, help me with You to have a greater affinity.
Holy Spirit, I want to know You as Jesus did.
Holy Spirit, please see what hint of sin in my heart is hid.
Holy Spirit, strengthen my soul to overlook insults.
Holy Spirit, grant me favor to live for deep spiritual results.
Holy Spirit, I am Yours to make and mold.
Holy Spirit, for ABBA, Father keep me faithfully bold!

"And whether you turn to the right or to the left, your ears will hear this command behind you: "This is the way. Walk in it" (Isa. 30:21).

"The Holy Spirit said to Philip, 'Go over and walk along beside the carriage'" (Acts 8:29).

In the Word that the unlearned were used much by the Spirit as needed.

Jesus by the Spirit wants all the Word to be heeded!

FOLLOW JESUS 1

When we follow Jesus, there is much to learn.
As we follow Jesus, one can see that the Kingdom He yearns.
Follow Jesus and there is not much fanfare.
Follow Jesus and even doubters can sense ABBA, Father there.
Following Jesus will surprise the lack of luxury.
Those that follow Jesus saw much recovery.
Following Jesus, all could see that He did thirst.
Follow Jesus as in the Word He was daily immersed.
Follow Jesus as He called disciples from the ordinary.
All that follow Jesus knew there was no salary.
Follow Jesus as He makes His bedding near the willow.
Follow Jesus as He lays minus a pillow.

"But Jesus answered, 'It is written: Man shall not live on bread alone, but on every word that comes from the mouth of God'" (Matt. 4:4).

"But Jesus replied, 'Foxes have dens to live in, and birds have nests, but the Son of Man has no place even to lay his head'" (Luke 9:58).

God from heaven can best our life direct.
Jesus by the Spirit shows every human the highest respect!

E: CLOSET TIME 208

ABBA, Father, I come my heart to render.
ABBA, Father, deliver me from being a pretender.
ABBA, Father, I come that You can take me deeper.
ABBA, Father, by the Spirit come be my Keeper.
ABBA, Father, restore my heart to Your perfect will.
ABBA, Father, in Jesus I ask for a Holy Spirit refill.
ABBA, Father, search my soul and see what prevents.
ABBA, Father, give me a mindset that easily repents.
ABBA, Father, help me to live faithfully humble.
ABBA, Father, strengthen me to help those that stumble.
ABBA, Father, I ask for help to walk in the Spirit and fire.
ABBA, Father, help me act on all that You require.

"I know that You can do all things, And that no purpose of Yours can be thwarted" (Job 42:2).
"Whatever the Lord pleases, He does, In heaven and in earth, in the seas and in all deeps" (Ps. 135:6).

The Lord overlooks all the earth.
Jesus by the Spirit wants to show what to God we are worth!

PM: Thank-You Note 116

Thank you, ABBA, Father, for sending power from on high.
Thank you, ABBA, Father, in Jesus drawing me nigh.
Thank you, ABBA, Father, for love and protection.
Thank you, ABBA, Father, that You keep me looking in heaven's direction!
Thank you, Lord Jesus, for sending the Holy Spirit daily.
Thank you, Lord Jesus, that in Your name I will trust plainly.
Thank you, Lord Jesus, for a Spirit refilling.
Thank you, Lord Jesus, for blessings that You're willing.
Thank you, Holy Spirit, for helping to rid my past.
Thank you, Holy Spirit, for changes that last.
Thank you, Holy Spirit, for daily new beginnings.
Thank you, Holy Spirit, that our walk is never ending!

"Now the Lord is the Spirit, and where the Spirit of the Lord is, there is freedom" (2 Cor. 3:17).
"For in Christ all the fullness of the Deity lives in bodily form" (Col. 2:9).

Thankfulness to God daily pays in the long run.
Jesus by the Spirit wants our life with thanksgiving to have begun!

A: CLOSET TIME 208

Holy Spirit, I need Your power to make this day.
Holy Spirit, I look to You for things I have to do and say.
Holy Spirit, my emotions and heart need renovation.
Holy Spirit, I need a new touch of revelation.
Holy Spirit, anoint my soul to overcome the enemy's tricks.
Holy Spirit, I look to You as my Guiding pick!
Holy Spirit, come and be my Coach.
Holy Spirit, with submission You I humbly approach.
Holy Spirit, help me retain tender and kind ways.
Holy Spirit, enhance how and when I pray.
Holy Spirit, come possess me that You may control.
Holy Spirit, keep me humbly in the fold!

"The Spirit of the LORD will rest on him—the Spirit of wisdom and of understanding, the Spirit of counsel and of might, the Spirit of the knowledge and fear of the LORD" (Isa. 11:2).

"And Peter said to them, 'Repent and be baptized every one of you in the name of Jesus Christ for the forgiveness of your sins, and you will receive the gift of the Holy Spirit'" (Acts 2:38).

FOLLOW JESUS 9

Follow Jesus as the Sermon on the Mount He is preaching.

Follow Jesus from the gutter of life a soul He is reaching.

Follow Jesus telling Sadducees, "Know not the Scripture nor God's power."

Follow Jesus as crowds flocked to Him all hours!

Follow Jesus as He speaks of His betrayer.

Follow Jesus as He shared the "Lord's Prayer."

Follow Jesus as He fights Satan in the wilderness.

Follow Jesus as He never forgets to be about ABBA's business.

Follow Jesus as disciples know the Holy Spirit is to come.

Follow Jesus as He tells them that godly they will become.

Follow Jesus as He washes their feet.

Follow Jesus when a God seeker He meets!

"'Who is He, Sir?' he replied. 'Tell me so that I may believe in Him.' 'You have already seen Him,' Jesus answered. 'He is the One speaking with you'" (John 9:36–38).

The Lord will always find those that wanting to be found.

Jesus by the Spirit has the power from sin to unbound!

Follow Jesus 8

Follow Jesus as He makes a market observation.
Follow Jesus as He starts a healing conversation.
Follow Jesus as leadership tries to set a speaking trap.
Follow Jesus as He responds with wisdom in a snap.
Follow Jesus as He pulls the disciples aside.
Follow Jesus when He tells them in Him they most abide.
Follow Jesus as He tries with ABBA, Father to barter.
Follow Jesus as He hears the request is going no farther.
Follow Jesus as He attempts to get disciples to pray.
Follow Jesus coming back as weary and sleepy they lay!
Follow Jesus as He protects His from harm.
Follow Jesus as He heals an ear to ease all alarm!

FOLLOW JESUS 7

Follow Jesus as tables are turned in disgust.
Follow Jesus when He pointed to a faith considered a must.
Follow Jesus as the blind to Him did come.
Follow Jesus as He marbled of ten healed there was only one!
Follow Jesus as He refuses religious speculations.
Follow Jesus as He highlights Spirit-led conversations.
Follow Jesus coming to the aid of a reject.
Follow Jesus as at the well living water she did accept.
Follow Jesus as He ridiculed religious pretense.
Follow Jesus as for the least of these He came to their defense.
Follow Jesus as He concerned for the shepherdless crowd.
Follow Jesus as celebrating ABBA, Father He did allow!

"When He saw the crowds, He felt empathy for them. They were confused and helpless, like sheep without a shepherd" (Matt. 9:36).

"Were not all ten cleansed?" Jesus asked. "Where then are the other nine?" (Luke 17:17).

Follow Jesus in the Gospel helps in "what would Jesus do?"
Jesus by the Spirit wants all in training too!

FOLLOW JESUS 6

Follow Jesus as He is awakened by the Spirit to go pray.
Follow Jesus as He leaves home for a prayer place away.
Follow Jesus to a dark area that was solitary.
Follow Jesus as in a still dark place He prayed unwary.
Follow Jesus as He exemplified the faith of a child.
Follow Jesus as He wouldn't allow children to be reviled.
Follow Jesus as He goes to retrieve from the tomb.
Follow Jesus as He saw the dead child in the room.
Follow Jesus as He taught the many what to believe.
Follow Jesus celebrating those that faith did receive!
Follow Jesus as the hypocrites He sternly rejected.
Follow Jesus as the meek and humble He gladly accepted!

"Very early in the morning, while it was still dark, Jesus got up, left the house and went off to a solitary place, where He prayed" (Mark 1:35).

"But Jesus called the children to Him and said, 'Let the little children come to Me, and do not hinder them! For the kingdom of God belongs to such as these'" (Luke 18:16).

As we look at an earthly Lord, He pointed to a Heavenly Father.
Jesus by the Spirit points to our Creator as no other!

Follow Jesus 5

Follow Jesus in the temple the smart He was confounding.
Follow Jesus not answering when it came demanding.
Follow Jesus at the wilderness Satan He engaged.
Follow Jesus as by quoting the Word heaven He paged!
Follow Jesus when He said, "You must be born again."
Follow Jesus when He scolded those acting vain.
Follow Jesus leaving Jerusalem crying.
Follow Jesus as He informed the disciples He was dying.
Follow Jesus when abruptly He came through the walls.
Follow Jesus as the disciple in awe on his knees falls.
Follow Jesus the infirm He daily heals.
Follow Jesus as with demons He quickly deals!

"You hypocrites! You know how to interpret the appearance of the earth and sky. Why don't you know how to interpret the present time?" (Luke 12:56).

"And Thomas answered and said to Him, 'My Lord and my God!'" (John 20:28).

The time of salvation is in its late stage.
Jesus by the Spirit from heaven continues to page!

FOLLOW JESUS 4

Follow Jesus as He multiplies the fish and loaves.
Follow Jesus as He quietly brings out people in droves.
Follow Jesus as the Holy Spirit come upon Him in full power.
Follow Jesus as Satan tried wiles at all hours.
Follow Jesus as the crowds to Him took.
Follow Jesus as His power the Romans couldn't overlook.
Follow Jesus as the woman made a daughter's appeal.
Follow Jesus as He pointed to her faith as being real.
Follow Jesus as the tax man was forgiving.
Follow Jesus as He questioned the disciples for not believing.
Follow Jesus as He tries to get a change of ending script.
Follow Jesus when His betrayal He did predict!

"He said to them, 'Why are you so afraid? Have you still no faith?'" (Mark 4:40).

"And the centurion standing opposite of Him, having seen that He breathed His last, thus said, 'Truly this man was *the* Son of God!'" (Mark 15:39).

A soldier boldly claims, "Truly this man was the Son of God," He was then and now.

Jesus by the Spirit ask believers to reach the lost somehow!

FOLLOW JESUS 3

Follow Jesus as He gets the Sadducees' attention.
Follow Jesus as He shows giving is not about pretension.
Follow Jesus as He rebukes for wrong teaching.
Follow Jesus as He assures that heaven salvation is releasing.
Follow Jesus as He heals a mother in bed.
Follow Jesus as He sits with drinkers instead.
Follow Jesus as He goes to the mount of transfiguration.
Follow Jesus at the well as He imparts salvation.
Follow Jesus as He directed a fisherman for tax money.
Follow Jesus in casting out demons how it seems funny.
Follow Jesus as He warned a sister of what was important.
Follow Jesus as He encouraged the reluctant!

"Later, as Jesus was dining at Matthew's house, many tax collectors and sinners came and ate with Him and His disciples" (Matt. 9:10).

"And He was transfigured before them; and His face shone like the sun, and His garments became as white as light" (Matt. 17:2).

Our Father did send heaven's best in Jesus.
Jesus by the Spirit wants to put back all our broken pieces!

FOLLOW JESUS 2

Follow Jesus as crowds pressed Him to a boat.
Follow Jesus as the multitude He taught on a float.
Follow Jesus as He consoled the widow with the dead son.
Follow Jesus as water turns to wine where He began.
Follow Jesus who speaks to the damsel to rise.
Follow Jesus as He habitually listens to Holy Spirit's advice.
Follow Jesus as He models abundant life living.
Follow Jesus as the Kingdom He gave to those receiving.
Follow Jesus as He rebukes disciples for unbelief.
Follow Jesus as to the destitute He brings relief.
Follow Jesus when He feeds the hungry.
Follow Jesus as the Pharisees with Him get angry.

"Then the disciples came to him and asked, 'Do you know that the Pharisees were offended when they heard this?'" (Matt. 5:12).

"Jesus got into the boat belonging to Simon and asked him to put out a little from shore. And sitting down, He taught the people from the boat" (Luke 5:3).

Our Lord has prepared the stage for eternal security.
Jesus by the Spirit has made God's gifts a reality!

TODAY...69

Today, I will be more concern for the shepherdless crowd.
Today, I will move away from the carnally loud.
Today, I will seek to be in ABBA, Father's view.
Today, I will ask the Holy Spirit to make me Christlike new.
Today, I will forgive anyone who sins against me.
Today, I will hope that Jesus in my ways they see.
Today, I will look to diligently obey.
Today, I will do whatever the Holy Spirit has to say.
Today, I will seek to renew a repentant mindset.
Today, I will deny myself and following Jesus not forget.
Today, I will listen to others with full attention.
Today, I will process listening for retention.

"This is the day that the LORD has made; we will rejoice and be glad in it" (Ps. 118:24).

"For God says, 'At just the right time, I heard you. On the day of salvation, I helped you. Indeed, the "right time" is now. Today is the day of salvation'" (2 Cor. 6:2).

The multitudes need to know that salvation has arrived.
Jesus by the Spirit tells us that the promises of God can be relied!

DEAR ABBA, FATHER 38

I come with a heart lifted to honor and exalt.
I come to serve, submit, and gain humility as a result.
I come to walk in the Spirit, not the flesh.
I come that my spirit and soul are afresh.
I come to be restored to a mindset easy to repent.
I come to strengthen my spirit for sinning to prevent.
I come to hate sin the way that You in the Word say.
I come to be refilled by the Holy Spirit for the Word to convey.
I come my heart to expose for Your perusal.
I come to confess and renounce hints of sin without refusal.
I come be rid of past strongholds that are a carryover.
I come by the Spirit in Jesus to fully recover!

"I am the LORD, and there is no other; there is no God but Me. I will equip you for battle…" (Isa. 45:5a).
"Let us therefore come boldly unto the throne of grace, that we may obtain mercy, and find grace to help in time of need" (Heb. 4:16).

God has an open-door policy to even to sinners.
Jesus by the Spirit wants the many to be saved beginners!

AM: THANK-YOU NOTE 116

Thank you, ABBA, Father, that I have faith to believe.
Thank you, ABBA, Father, that a new infilling I will receive.
Thank you, ABBA, Father, for a life worthy of blessings.
Thank you, ABBA, Father, that You keep me from regressing!
Thank you, Lord Jesus, for help to stay the faithful course.
Thank you, Lord Jesus, that You are my eternal Source!
Thank you, Lord Jesus, for the gift of being thankful.
Thank you, Lord Jesus, for making me graceful!
Thank you, Holy Spirit, that You are daily in me.
Thank you, Holy Spirit, for helping my spiritual eyes see.
Thank you, Holy Spirit, that You are faithful to convict.
Thank you, Holy Spirit, for helping me sin to quickly evict!

"To You, O God of my fathers, I give thanks and praise, For You have given me wisdom and power; Even now You have made known to me what we requested of You" (Dan. 2:23).

"I shall give thanks to You, for You have answered me, And You have become my salvation" (Ps. 118:21).

God still hears and answers sincere prayer request.
Jesus by the Spirit reminds us that God has the best!

M: Closet Time 208

Lord Jesus, You are the Pillar of my foundation.
Lord Jesus, You saved me from hell and damnation.
Lord Jesus, You rescued me from drugs and prison.
Lord Jesus, You set me in heavenly places and gave me reason.
Lord Jesus, You blessed my life for years.
Lord Jesus, today my utmost desire is to You be near.
Lord Jesus, I come to confess how You I failed.
Lord Jesus, possess me for You to best prevail.
Lord Jesus, anoint me to be gentle and kind.
Lord Jesus, lift my heart to what is holy and divine.
Lord Jesus, by the Spirit come and quiet my soul.
Lord Jesus, I ask to be made totally whole.
Lord Jesus, You are the Potter, I am the clay.
Lord Jesus, I go to the altar as a sacrifice I lay!

"When they had brought their boats to land, they left everything and followed Him" (Luke 5:11).

"Now this He said, signifying by what kind of death He would glorify God. And when He had spoken this, He said to him, 'Follow Me!'" (John 21:19).

Living with the best benefits heaven offers we must sell out.
Jesus by the Spirit allows testing for us to see what we are about!

E: Closet Time 207

ABBA, Father, You I worship and adore.
ABBA, Father, today I exalt and praise You more than before.
ABBA, Father, be my strength and Defender.
ABBA, Father, deliver me from being a pretender.
ABBA, Father, come renew my loyalty.
ABBA, Father, help me live in the truth that I am royalty.
ABBA, Father, search me from things that hinder.
ABBA, Father, restore my faith and soul by Thy finger.
ABBA, Father, take me to that Holies of Holies.
ABBA, Father, help me walk with a heart that is lowly.
ABBA, Father, refurbish in me a repentant mindset.
ABBA, Father, help me live each daily without regret.

"Guide me in your truth and teach me, for You are God my Savior, and my hope is in You all day long" (Ps. 25:5).

"Peace I leave with you; my peace I give you. I do not give to you as the world gives. Do not let your hearts be troubled and do not be afraid" (John 14:27).

There is peace, grace, and truth for the daily asking.

Jesus by the Spirit doesn't want worry when the enemy is attacking!

PM: THANK-YOU NOTE 115

Thank you, ABBA, Father, for a day of peace.

Thank you, ABBA, Father, for guilt that confession made at ease.

Thank you, ABBA, Father, for a love that is unconditional.

Thank you, ABBA, Father, that earth life is transitional.

Thank you, Lord Jesus, for angels that hear my name.

Thank you, Lord Jesus, that in forgiving You are the same.

Thank you, Lord Jesus, that You love the childlike humble.

Thank you, Lord Jesus, that You pick up those that stumble.

Thank you, Holy Spirit, that You advance the will of Jesus.

Thank you, Holy Spirit, for healing my broken pieces.

Thank you, Holy Spirit, for Your gentle outreach.

Thank you, Holy Spirit, for helping me to still preach!

"Be strong and courageous. Do not be afraid; do not be discouraged, for the LORD your God will be with you wherever you go" (Josh. 1:9).

"So do not fear, for I am with you; do not be dismayed, for I am your God. I will strengthen you and help you; I will uphold you with My righteous right hand" (Isa. 41:10).

Every possible insurance the Lord does provide.

Jesus by the Spirit wants all in Him to abide!

A: Closet Time 207

Holy Spirit, I come Your will and ways to seek.
Holy Spirit, I committed to hear when in my ears You speak.
Holy Spirit, I confess and renounce as all that offends.
Holy Spirit, on Your wisdom and revelation I depend.
Holy Spirit, increase in my spirit eternal hope.
Holy Spirit, grant me mercy and grace to cope.
Holy Spirit, search for what in me is needing purging.
Holy Spirit, I come Your will and guidance urging.
Holy Spirit, come possess me to be diligent.
Holy Spirit, in Jesus help me be spiritually vigilant.
Holy Spirit, redirect my steps in ABBA, Father's will.
Holy Spirit, make me quiet, confident and still!

"In you, Lord my God, I put my trust. I trust in you; do not let me be put to shame, nor let my enemies triumph over me" (Ps. 25:1–2).

"But me? I trust you, LORD! I affirm, 'You are my God'" (Ps. 31:14).

For God to work from His best, trusting must be a daily occurrence.

Jesus by the Spirit gives all promises God's assurance!

Dear Abba, Father 37

I come to bring You worship and glory.
I come in Your presence to take my spiritual inventory.
I come from sinful attitudes to be disarmed.
I come to empty my heart from all that is alarmed.
I come to be renewed in my spiritual thinking.
I come that from the well of eternity I am drinking!
I come to reject all the lies of hell.
I come to strengthen the things of God to tell.
I come to be empowered for facing the enemy's wiles.
I come to follow the Holy Spirit for Jesus all the while.
I come to be in sync with what are Your commands.
I come with a godly attitude meet life's demands!

TODAY...68

Today, I will look to the Lord who is my shield.
Today, I will the Holy Spirit for help in how I feel.
Today, I will be ABBA, Father's diligent seeker.
Today, I will allow the Holy Spirit to make me a better speaker.
Today, I will forgive no matter the infraction.
Today, I will trust You by the Spirit to be my point of action.
Today, I will ask for strengthening of my repentant mindset.
Today, I will seek the Holy Spirit to keep me from regret.
Today, I will lift Jesus as Lord of all.
Today, I will readily answer God's heavenly call.
Today, I will walk quiet, confident and still.
Today, I will ask, seek, and knock for a Holy Spirit refill!

"I said to myself, 'I will watch what I do and not sin in what I say. I will hold my tongue when the ungodly are around me'" (Ps. 39:1).

"Show me, LORD, my life's end and the number of my days; let me know how fleeting my life is" (Ps. 39:4).

Living for the Lord one day at time leads to years of learning.

Jesus by the Spirit wants us for the Kingdom of God to be yearning!

TALKING TO GOD

ABBA, Father, deliver me from Your wrathful rebuke.
When You discipline me, help me keep a godly attitude.
For when You do in anger the hurting goes deeply.
Your hand presses me down steadily.
In Your wrath, my flesh is sapped to its core.
Makes me repentant and never sin anymore.
My guilty sin has overwhelmed my head.
The weight of the guilt has made me a prisoner instead.
The wounds of my soul are sharp and festering.
All this as I hid my sin while in my heart was pestering.
I was troubled bowed down greatly.
There I was walking around in my sin vainly.
Deep within my loins, there was a hurting inflammation.
My failure to repent left my flesh in a state of consternation.
I am spiritually feeble and within severely broken.
Turmoil of heart all because with You I haven't spoken!

"Do not forsake me, O LORD; be not far from me, O my God. Come quickly to help me, O Lord my Savior" (Ps. 38:21–22).

It does not matter how far we stray, He is there to see how close we get.

Jesus by the Spirit of God's forgiveness He doesn't want us to forget!

176

AM: THANK-YOU NOTE 115

Thank you, ABBA, Father, for truth to live by.
Thank you, ABBA, Father, for daily wisdom on which to rely.
Thank you, ABBA, Father, that You never forsake.
Thank you, ABBA, Father, for a new Kingdom You did make!
Thank you, Lord Jesus, for blood that cover my vile sins.
Thank you, Lord Jesus, for help to expunge my heart within.
Thank you, Lord Jesus, that I am a new creation.
Thank you, Lord Jesus, for daily wisdom and revelation.
Thank you, Holy Spirit, for helping me to enjoy abundant living.
Thank you, Holy Spirit, for the new insights I'm receiving.
Thank you, Holy Spirit, that You are here to stay.
Thank you, Holy Spirit, for power to testify in Christlike Way!

"For such is God, Our God forever and ever; He will guide us until death" (Ps. 48:14).
"I will give thanks to You, O Lord my God, with all my heart, And will glorify Your name forever" (Ps. 86:12).

Daily thanksgiving will make us appreciate God for sure.
Jesus by the Spirit wants us to know diligence keeps salvation secure!

M: Closet Time 207

Lord Jesus, I come because You are the lifter of my head.
Lord Jesus, when trouble comes, I trust You instead.
Lord Jesus, help me not think of my troublers.
Lord Jesus, I look to You as my shield and Comforter.
Lord Jesus, I praise You for being the resurrection.
Lord Jesus, I exalt and worship You for salvation.
Lord Jesus, I honor Your work of recovery.
Lord Jesus, by the Spirit there is daily recovery.
Lord Jesus, anoint my mind as of You I testify.
Lord Jesus, by the Spirit my efforts verify.
Lord Jesus, I come to totally surrender.
Lord Jesus, I look to You as my Defender!

"My heart is steadfast, God, my heart is steadfast. I will sing, yes, I will sing praises" (Ps. 57:7).

"You, my brothers and sisters, were called to be free. But do not use your freedom to indulge the flesh; rather, serve one another humbly in love" (Gal. 5:13).

The Lord is nearer to those who sincerely call.
Jesus by the Spirit wants us to learn on our knees to fall!

LORD, I COME

Lord, I come as many have turned on me for no cause.
I daily check my heart as I spiritually pause.
Many have conspired to shut me down.
The faithful friends I have are few that I found.
But You are my Friend and my righteous shield.
As my troublers increase to You, I come with what I feel.
You are my glory and the lifter of my head.
Others want my demise, but You fill me with confidence instead.
Early morning, I call to You upon the throne.
As I continue in Your presence, I never feel alone!
Lord, I do pray for those who turn on me for no reason.
Lord, help them come to a genuine repentance season!
Thank you, Lord, for daily giving me sound sleep.
This morning, I turn to You my spirit and soul to keep!

"LORD, how they have increased who trouble me! Many *are* they who rise up against me. Many *are* they who say of me, '*There is no help for him in God*'" (Ps. 3:1–2).

When the many turn against you, the Lord is there.
Jesus by the Spirit always shows that God does care!

179

E: Closet Time 206

Holy Spirit, I come to know You for sure.
Holy Spirit, knowing Your near makes me feel secure.
Holy Spirit, I ask for ears to hear Your voice.
Holy Spirit, help me continue to make the Christlike choice.
Holy Spirit, anoint my mind to think on heaven above.
Holy Spirit, rekindle in me ABBA, Father's love.
Holy Spirit, strengthen my faith and believe.
Holy Spirit, empower my spirit from You to receive.
Holy Spirit, possess this temple to better serve.
Holy Spirit, grant me a mindset the will of God to best observe.
Holy Spirit, my devotion to seeking You is never ending.
Holy Spirit, so wait for the inner power You are sending!

"When the Advocate comes, whom I will send to you from the Father—the Spirit of truth who proceeds from the Father—He will testify about Me" (John 15:26).

"However, when the Spirit of truth comes, He will guide you into all truth. For He will not speak on His own, but He will speak what He hears, and He will declare to you what is to come" (John 16:13).

The Holy Spirit is a Person who wants to Help, especially believers.

Jesus by the Spirit teaches that the Holy Spirit can keep us from deceivers!

PM: Thank-You Note 114

Thank you, ABBA, Father, for love to win me over.
Thank you, ABBA, Father, that Jesus in me You will recover.
Thank you, ABBA, Father, for help to serve with honesty.
Thank you, ABBA, Father, for the Spirit with me constantly.
Thank you, Lord Jesus, for grace to live forgiving.
Thank you, Lord Jesus, that Your love I keep receiving!
Thank you, Lord Jesus, for life on the straight and narrow.
Thank you, Lord Jesus, that Your eyes my life follows.
Thank you, Holy Spirit, for wisdom to write well.
Thank you, Holy Spirit, for counsel in the Gospel to tell.
Thank you, Holy Spirit, that You wake me to pray.
Thank you, Holy Spirit, for helping me to follow the Way!

"One of them, when he saw he was healed, came back, praising God in a loud voice. He threw himself at Jesus' feet and thanked Him—and he was a Samaritan" (Luke 17:15–17).

Thanksgiving is a desired learned behavior.
Jesus by the Spirit teaches to always thank the Savior!

RRSS

Rise, Rejoice, Serve, and Seed!
Rise, Rejoice, Serve, and Seed.
Spreading the Gospel is our greatest deed.
In the Spirit, Satan cannot interrupt.
Shining the Light repels the corrupt.
Rising means with Jesus power.
Rejoicing starts at that first prayer hour.
Serving is the result of given grace.
Seeding we do at the Holy Spirit's pace.
The armor of God evil cannot penetrate.
Testifying is to be done and not hesitate.
By the Holy Spirit, we have a Christ mind.
At rise, rejoice, serve, and seed, Jesus we can find!

"Then they left the presence of the council, rejoicing that they were counted worthy to suffer dishonor for the name" (Acts 5:41).

"But Stephen, full of the Holy Spirit, looked intently into heaven and saw the glory of God and Jesus standing at the right hand of God" (Acts 7:55).

A godly attitude will help over the worse of testing.
Jesus by the Spirit helps us that it is good to come away resting!

SPIRITUAL FACTS

Fact: Christ came.
Fact: He died for the spiritually lame.
Fact: He resurrected!
Fact: In repentance, all forgiveness accepted.
Fact: All become a new creation.
Fact: Many benefits to Christ salvation.
Fact: Believers are free from sinful strife.
Fact: Jesus gives abundant life.
Fact: Jesus from heaven He looks.
Fact: He keeps names in His personal books.
Fact: All will be judged for their deeds.
Fact: It pays to daily plant Gospel seeds!

Fact: "Everyone the Father gives Me will come to Me, and the one who comes to Me I will never drive away" (John 6:37).
Fact: "Jesus answered, 'I am the way and the truth and the life. No one comes to the Father except through Me'" (John 14:6).

Spiritual facts are unchanging Truth.
Jesus by the Spirit send the Word just for you!

HEART CONFESSIONS

ABBA, Father, with You, all things are possible.
ABBA, Father, by the Blood of Jesus, all sins are washable.
ABBA, Father, in the Spirit, I come to confess and renounce.
ABBA, Father, by the Spirit, I want all hidden sin to denounce.
ABBA, Father, by the Spirit, expose sins to my mind.
ABBA, Father, in Jesus, come and see what You find.
ABBA, Father, I confess sexual sins within my soul.
ABBA, Father, I long to be made spiritually whole.
ABBA, Father, nothing is hidden from Your sight.
ABBA, Father, I ask in Jesus to be made right.
ABBA, Father, I will do what is needed.
ABBA, Father, in the Spirit let the healing be completed.

"Confess your sins to each other and pray for each other so that you may be healed. The earnest prayer of a righteous person has great power and produces wonderful results" (James 5:16).

"If we confess our sins, He is faithful and just and will forgive us our sins and purify us from all unrighteousness" (1 John 1:9).

Authentic heart confessions bring quick relief.
Jesus by the Spirit wants to strengthen what we belief!

OBEDIENCE: I MUST

Obedience is the building block to vibrant faith.
Obedience will help to the Holy Trinity relate.
I must learn to disregard what is convenient.
I must practice to be a servant that is Word obedient.
Obedience will make you pick up the cross.
Obedience will make us morn the wandering loss.
I must initiate obedience for grace to act it out.
I must exemplify obedience that others see what Christ is about.
Obedience is hard at first.
Obedience happens as for God we hunger and thirst.
Obedience is a most worthy sacrifice.
Obedience brings the best Holy Spirit advice!

"Walk in obedience to all that the Lord your God has commanded you, so that you may live and prosper and prolong your days in the land that you will possess" (Deut. 5:33).

"But Samuel replied, 'What is more pleasing to the LORD: your burnt offerings and sacrifices or your obedience to his voice? Listen! Obedience is better than sacrifice, and submission is better than offering the fat of rams'" (1 Sam. 15:22).

Obedience is prerequisite to being born again.
Jesus by the Spirit show that God blessings upon us will rain!

JESUS: LORD OF ALL!

Jesus: Lord of All!
Jesus changed the paradigm.
Jesus came that all in God live a long time.
Jesus came as all was prepared.
Jesus was born in a stable needing repair.
Jesus was visited by the very wise.
Jesus by the Spirit still gives perfect advice.
Jesus by ABBA, Father was protected.
Jesus as a child was well respected.
Jesus grew and died to save the world.
Jesus resurrecting His love unfurled.
Jesus in heaven daily will intercede.
Jesus saves and the enemy can't impede.

"God sent His Son into the world not to judge the world, but to save the world through Him" (John 3:17).

"But when the fullness of the time had come, God sent forth His Son, having been born of a woman, having been born under the Law" (Gal. 4:4).

As a child, He came as a Savior He resurrected.
Jesus by the Spirit tells all that only God's best is to be expected!

DARING TO OBEY 3

Daring to obey is an act of the will.
Daring to obey makes the Holy Spirit a heart fill.
In daring to obey, you invite God's best.
The person daring to obey in a storm finds rest.
Daring to obey is not for the uncommitted.
Daring to obey freedom in Jesus in totally permitted.
Those daring to obey are a rare kind of believer.
A benefit of daring to obey is easier to detect the deceiver.
Daring to obey by practice becomes second nature.
Daring to obey brings ABBA, Father in Jesus great pleasure!
Those daring to obey make winning souls a priority.
The daring to obey know who has ultimate authority.

"Remember, O LORD, your compassion and unfailing love, which you have shown from long ages past" (Ps. 25:6).
"But Peter and the apostles replied, 'We must obey God rather than any human authority'" (Acts 5:29).

Nothing advances spiritual growth like obeying.
Jesus by the Spirit ABBA's will is constantly relaying!

DARING TO OBEY 2

Daring to obey will take its toll.
Daring to obey will prompt others to be bold.
Daring to obey makes some believers full of cynicism.
Daring to obey often results in much criticism.
Daring to obey takes you in Jesus deeper.
Daring to obey makes clearer that Jesus is our Keeper.
Daring to obey helps to see heaven with clarity.
Daring to obey makes heaven's Book a reality.
Daring to obey will alter our spiritual perspective.
Daring to obey helps rid what in the heart is defective.
Daring to obey prevents from willful sin to stumble.
Daring to obey will increase the propensity to be humble!

"He guides the humble in what is right and teaches them his way" (Ps. 25:9).

"And He gives grace generously. As the Scriptures say, 'God opposes the proud but gives grace to the humble'" (James 4:6).

Practicing genuine humbleness has great heavenly rewards.
Jesus by the Spirit never forgets to give earned awards!

DARING TO OBEY 1

The earthly journey is tough when daring to obey.
Daring to obey has to be an inner aspiration every day.
God's promises are sure when daring to obey is the intent.
For the daring to obey miracles from heaven will be sent.
Daring to obey must have a "God first" motivation.
Daring to obey look for God's intervention.
The act of "daring to obey" will bring hell's fury.
God in Jesus will always be judge and jury!
Daring to obey welcomes when by God corrected.
Daring to obey, when disciplined by God will be accepted.
Daring to obey will avoid earthly strife.
Daring to obey will enjoy God's abundant life!

"All these blessings will come on you and accompany you if you obey the LORD your God" (Deut. 28:2).

"The thief's purpose is to steal and kill and destroy. My purpose is to give them a rich and satisfying life" (John 10:10).

Daring to daily obey makes for a childlike mindset.
Jesus by the Spirit reinforces obedience without regret!

LIES, LYING: LIAR 2

Lying is intended to hurt its recipient.
The liar is always a conniving participant.
Those that by design are liars do not consider the effect.
Liars are narcissistic and for others have no respect.
Liars push God far from time and mind.
Lying and liars look for friendship with those one of a kind.
Lying keeps the practitioner in Satan's grip.
Lies, lying and liars will all into hell's gate slip.
Lies, lying and liars opened the doors of sinful DNA.
Lying and liars, religious leaders misleading the way.
Lying and liars, Jesus by the Spirit did expose.
Lying and liars, repenting in Jesus can sins be dispose!

"You must not steal. You must not lie or deceive one another"
(Lev. 19:11).
"Don't lie to each other, for you have stripped off your old sinful
nature and all its wicked deeds" (Col. 3:9).

Habits of the past can impede Christlike growing.
Jesus by the Spirit wants our light to keep showing!

LIES, LYING: LIAR 1

When a lie is told, the enemy is manipulating.
Lies lead to being introspectively hating.
Lying is practicing what our heart has inclined.
In becoming a liar, your carnal senses have been refined.
Lying unchecked is habitually willful.
Liars judge others and lie very skillful.
Lie, lies, and lying are to a liar second-nature.
Liars disregard consequences as in lying they take pleasure.
Lie, lies, and lying leads the lying novice to fear.
Practicing any lying invites the enemy near.
Lying stunts any and all spiritual traction.
Lying makes the liar to live in constant reaction.

"You shall not give false testimony against your neighbor"
(Exod. 20:16).

"You belong to your father, the devil...refusing to uphold the
truth, because there is no truth in him. When he lies, he speaks his
native language, because he is a liar and the father of lies" (John
8:44).

Lying is part of the fallen nature to be eradicated.
Jesus by the Spirit being free from past sins is a plan God created!

DAILY INVENTORY 4

Daily inventory prevents an anemic godly life.
Daily inventory help foreseeing oncoming strife.
Daily inventory prepares for the worse.
Daily inventory meditates at least on one verse.
Daily inventory uses words with restrain.
Daily inventory in speaking aims to heal pain.
Daily inventory attempts to be all things to all men.
Daily inventory's objective is winning souls at the end.
Daily inventory works to live a life without reproach.
Daily inventory invites the Holy Spirit as their Coach.
Daily inventory increases a Christlike hunger and thirst.
Daily inventory seeks ABBA, Father in Jesus first!

"Search me, God, and know my heart; test me and know my anxious thoughts" (Ps. 139:23).

"But seek His kingdom, and these things will be added unto you" (Luke 12:31).

Whatever God wants out the replacement is outstanding.
Jesus by the Spirit wants believers in Kingdom life expanding!

DAILY INVENTORY 3

Daily inventory makes for a vibrant Christlike walk.
Daily inventory helps avoid all carnal talk.
Daily inventory is willing to make any sacrifice.
Daily inventory looks on how God's will to faithfully suffice.
Daily inventory gets to know the Holy Spirit firsthand.
Daily inventory trains to obey every command.
Daily inventory learns to esteem others more than self.
Daily inventory puts feelings on a shelf.
Daily inventory wants a new anointing and grace.
Daily inventory helps with the Holy Spirit to keep pace.
Daily inventory looks towards higher spiritual ground.
Daily inventory culminating desire is in Christ to be found!

"To the weak I became weak, to win the weak. I have become all things to all people so that by all possible means I might save some" (1 Cor. 9:22).

"For this reason, even though I suffer as I do, I am not ashamed; for I know whom I have believed, and I am convinced that He is able to guard what I have entrusted to Him for that day" (2 Tim. 1:12).

Self-inventory will manifest where Christlikeness is low.
Jesus by the Spirit wants God's changing power to show!

DAILY INVENTORY 2

Daily inventory of our spiritual walk is necessary.
Daily inventory helps to prepare for our adversary.
Daily inventory allows staying updated on our spiritual stock.
Daily inventory helps in prayer to ask, seek, and knock.
Daily inventory makes for facing our deficiencies.
Daily inventory upgrades for prayer closet efficiencies.
Daily inventory looks to the Word for prayer closet enhancing.
Daily inventory wants intimacy with the Trinity advancing.
Daily inventory is yearning with God to go deeper.
Daily inventory desires proximity to Jesus as Keeper.
Daily inventory ultimately cleanses the soul.
Daily inventory stays focused on becoming whole!

"So I say, let the Holy Spirit guide your lives. Then you won't be doing what your sinful nature craves" (Gal. 5:16).

"Work hard to show the results of your salvation, obeying God with deep reverence and fear" (Phil. 2:12b).

We are to bear fruit in our daily labor.
Jesus by the Spirit shows us we have godly favor!

DAILY INVENTORY 1

Every day, we could take spiritual inventory.
Did we prepare to go tell the Gospel story?
Is our hearing of the Word sufficient?
When meditating on the Word, is it efficient?
Are we aware that faith is assured by hearing it?
In the prayer closet, did we speak with the Holy Spirit?
Are we making the right prayer closet choices?
Are we distinguishing whose are the voices?
In the prayer closet are we to the Trinity drawing near?
Have we lost the universal "I can't pray" fear?
Taking inventory should be done every day.
Inventory helps develop prayer power the enemy to slay!

"Teach us to number our days, that we may gain a heart of wisdom" (Ps. 90:12).
"So be careful how you live. Don't live like fools, but like those who are wise. Make the most of every opportunity in these evil days" (Eph. 5:15–16).

Taking spiritual inventory is best done with God above.
Jesus by the Spirit majors in us doing the command of love!

TODAY...32

Today, I will be careful to speak with grace.
Today, I will keep my heart in a humble place.
Today, I will stay my distance from the crowd.
Today, I will train my soul not to be loud.
Today, I will boast only on the Lord.
Today, I will share Jesus hoping they come aboard.
Today, I will tell of what the Lord has done.
Today, I will rejoice that yesterday's sins are gone.
Today, I will declare how the Lord gave me mercy.
Today, I will share of forgiveness from deadly controversy.
Today, I will meditate on being set eternally free.
Today, I will seek to uplift and bring honor to Thee!

"But Jesus would not allow him. 'Go home to your own people,' He said, 'and tell them how much the Lord has done for you, and what mercy He has shown you'" (Mark 5:19).

"Therefore, if anyone is in Christ, the new creation has come: The old has gone, the new is here!" (2 Cor. 5:17).

Telling what God has done personally is faith in action.
Jesus by the Spirit wants us to gain Spirit-led traction!

Humbly Ask

Jesus is aware of the hurt and how we're broken.
Jesus will heal by His command spoken.
He is faithful to see how we are doing.
He waits for an invite to take charge where we are going.
Jesus is an ever-present Friend.
We need not wait to ask till it is almost the end.
Daily ask for grace to handle with the mindset of Jesus.
Ask the Holy Spirit to help pick up the pieces.
The undertaking will be a sensitive task.
Remember that all we need is to ask.
Asking will get prayer answers quick at all hours.
Jesus loves to showcase His eternal powers!

"That night God appeared…and said, 'What do you want? Ask, and I will give it to you!'" (2 Chron. 1:7).
"You want what you don't have, so you scheme…to get it… Yet you don't have what you want because you don't ask God for it" (James 4:2).

Any significant change is just a matter of asking.
Jesus by the Spirit wants our sins to continue unmasking!

CHANGING CLOTHES

The prayer closet is for changing clothes.
Yesterday's attire needs change for others to behold.
Changing clothes is a daily task.
In the prayer closet, we change clothes as we learn to ask.
The closet is full of clothes that are tailored made.
At the clothing exchange, the price has been paid.
Changing clothes daily in the prayer closet is essential.
Changing clothes can enhance a spiritual potential.
Changing clothes will never incur shame.
Changing clothes happens without any blame.
Changing clothes for the day ahead will take time to equip.
Changing clothes will take adjusting to fit.
Changing clothes in the prayer closet is never the same.
Changing clothes is all readied in His name!

"You were taught, with regard to your former way of life, to put off your old self, which is being corrupted by its deceitful desires; to be made new in the attitude of your minds; and to put on the new self, created to be like God in true righteousness and holiness" (Eph.4:22–24).

A new way of living happens when we get rid ways that are old.
Jesus by the Spirit wants to make us obedient to what we are told!

WHY?

Why a devout Abel is murdered by his brother?
Why Joseph's siblings rescuing him did not bother?
Why did Job have to suffer so unnecessary?
Why did Elijah have to leave town in a hurry?
Why so many babies slaughtered trying to find baby Jesus?
Why was Jerusalem (with humans) had to be broken to pieces?
Why did so many have to die in the flood?
Why did Jesus have to shed His blood?
Why did Peter and others died being killed?
Why did Jesus dying at the cross needed to be fulfilled?
Why did Lazarus have to die to be resurrected?
Why is it that to have eternal life Jesus has to be accepted?

"The LORD observed the extent of human wickedness on the earth, and he saw that everything they thought or imagined was consistently and totally evil" (Gen. 6:5).

"I have told you these things so that in Me you may have peace. In the world you will have tribulation. But take courage; I have overcome the world!" (John 16:33).

Our Father is a God of mercy and justice for all.
Jesus by the Spirit answers when in His name we call!

TODAY...42

Today, I will avoid all semblances of doubt.
Today, I will listen to the Word for greater faith to find out.
Today, I will encourage the weak.
Today, I will accept evil by turning the other cheek.
Today, I will not ponder on evil others have to say.
Today, I will by the Spirit do things God's way.
Today, I will not think or speak of the past.
Today, I will consider when in heaven I'm at last.
Today, I will not fret or despair.
Today, I will the Gospel share.
Today, I will not be ashamed to confess sin.
Today, I will in the prayer closet my day begin!

"For as he thinks in his heart, so is he..." (Prov. 23:7a)
"What you say flows from what is in your heart" (Luke 6:45b).

The eyes of God are for the diligent who obey.
Jesus by the Spirit will always be the only Way!

A: Closet Time 206

ABBA, Father, increase my trust.
ABBA, Father, help increase my prayer closet which is a must.
ABBA, Father, renew my sense of devotion.
ABBA, Father, in Jesus I look to You for promotion.
ABBA, Father, I want to You be pleasing.
ABBA, Father, I ask Your power in me to be releasing.
ABBA, Father, strengthen my will to be God fearing.
ABBA, Father, by the Spirit to You I want to be nearing.
ABBA, Father, make me like Your only Begotten.
ABBA, Father, by the Spirit Your perfect will in me is not forgotten.
ABBA, Father, by the Spirit help me to serve You only.
ABBA, Father, as You are holy help me to be holy!

"After this manner therefore pray ye: Our Father which art in heaven, Hallowed be Thy name" (Matt. 6:9).
"Jesus replied: 'Love the Lord your God with all your heart and with all your soul and with all your mind'" (Matt. 22:37).

Transferring all our devotions to God is always the best deal.
Jesus by the Spirit makes certain that loving God first is real!

M: Closet Time 180

ABBA, Father, I worship and exalt You this day.
ABBA, Father, Your presence is where I want to stay.
ABBA, Father, my heart is fixated on Your perfect will.
ABBA, Father, I come to learn being quiet and still.
ABBA, Father, to You my sins I do confess.
ABBA, Father, by the Spirit advance my holiness.
ABBA, Father, let no semblance of sin in me reside.
ABBA, Father, in Your shadow I am prepared to hide.
ABBA, Father, Your protection for me is rewarding.
ABBA, Father, the Word in my heart I will continue hoarding.
ABBA, Father, accumulating the Word is fulfilling.
ABBA, Father, I ask for a Holy Spirit refilling.

"Our God is in heaven; He does whatever pleases Him" (Ps. 115:3).
"The heart of man plans His way, but the Lord establishes His steps" (Prov. 16:9).

Our Father is extremely watchful of faithfully devote.
Jesus by the Spirit wants all to know what God's power is about!

DISTRACTIONS 2

Distractions is fighting with leadership.
Distractions is when making God first we slip.
Distractions happen when we decide our own offering.
Distractions is not having solid spiritual covering.
Distractions is in a spiritual desert complaining.
Distractions is when judging we justify remaining.
Distractions is playing the blame game.
Distractions is years later you are spiritually the same.
Distractions come easy to those gullible to receive.
Distractions are the enemy's ways to deceive.
Distractions are by some done when projecting.
Distractions come when the full Word we are not accepting!

"'You will not certainly die,' the serpent said to the woman" (Gen. 3:4).
"The thief comes only to steal and kill and destroy; I have come that they may have life, and have it to the full" (John 10:10).

The enemy will always focus on delaying our potential.
Jesus by the Spirit teach us what is spiritually essential!

Distractions 1

The enemy distracted Adam from God's declaration.
Distractions manifest as we add to God's expectation.
The distractions were further magnified.
Distractions come when the enemy's wisdom is relied.
The enemy distracted by appealing to the emotions.
Distractions can make one feel they are worthy devotions.
Ultimately, the distraction was physically consummated.
Distractions are strengthened when we have "ate it."
Distractions come listening and looking.
Distractions are baits the enemy wants someone hooking.
Distractions is not wanting Jesus to go to the cross.
Distractions are talks that does not help someone loss!

"For God knows that when you eat from it your eyes will be opened, and you will be like God, knowing good and evil" (Gen. 3:5).

"And ought not this woman…whom Satan bound for eighteen years, be loosed from this bond…" (Luke 13:16).

Lies and deceptions are keeping many bound.
Jesus by the Spirit details that in salvation healing is found!

Betrayers Come

Betrayers come with much disguise.
Betrayers come to act like they are on your side.
Betrayers come to strike when you least expect.
Betrayers come while giving their target respect.
Betrayers come as creative in their approach.
Betrayers come to engage the crowd much.
Betrayers come to see if they subtly can recruit.
Betrayers come to inspect all willing fruit.
Betrayers come prepared to be filled.
Betrayers come for the moment when by Satan they're willed!
Betrayers come until their final act.
Betrayers come to live a miserable life and that's a fact.

"Then Satan entered Judas Iscariot, who was one of the Twelve" (Luke 22:3).

"Arise, let's be going. Behold, he who betrays Me is at hand" (Matt. 26:46).

Betrayal is Satan's most heinous ploy.
Jesus by the Spirit will show how in all circumstances we can have eternal joy!

BETRAYAL

Betrayal wants you on the cross for wrong reasons.
Betrayal is fashionable at all seasons.
Betrayal is a hellish perfected wile.
Betrayal is often done with a blatant smile.
Betrayal is always ready to spring the trap.
Betrayal is often done in a mindset of recap.
Betrayal is definitely a carnal sin like no other.
Betrayal once done is hard from it to recover.
Betrayal will lead to a life of double-mind at best.
Betrayal will leave the perpetrator without rest.
Betrayal will take you to a spiritual ledge.
Betrayal keeps you living at hell's edge!

"For it is not an enemy who insults me; that I could endure. It is not a foe who rises against me; from him I could hide. But it is you, a man like myself, my companion and close friend" (Ps. 55:12–13).

Betrayal is harsh to process and heal.
Jesus by the Spirit knows in all circumstances how you feel!

TODAY...67

Today, I will forgive even when betrayed.
Today, I will show how forgiving is daily portrayed.
Today, I will focus on who I am in Christ.
Today, I will seek direct Holy Spirit advice.
Today, I will shed any hint of sinful behavior.
Today, I will look intently at my Savior.
Today, I will esteem others more than myself.
Today, I will leave my feelings on a sacrificial shelf.
Today, I will be slow to speak and fast to hear.
Today, I with let the speaker know that I'm all ear.
Today, I will look to be Holy Spirit refilled.
Today, I will sacrifice being self-willed!

"He will call on Me, and I will answer him; I will be with him in trouble, I will deliver him and honor him" (Ps. 91:5).
"I will save you from the hands of the wicked and deliver you from the grasp of the cruel" (Jer. 15:21).

Honesty with God will get you what you need.
Jesus by the Spirit motivates the devote to plant a daily seed!

DEAR ABBA, FATHER 36

I come this morning my heart to You expose.
I come my sins and faults to openly disclose.
I come to walk today honoring You deep within.
I come to purge and flush out all hint of sin.
I come to walk in the Spirit and not the flesh.
I come to be forgiving, renewed, and refreshed.
I come to rekindle Word and Your deeds meditation.
I come to solidify commitment to sanctification.
I come to be restored to the faith of a child.
I come to forgive betrayers who do it with a smile.
I come to gain my spiritual equilibrium.
I come to ask for the faith of heaven that is premium!

"Purify me from my sins, and I will be clean; wash me, and I will be whiter than snow" (Ps. 51:7).

"I, the LORD, invite you to come and talk it over. Your sins are scarlet red, but they will be whiter than snow or wool" (Isa. 1:18).

God is not interested how bad you are, He is interested in how good you will become.

Jesus by the Spirit will never leave a believer alone!

AM: THANK-YOU NOTE 114

Thank you, ABBA, Father, for Your eternal assurance.
Thank you, ABBA, Father, by the Spirit I've gained endurance.
Thank you, ABBA, Father, that of me You are protective.
Thank you, ABBA, Father, that all Your ways are effective!
Thank you, Lord Jesus, that You shed blood for me.
Thank you, Lord Jesus, for going to Calvary!
Thank you, Lord Jesus, for Your resurrection.
Thank you, Lord Jesus, for securing my sanctification!
Thank you, Holy Spirit, for always helping even when I fail.
Thank you, Holy Spirit, that Your intervention prevails.
Thank you, Holy Spirit, for possessing me.
Thank you, Holy Spirit, for forging in me Jesus that others can see!

Was there no one found to return and to give thanks *and* praise to God, except this foreigner?" (Luke 17:18).
"However, those the Father has given me will come to me, and I will never reject them" (John 6:37).

Thankfulness is an indicator of a genuine transformation.
Jesus by the Spirit continues to promote great expectations!

M: Closet Time 206

Lord Jesus, help me to throw caution to the wind.
Lord Jesus, for Your perfect will I'm all in.
Lord Jesus, purge what needs to be extracted.
Lord Jesus, flush out all hint of sin I am still attracted.
Lord Jesus, restore what the locust has eaten.
Lord Jesus, help conquer mind sins of which I feel beaten!
Lord Jesus, help me Holy Spirit filled.
Lord Jesus, deliver me of taking for granted what You have willed!
Lord Jesus, anoint me to be more gentle and kind.
Lord Jesus, bless me in helping others salvation to find.
Lord Jesus, deliver me from the sin of not interceding.
Lord Jesus, release in me a deeper sense of believing!

"Jesus…said, 'I am the light of the world. Whoever follows Me will never walk in the darkness, but will have the light of life'" (John 8:12).

"All the people saw this and began to mutter, 'He has gone to be the guest of a sinner'" (Luke 19:7).

God will break any norm that impedes testifying.
Jesus by the Spirit the Word is always verifying!

E: Closet Time 205

ABBA, Father, my spirit longs to know You with intimacy.
ABBA, Father, I want to know You literally.
ABBA, Father, show me Your glory.
ABBA, Father, strengthen my soul to better tell Your story.
ABBA, Father, release me from all strongholds of the past.
ABBA, Father, develop in me intimacy that will last.
ABBA, Father, help me to be quiet, confident and still.
ABBA, Father, in Jesus grant a Holy Spirit refill.
ABBA, Father, renew in me to be kind and humble.
ABBA, Father, help me that my faith I do not fumble.
ABBA, Father, take me to Your secret place.
ABBA, Father, I yearn to look upon Your face.
ABBA, Father, heal me from all that You I offend.
ABBA, Father, in Jesus by the Spirit on You I depend!

"My help comes from the LORD, the Maker of heaven and earth" (Ps. 121:2).
"I called on the LORD, who is worthy of praise, and He saved me from my enemies" (Ps. 18:3).

Staying focus on God even from our enemies we are secure.
Jesus by the Spirit wants our hearts on things above for sure!

PM: THANK-YOU NOTE 113

Thank you, ABBA, Father, for the treasure of Your Word.
Thank you, ABBA, Father, for favor to believe what I heard.
Thank you, ABBA, Father, for all others provisions.
Thank you, ABBA, Father, that in Jesus I have eternal permission.
Thank you, Lord Jesus, for being my Substitute.
Thank you, Lord Jesus, there is no other like You.
Thank you, Lord Jesus, for help to daily trust.
Thank you, Lord Jesus, that You helped me beyond sinful lust.
Thank you, Holy Spirit, for helping to live above the crowd.
Thank you, Holy Spirit, for making me for ABBA, Father loud!
Thank you, Holy Spirit, that of the Gospel I am not shame.
Thank you, Holy Spirit, for helping me be free from sin's blame!

"Blessed is the man to whom the Lord will not impute sin" (Rom. 4:8).

"For the gospel reveals the righteousness of God that comes by faith from start to finish, just as it is written: "The righteous will live by faith" (Rom. 1:17).

Thanking God every day reduces the cares of this world.
Jesus by the Spirit gives clarity to the love ABBA has unfurl!

LISTEN TO ME 15

Listen to Me, the promises are by God told.
Listen to Me, they are sure and bold.
Listen to Me, I trusted all promises when I came.
Listen to Me, the promises are the same.
Listen to Me, don't get distracted.
Listen to Me, meditate until to you they are attracted.
Listen to Me, at age twelve I knew my stuff.
Listen to Me, that is how I made Satan's life rough.
Listen to Me, the Word in you equips the Spirit best.
Listen to Me, promises in you give much rest.
Listen to Me, the Word doesn't return void.
Listen to Me, meditating on promises is best the choice!

"But whose delight is in the law of the LORD, and who meditates on his law day and night" (Ps. 1:2).

"Jesus answered and said to them, 'This is the work of God, that you believe in Him whom He has sent'" (John 6:29).

Meditating on the Word comes loaded with great results.
Jesus by the Spirit will in getting rid of all faults!

LISTEN TO ME 14

Listen to Me, meditation of the Word is compulsory.
Listen to Me, failure to meditate is spiritual slumbery.
Listen to Me, lack of meditation makes believers weak.
Listen to Me, daily meditation makes the proud meek.
Listen to Me, meditation kept Me in the straight and narrow.
Listen to Me, meditation made it easy the Holy Spirit to follow.
Listen to Me, meditation allows ABBA, Father to intercede.
Listen to Me, meditation gives the Holy Spirit ability to lead.
Listen to Me, meditation fends off the enemy's attacks.
Listen to Me, meditation keeps you on godly tracks.
Listen to Me, meditation is excellent for the soul.
Listen to Me, meditation will make a broken person whole!

"I will meditate on Your precepts, And regard Your ways. I shall delight in Your statutes; I shall not forget Your word" (Ps. 119:15–16).
"Practice these things, immerse yourself in them, so that all may see your progress" (1 Tim. 4:15).

Daily meditation will keep the enemy away.
Jesus by the Spirit works hard to get us to daily pray!

LISTEN TO ME 13

Listen to Me, all is prepared for Your success.
Listen to Me, intimacy with the Spirit the greater I bless.
Listen to Me, at the baptism the Holy Spirit came in full power.
Listen to Me, my ability to act was altered that very hour.
Listen to Me, at that moment, the Holy Spirit had full control.
Listen to Me, I could hear better and easier to be bold.
Listen to Me, the Holy Spirit's power has not diminished.
Listen to Me, the Helper directed until I said, "It is finished."
Listen to Me, then as Comforter He raised Me from the dead.
Listen to Me, as I got to heaven I sent Him back instead.
Listen to Me, the Spirit can possess you as He did Me.
Listen to Me, only by possessing you, then you too like Me will be!

"I will pray to the Father, and He will give you another Counselor, that He may be with you forever" (John 14:16).

"I will not leave you as orphans; I will come to you" (John 14:18).

Besides salvation, He modeled what abundant life was like.
Jesus by the Spirit will take on a long spiritual hike!

LISTEN TO ME 12

Listen to Me, I have called you to eternal living.
Listen to Me, stop letting the enemy keep deceiving.
Listen to Me, by the Holy Spirit, I am always near.
Listen to Me, the Spirit will tell what you need to hear.
Listen to Me, let my Word in You abide.
Listen to Me, as you abide from Me you won't hide.
Listen to Me, know the Holy Spirit well.
Listen to Me, all My strategies to you He will tell.
Listen to Me, as trials and testing come don't despair.
Listen to Me, the Holy Spirit will be there!

"Abide in Me, and I in you. As the branch cannot bear fruit of itself, unless it abides in the vine, neither can you, unless you abide in Me" (John 15:4).

"However, when the Spirit of truth comes, He will guide you into all truth. For He will not speak on His own, but He will speak what He hears, and He will declare to you what is to come" (John 16:13).

The greater attention we pay to the Word the better off we are. Jesus by the Spirit will not allow to stray far!

LISTEN TO ME 11

Listen to Me, from the throne, nothing escapes My vision.
I am prepared to assist servants fulfill their commission.
Listen to Me, in heaven, I speak of those who openly share.
Listen to Me, the Holy Spirit will always be there.
He knows how to best fulfill your prepared perfect will.
Listen to Me, the Spirit helps you be quiet, confident, and still.
Listen to Me, resources in heaven have not diminished.
Listen to Me, I will not leave you till all is finished.
Listen to Me, don't become lukewarm!
Listen to Me, warnings are to keep you focus not harm.
ABBA Father in My name is jubilant to receive you!
Listen to Me, I look for your coming, too!

"Do not fear, for I have redeemed you; I have called you by your name; you are Mine!" (Isa. 43:1b).
"The Lord knoweth them that are His. And, let every one that nameth the name of Christ depart from iniquity" (2 Tim. 2:19b).

Pretense is obsolete with God since He knows the elect.
Jesus by the Spirit will show all the Kingdom and what to expect!

LISTEN TO ME 10

Listen to Me, caring for you will never decrease.
I am delighted by those ABBA, Father want to please.
Listen to Me, there is special favor for diligent seekers.
Listen to Me, those planting will become reapers.
Listen to Me, witnessing is a matter of knowing Me.
Sharing a testimony is what I have done that others see.
Listen to Me, I will give you beyond your necessities.
The Holy Spirit will advance your spiritual realities.
Listen to Me, at the closet, give the Spirit your will.
Listen to Me, He will increase Me in you to be fulfill.
Listen to Me, the Holy Spirit has much to say.
Listen to Me, by the Holy Spirit continue to pray!

"And your ears shall hear a word behind you, saying, 'This is the way, walk in it,' when you turn to the right or when you turn to the left" (Isa. 30:21).

"Behold, I send forth the promise of my Father on you. But wait...until you are clothed with power from on high" (Luke 24:49).

The relentless seekers of God enjoy be Holy Spirit guided.
Jesus by the Spirit looks for those that for God are decided!

LISTEN TO ME 9

Listen to Me, trials, traps, and testings I felt the likes.
Listen to Me, the pain was searing as they hit the spikes.
Listen to Me, on earth, I dodged sin everywhere.
Listen to Me, ABBA, Father and Spirit was always there.
Listen to Me, Spirit guided control kept Me above the fray.
Listen to Me, Holy Spirit always knew the best way.
Listen to Me, "Render to Caesar" was from the Spirit's mind.
He was faithful to deliver Me from the evil and unkind.
Listen to Me, the Holy Spirit the highest credentials.
He will accomplish changes that are prerequisite and essential.
My child, the baptism in and with the Holy Spirit will not expire.
Listen to Me, this baptism will endue power and holy fire.
Listen to Me, the Spirit can extract heart impurities.
His expertise will expedite all essential growth and maturities.

"'Come, follow Me,' Jesus said, 'and I will make you fishers of men'" (Matt. 4:19).

"Jesus answered, 'I am the way and the truth and the life. No one comes to the Father except through Me'" (John 14:6).

Beyond salvation there is much to enjoy and achieve.
Jesus by the Spirit wants our faith ready to always receive!

LISTEN TO ME 8

Daily I knock on the door of your heart for accessibility.
Letting Me into your heart allows Me to extract deformities.
You accepted Me as Savior, I must be your Lord.
There are things in your heart that you cannot afford.
Listen to Me, the Holy Spirit can right the wrong.
Listen to Me, allow Him access, it won't take long.
Listen to Me, testifying advances the healing.
Listen to Me, all is by faith, not by feelings.
Listen to Me, the Holy Spirit must have total control.
Listen to Me, submit your will and you'll be lovingly bold.
Listen to Me, walk in the Spirit and avoid the flesh.
Listen to Me, the Trinity will keep you spiritually afresh!

"Jesus said to the people who believed in him, 'You are truly my disciples if you remain faithful to my teachings'" (John 8:31).
"My sheep listen to My voice; I know them, and they follow Me" (John 10:27).

All for believers has been prepared and tested.
Jesus by the Spirit on His authority has rested!

LISTEN TO ME 7

Listen to Me, in resurrecting, I have all power and authority.
Listen to Me, abiding in Me and My Word, you are priority.
Listen to Me, I gave Gideon a complete makeover.
Listen to Me, I was there to help Joshua recover.
Listen to Me, I gave strength to Job in temptations.
Listen to Me, I made Daniel great in public relations.
Listen to me, Solomon just asked and got over and above.
Listen to Me, obey and I will tackle you with love.
Listen to Me, I rescued Jabez from a life of despair.
Listen to Me, as he prayed his life, I did repair.
Listen to Me, for I am Lord of all.
Listen to Me, even the "least of these," I answer the call!

"Then Jesus came to them and said, 'All authority in heaven and on earth has been given to Me'" (Matt. 28:18).
"Behold, I have given you authority to tread on snakes and scorpions, and over all the power of the enemy. Nothing will harm you" (Luke 10:19).

In His name, we have the same power.
Jesus by the Spirit works to remind us who we are all hours!

LISTEN TO ME 6

Listen to Me, remember that I called you My friend.
Listen to Me, disciples knew that I was there till the end.
Listen to Me, after Peter denied, I came to restore.
Listen to Me, as he repented, his sin was no more.
Listen to me, I sent him to "feed My sheep."
Listen to Me, in my vision, disciples I keep.
Listen to Me, I came to Thomas who was full of doubt.
Listen to Me, he said, "My Lord and My God," with a shout.
Listen to Me, I came through walls as they cowered with fear.
Listen to Me, their fear left as I came near.
Listen to Me, I am forever Lord of all!
Listen to Me, by the Holy Spirit continue to call!

"But those who wait upon the LORD will renew their strength; they will mount up with wings like eagles; they will run and not grow weary, they will walk and not faint" (Isa. 40:31).

"I will not leave you as orphans; I will come to you" (John 14:18).

Those that are relentless for Him have all of His resources.
Jesus by the Spirit will provide all of heaven's forces!

LISTEN TO ME 5

Listen to Me, daily I intercede for you to be wiser and bold.
Listen to Me, failure to testify will make you cold.
Listen to Me, while on earth, I went around doing good.
Listen to Me, the Spirit took Me to planting seeds were I could.
Listen to Me, the Spirit knows all My plans just for you.
Listen to Me, the is your Coach, too!
Listen to Me, He coached the disciples in what to say.
Listen to Me, baptized in the Holy Spirit, they could follow His way.
Listen to Me, you need to ask for the baptism in the Spirit and fire.
Listen to Me, baptizing devoted disciples is My utmost desire.
Listen to Me, I will only give what is best.
Listen to Me, as sheep humbly come and find rest!

"I said, 'Oh, that I had the wings of a dove! I would fly away and be at rest'" (Ps. 55:6).
"Come to Me, all you who are weary and burdened, and I will give you rest" (Matt. 11:28).

Those that Spirit guided know when to rest.
Jesus by the Spirit for devoted believers has His best!

LISTEN TO ME 4

Listen to Me, the promises I left you are time tested.
Listen to Me, real disciples hope and faith on My Word rested.
Listen to Me, all promises are with prerequisite conditions.
Listen to Me, as conditions are met you have My permission.
Listen to Me, not one promise of My will ever fail.
Listen to Me, all things humbly done in My name will prevail.
Listen to Me, all promises are for those that are pure in heart.
Listen to Me, you must rid self of any hint of sin from the start.
Listen to Me, submit to the Holy Spirit as He knows what to do.
Listen to Me, the Holy Spirit came to be the perfect Friend for you.
Listen to Me, the journey to heaven is arduous at time.
Listen to Me, you can trust on every promise that is Mine!

"Then Yahweh said to me, 'You have seen well; for I watch over my word to perform it'" (Jer. 1:12).

"For...promises God has made, they are 'Yes' in Christ. And so through Him the 'Amen' is spoken by us to the glory of God" (2 Cor. 1:20).

The promises of God are backed by His assurance.

Jesus by the Spirit commits to promises by His name as insurance!

LISTEN TO ME 3

I Am before anything that was created.
I Am when all has burned and faded.
I Am the One who made you in my imagination.
I Am the One who saw you at conception.
I Am the One who has eternal plans.
I Am the One who wants you following my commands.
I Am the One who daily puts You to rest.
I Am the One who will always want your perfect best.
I Am the One who knows it all.
I Am the One who daily yearns for your faithful call.
I Am the One that for you died and resurrected.
I Am the One you will see with the elected.

"God said…, 'I AM WHO I AM. This is what you are to say… I AM has sent me to you'" (Exod. 3:14).

"Jesus said to them, 'Most assuredly, I say to you, before Abraham was, I AM'" (John 8:58).

The Creator of all wants to use the least of us while blessing.
Jesus by the Spirit does not want anyone regressing!

LISTEN TO ME 2

Listen to Me, as I Am the First and the Last.
Listen to Me, so I can show you were the net should be cast.
Listen to Me, I will still the storms raging with demand.
Listen to Me, even a fish knows to obey My command.
Listen to Me, I will heal betrayals, rejection, and much more.
Listen to Me, in your behalf I keep, I will even the score.
Listen to Me, I maintain the exclusive power to resurrect.
Listen to Me, I pay close attention to My blood bought elect!
Listen to Me, I can uproot a tree with My voice.
Listen to Me, when trials come you will always be poised.
Listen to Me, come drink from the well of renewal.
Listen to Me, I paid for you, making you My crown jewel!

"My word…will not return to Me empty, but it will accomplish what I please, and it will prosper where I send it" (Isa. 55:11).
"God will supply all your needs according to His glorious riches in Christ Jesus" (Phil. 4:19).

There is a place of assurance that all He will provide.
Jesus by the Spirit lets us know the prayer closet is the best morning place to hide!

LISTEN TO ME 1

Truly I AM the beginning and the end.
In My power to a hurting world, you I did send.
Not forsaking you means I will be there.
I stood up in heaven for Stephen out of My eternal care.
Nothing happens to you that passes My sight.
As the elect, you inherited being an eternal light.
All of My power by the Holy Spirit can bring great results.
As you confess and renounce sin, I release you from faults.
You have a heavenly tailor-made perfect will.
As your Lord, beyond the prayer closet, be quiet and still.
You see, the Holy Spirit speaks at all times.
In a quiet and still spirit He can easily align!

"The LORD your God will raise up for you a prophet like me from among you, from your fellow Israelites. You must listen to Him" (Deut. 18:15).

"The Spirit is the one who gives life! Human strength can do nothing. The words that I have spoken to you are from that life-giving Spirit" (John 6:63).

The Lord speaks to elevate our spirit to a higher perspective.
Jesus by the Spirit gives us Word directive!

SPECIAL DELIVERY!

Serving God in Christ is a lot of fun.
Only as our day in the prayer closet has begun.
Listening to the Word has to be a must.
Walking by faith is how in God we trust.
We must daily go about doing good.
Honoring the Trinity we should.
There is ABBA, Father answering our call.
The Lord Jesus is worth on our knees to fall.
The Holy Spirit is ready to take us on mission.
The Holy Spirit opens eyes to see the vision.
Serving is fun if we keep a heavenly attitude.
Come to the prayer closet with gratitude.

"Enter His gates with thanksgiving and His courts with praise; give thanks to Him and bless His name" (Ps. 100:4).

"I have hidden your word in my heart, that I might not sin against you" (Ps. 119:11).

The best way to not sin against God is putting the Word in our heart.

Jesus by the Spirit will help love the Word from the start!

Penetrating Words!

Words that penetrate from eternity had to be written.
Words that penetrate help those heart smitten.
Words that penetrate are God's original intent.
Words that penetrate help those that genuinely repent.
Words that penetrate help as to God we are submitted.
Words that penetrate will heal from all sins committed.
Words that penetrate divides the spirit and intellect.
Words that penetrate deserves the highest respect.
Words that penetrate had been sinfully overlooked.
Words that penetrate God found a way to get man hooked.
Words that penetrate dwelled among creation.
Words that penetrate in Jesus can bring eternal salvation!

"But the word is very near to you, in your mouth, and in your heart, that you may do it."

"For the word of God *is* living and active, and sharper than any two-edged sword, penetrating even as far as *the* division of soul and spirit, and of joints and marrows, and able to judge *the* thoughts and intentions of *the* heart" (Heb. 4:12).

Genuinely calling out to God will always bring a respond.
Jesus by the Spirit teach the faithful to follow every command!

TROUBLED HEART

ABBA, Father, I come to release my heart's turmoil.
Holy Spirit, come in power and the accusations foil.
Lord Jesus, in Your name, quell my inner despair.
ABBA, Father, horrendous thinking avalanche from nowhere.
Holy Spirit, I appeal to Your expertise.
Holy Spirit, possess this temple and dwell in me.
Lord Jesus, help me live in the abundant life today.
ABBA, Father, come in wisdom and might to have the last say!
Holy Spirit, help me battle this last stronghold.
Lord Jesus, I am fully prepared to do what I am told!
ABBA, Father, speak by the Spirit to my weary mind.
Holy Spirit, in Jesus may this day in Your counsel peace I find!

"He heals the brokenhearted and binds up their wounds" (Ps. 147:3).

Then Jesus said to her, 'Daughter, your faith has healed you. Go in peace and be freed from your suffering'" (Mark 2:17).

God's ability to heal will never decrease.
Jesus by the Spirit showing His love will never cease!

HOLY SPIRIT

Holy Spirit, hear my daily appeal.
Holy Spirit, I don't want to live on how I feel.
Holy Spirit, help me know that You are my Guide.
Holy Spirit, I ask You to come possess me inside.
Holy Spirit, help me live with the confidence that exudes power.
Holy Spirit, fill this temple to overflowing every hour.
Holy Spirit, work in me to have a vessel clear of sins residue.
Holy Spirit, I call out because I truly trust You.
Holy Spirit, show me what is clogging the potential.
Holy Spirit, please show me what I need to do that is essential.
Holy Spirit, I call upon You to be my intimate Friend.
Holy Spirit, come complete the mission the Lord did send!

"Then the Spirit of the LORD clothed Gideon with power" (Judg. 6:34a).
"And now I will send the Holy Spirit, just as my Father promised. But stay…until the Holy Spirit…fills you with power from heaven" (Luke 24:49).

God's promises are irrevocable even "to the least of these."
Jesus by the Spirit imparts power to put all at ease!

BECOMING 8

Becoming is what Enoch sought.
Becoming acquainted with the real God he fought.
Becoming was the battle to know which God was real.
Becoming for years to Enoch was just a feel.
Becoming happened one day as he least expected.
Becoming is knowing the God needing to be respected.
Becoming happened to Enoch as he turned sixty-five.
Becoming is when the God of heaven shows He is alive!
Becoming is Enoch experiencing ABBA's gentle fingers.
Becoming is Enoch now in His presence lingers!
Becoming will make for in His presence to stay.
Becoming is God sending a chariot to hall you away!

"When Enoch had lived 65 years, he...walked with God,... Thus all the days of Enoch were 365 years. Enoch walked with God, and he was not, for God took him" (Gen. 5:21–24).

All diligently seeking to honor God will also be taken.
Jesus by the Spirit to the resurrection wants all awakened!

BECOMING 7

Becoming happens as with God, we are forthcoming.
Becoming looks to rid heart of all foreign belongings.
Becoming by the Spirit learns the art of introspection.
Becoming is expedited by Word meditation.
Becoming is a continuous end result.
Becoming by the Spirit relinquish any soulish fault.
Becoming needs to be aided by the Spirit's ability.
Becoming peaks when by the Spirit in Jesus there is docility!
Becoming makes it easier to be used in the gifts.
Becoming empowers to give others a spiritual lift.
Becoming is not for the wavering and faint of heart.
Becoming embraces the Trinity right from the start!

"And Jabez called out to the God of Israel, 'If only You would bless me and enlarge my territory! May Your hand be with me and keep me from harm, so that I will be free from pain.' And God granted the request of Jabez" (1 Chron. 4:10).

"Therefore, having been justified by faith, we have peace with God through our Lord Jesus Christ" (Rom. 5:1).

Even from the lowest point God hears because He cares.
Jesus by the Spirit God's perfect will clearly shares!

Becoming 6

Becoming requires spirit and soul consensual training.
Becoming redeems the time for much gaining.
Becoming makes the altar a place of self-sacrifice.
Becoming seeks early Holy Spirit advice.
Becoming studies to be by the Trinity approved.
Becoming is submissive to hint of sin removed.
Becoming learns to meditate and deeply ponders.
Becoming thinks on the Word and delightfully wonders.
Becoming uses the armor for the enemy's defeat.
Becoming makes the prayer closet a daily repeat.
Becoming receives correction in stride.
Becoming listens to the Holy Spirit for caution of pride!
Becoming acknowledges Jesus everywhere.
Becoming saints giving Jesus glory is a priority care!

"He must increase, but I *must* decrease" (John 3:30).

"I have been crucified with Christ, and I no longer live, but Christ lives in me. The life I live in the body, I live by faith in the Son of God, who loved me and gave Himself up for me" (Gal. 2:20).

Living directed by the Holy Spirit is lots of fun.
Jesus by the Spirit guiding us has just begun!

BECOMING 5

Becoming see the possibilities and are relentless.
Becoming in Jesus by the Spirit see the outcome of greatness.
Becoming believers will never drown.
Becoming saints are looking unto Jesus are always found.
Becoming servants shift quickly from Savior to Lord!
Becoming learn the Persons of the Trinity to stay in one accord.
Becoming severs serve a pauper and a King!
Becoming saints look to ABBA, Father for everything.
Becoming followers plant seeds while hoping on tomorrow.
Becoming believers will freely give and rarely borrow.
Becoming babes advance by leaps and bounds.
Becoming saints are ecstatic about the Master they found!

"You have been set free from sin and have become slaves to righteousness" (Rom. 6:18).

"So you are no longer slaves but God's children. Since you are God's children, God has also made you heirs" (Gal. 4:7).

Salvation sets the ground work a new way of living.
Jesus by the Spirit begins the process of a new nature retrieving!

BECOMING 4

Becoming motivates the one who pays attention.
Becoming is for the obedient with graceful intention.
Becoming learns a lesson from every fall.
Becoming happens listening to the Holy Spirit's call.
Becoming looks at Jesus as the model of possibilities.
Becoming owns up to their shortcoming realities.
Becoming rejoices at the insight of Kingdom affiliation.
Becoming can form into an addictive fixation.
Becoming stay looking in the mirror of the Word.
Becoming listens carefully to all they have heard.
Becoming makes the prayer closet a place to grow.
Becoming when needed put on a Christlike show!

"Simon Peter replied, 'Lord, to whom would we go? You have the words of eternal life'" (John 6:68).

"For to me, living means living for Christ, and dying is even better" (Phil. 1:21).

Becoming has a blissful eternal beginning.
Jesus by the Spirit will see to it that your life has no ending!

Becoming 3

Becoming is the journey of no return.
Becoming allows daily of God to learn.
Becoming takes willingness to change.
Becoming allows Jesus by the Spirit our thoughts to rearrange.
Becoming is daily doing what to Jesus is essential.
Becoming is a prayer closet that is highly confidential.
Becoming is disregarding all past religious teaching.
Becoming is asking for spiritual mew heights to be reaching.
Becoming learns to overcome look others faults.
Becoming daily looks to the Holy Spirit for results.
Becoming ask, seeks, and knocks to go deeper.
Becoming yearns to appreciate Jesus as our Keeper!

"The LORD Himself watches over you! The LORD stands beside you as your protective shade" (Ps. 121:5).
"My sheep listen to My voice; I know them, and they follow Me" (John 10:27).

The protective shield of God is for all days and seasons.
Jesus by the Spirit will rescue the drowning no matter the reasons!

Becoming 2

Becoming is the recovery from our past.
Becoming is God by the Spirit doing it to last.
Becoming is preparing for living in eternity.
Becoming is living unto Jesus cheerfully.
Becoming makes all things new to enjoy.
Becoming is Jesus continuing sinful ways to destroy!
Becoming is conquering habits needing to be uncurled.
Becoming is showing freedom from sin to the world.
Becoming is exalting Jesus without excuse!
Becoming is when invites to sinning we refuse.
Becoming keeps us in Jesus's will discovering.
Becoming helps trusting the Holy Spirit while recovering!

"That I may know Him, and the power of His resurrection, and the fellowship of His sufferings, being made conformable unto His death" (Phil. 3:10).

"The one who says he abides in Him ought himself to walk in the same manner as He walked" (1 John 2:6).

Mimicking the Lord is possible to the meek and humble.
Jesus by the Spirit will be there to help if we stumble!

BECOMING 1

Becoming is a promise without limitation.
Becoming starts at the minute of salvation.
Becoming takes the recipient to the original intent.
Becoming was in God's heart without relent.
Becoming is what the Trinity did decree.
Becoming is available to the likes of you and me.
Becoming has to be induced with eternal hope.
Becoming is provided with One that will help cope.
Becoming will be from heaven navigated.
Becoming will by the faithful be daily instigated.
Becoming is thwarted by hearing the enemy's reproof.
Becoming is in Jesus by the Spirit fail proof!

"But to all who believed Him and accepted Him, He gave the right to become children of God" (John 1:12).

"Whoever says he abides in him ought to walk in the same way in which he walked" (1 John 2:6).

The right to become children of God comes when Jesus as Savior is received.

The Holy Spirit is present to help the willing not be deceived!

TODAY...66

Today, I will seek ABBA, Father as my priority.
Today, I will enjoy the Holy Spirit avoiding frivolity.
Today, I will call upon Jesus my heart to rule.
Today, I will look at disaster and stay calm and cool.
Today, I will guard my heart from the enemy's distractions.
Today, I will return good for evil as my godly actions.
Today, I will not worry about what others say or do.
Today, I will honor God first as I was told to.
Today, I will serve in the Kingdom with expectation.
Today, I will tell of Jesus bringing eternal salvation.
Today, I will remove all that my faith hinders.
Today, I will look to be made whole by ABBA's fingers!

"When I consider Your heavens, the work of Your fingers, The moon and the stars, which You have ordained" (Ps. 8:3).
"But if I cast out demons by the finger of God, then the kingdom of God has come upon you" (Luke 11:20).

Every salvation is God's finger ordaining.
Jesus by the Spirit wants all believers to stay in training!

DEAR ABBA, FATHER 35

I come in search of renewal and revival.
I come for the baptism of the Spirit as a new arrival.
I come to relinquish my soul's inner battle.
I come that by the Spirit the enemy stops the rattle.
I come to explore what I need to expel.
I come that by the Spirit I will modify my behavior.
I come to do say and do what reflects my Savior!
I come to live in Your presence spiritually well.
I come to expose, confess, and renounce what obstruct.
I come in Jesus by the Spirit for You to reconstruct.
I come to maintain a conscience that is clear.
I come to walk in the Spirit and to You be near!

"Test me, O LORD, and try me; examine my heart and mind" (Ps. 27:2).
"Arise, shine, for your light has come, and the glory of the Lord has risen upon you" (Isa. 60:1).

Opening our heart to God's is beneficial.
Jesus by the Spirit providing conquering power is official!

AM: Thank-You Note 113

Thank you, ABBA, Father, for coming to my defense.
Thank you, ABBA, Father, that Your name is my offense.
Thank you, ABBA, Father, for being full of mercy.
Thank you, ABBA, Father, for delivering me from controversy!
Thank you, Lord Jesus, for calming my inner storm.
Thank you, Lord Jesus, by the Spirit to Your will I conform.
Thank you, Lord Jesus, for help in time of spiritual turmoil.
Thank you, Lord Jesus, by the Spirit all evil You do foil.
Thank you, Holy Spirit, for the work in my brain.
Thank you, Holy Spirit, for all the spiritual truth I gain.
Thank you, Holy Spirit, for setting me free of my past.
Thank you, Holy Spirit, for the work in me that will last!

"Give thanks to the God of heaven, for his steadfast love endures forever" (Ps. 136:26).
"Give thanks in all circumstances; for this is the will of God in Christ Jesus for you" (1 Thess. 5:18).

Thankfulness to God daily will increase spiritual maturity.
Jesus by the Spirit brings the fullness of spiritual reality!

M: CLOSET TIME 205

Lord Jesus, I enter Your presence with admiration.
Lord Jesus, my heart for You is full of joy and adoration.
Lord Jesus, help me this day to be most pleasing.
Lord Jesus, possess me that all impurities begin releasing.
Lord Jesus, create in me a vessel of gold.
Lord Jesus, rekindle obedience to do what I am told.
Lord Jesus, grant me a submitted will.
Lord Jesus, rebaptize me and in the Holy Spirit refill.
Lord Jesus, reestablish in me a heart of a child.
Lord Jesus, by the Spirit help me enjoy Your peace all the while.
Lord Jesus, give me a new joy in testifying.
Lord Jesus, this day only in Your power I am relying!

"Then I acknowledged my sin to You and did not hide my iniquity. I said, 'I will confess my transgressions to the LORD,' and You forgave the guilt of my sin…" (Ps. 32:5).

"Everyone who acknowledges Me publicly here on earth, I will also acknowledge before My Father in heaven" (Matt. 10:32).

Believers daily confess to God and to others of God's mercy.
Jesus by the Spirit make it clear that of praise God is worthy!

E: Closet Time 204

Holy Spirit, come fill this temple to overflowing.
Holy Spirit, make the Jesus in to be glowing!
Holy Spirit, I confess and renounce all hint of sin in me.
Holy Spirit, come anew to guide to better hear Thee.
Holy Spirit, renew a desire to know You firsthand.
Holy Spirit, anoint my spirit to follow Your command.
Holy Spirit, don't let sin in my heart dwell.
Holy Spirit, empower me that my heart sins ways repel.
Holy Spirit, possess me with full control.
Holy Spirit, bless my hearing to do as told.
Holy Spirit, I submit my will for death of the old nature.
Holy Spirit, come in me and function at pleasure!

"When he calls to Me, I will answer him; I will be with him in trouble; I will rescue him and honor him" (Ps. 91:15).
"For God gave us a spirit not of fear but of power and love and self-control" (2 Tim. 1:7).

The greatest joy in life is to know that you have been forgiving.
Jesus by the Spirit gives wisdom and insight for receiving!

PM: THANK-YOU NOTE 112

Thank you, ABBA, Father, for ordering my life.
Thank you, ABBA, Father, for a wonderful wife.
Thank you, ABBA, Father, for family and friends.
Thank you, ABBA, Father, that You will be there at the end.
Thank you, Lord Jesus, for help to live trusting.
Thank you, Lord Jesus, that to Your will I keep adjusting.
Thank you, Lord Jesus, for keeping me from all evil.
Thank you, Lord Jesus, for help to be quiet and confidently civil.
Thank you, Holy Spirit, that You never tire of me.
Thank you, Holy Spirit, for the things You help me see.
Thank you, Holy Spirit, for being my Coach.
Thank you, Holy Spirit, for being there when I approach!

"In all your ways acknowledge Him, and He will make straight your paths" (Prov. 3:6).

"Thus says the Lord, your Redeemer, the Holy One of Israel: 'I am the Lord your God, who teaches you to profit, who leads you in the way you should go'" (Isa. 48:18).

The guidance of God leads to abundant living.
Jesus by the Spirit enhances for faith believing!

TODAY...9

Today, by grace I will move about with caution.
Today, I will seek to be further healed in my emotions.
Today, I will listen and really hear.
Today, I will strengthen the weak and cast out fear.
Today, I will forgive the other people offenses.
Today, I will walk by faith and lower my defenses.
Today, I will deny myself and pick up the cross.
Today, I will have high concern for the wandering loss.
Today, my heart will seek genuine revival.
Today, I will seek Holy Spirit insightful arrival.
Today, I will meet the promises conditions.
Today, I will seek ABBA, Father in Jesus for permission!

"The heart of man plans his way, but the Lord establishes his steps" (Ps. 16:9).

"For God is the *One* working in you both to will and to work according to *His* good pleasure" (Phil. 2:13).

All is fine-tuned by God for all believers to be successful.
Jesus by the Spirit makes us see the value in being grateful!

TODAY...8

Today, I am determined to be a vessel of gold.
Today, my heart is available for what in the Word I am told.
Today, I want to appreciate even the least of these.
Today, ABBA, Father, it is You by the Spirit I want to please.
Today, Lord Jesus, I desire to honor Your name.
Today, Holy Spirit, help that my ways bring You no shame.
Today, I am determined to listen more attentive.
Today, in meditation of the Word, help me to be more retentive.
Today, I will die more to myself and esteem others.
Today, I will help the backslider recover.
Today, I will honor the Holy Trinity in what I say and do.
Today, I will seek less of me and more of You!

"I will instruct you and teach you in the way you should go; I will counsel you with My eye upon you" (Ps. 32:8).

"As it is said: 'Today if you should hear His voice, do not harden your hearts, as in the rebellion'" (Heb. 3:15).

Our Father has done His utmost best to recover everyone lost.

Jesus by the Spirit opens eyes to see that the Savior paid the ultimate cost!

TODAY...7

Today, I am determined to expand my faith boundaries.
Today, I am trusting You promises realities.
Today, I will seek the perfecting of my hearing.
Today, to Your throne I will be nearing.
Today, Holy Spirit, I will attempt to quickly obey.
Today, ABBA, Father, I will seek to do things Your way.
Today, Lord Jesus, my heart to You I gladly submit.
Today, Holy Trinity honoring You is what I commit.
Today, I need an abundance of grace Your will to perform.
Today, I ask that to Your ways I conform.
Today, Lord, I open the door of my heart.
Today, Lord Jesus, grant a me new start!

"You shall love the Lord your God with all your heart and with all your soul and with all your might" (Deut. 6:5).
"Jesus responded, 'Salvation has come to this home today, for this man has shown himself to be a true son...'" (Luke 19:9).

Connecting with God is not hard, if you do it right.
Jesus by the Spirit will teach only what brightens our light!

TODAY...6

Today, I will not allow my mind and heart to worry.
Today, to the prayer closet, I will all my cares carry.
Today, I must reject all inferences of unbelief.
Today, I will stay in the prayer closet until I get relief.
Today, Holy Spirit, show what in my heart is hidden.
Today, I will avoid what the Word has forbidden.
Today, Holy Spirit, Your promises I will receive.
Today, Lord Jesus, help me not let the enemy deceive.
Today, I will trust Your healing touch.
Today, I will call the Comforter when the pain is much.
Today, I focus on the Word to relearn.
Today, for ABBA, Father's presence, I will seek and yearn.
Today, by the Holy Spirit, being like Jesus is my mission.
Today, having more intimacy with the Trinity is my vision.

"In the morning, Lord, You will hear my voice; In the morning
I will present *my prayer* to You and be on the watch" (Ps. 5:3).
"Therefore I tell you, whatever you ask in prayer, believe that
you have received it, and it will be yours."

Answers to prayer is what God has His seal of approval.
Jesus by the Spirit works to strengthen faith by all sin removal!

TODAY...5

Today, unto You my worship will I raise.
Today, my lips will be full of exaltation and praise.
Today, the Trinity will I exalt along the way.
Today, I will encourage others with what I say.
Today, I will plant Gospel seeds.
Today, I will point all persons to Thee.
Today, I will intercede and pray for others.
Today, I will pray that my enemies recover.
Today, every moment You I will bless.
Today, in Your promises, I will rest.
Today, Holy Spirit, help me to honor ABBA in my behavior.
Today, with joy, I will direct others to my Exalted Savior.

"The LORD is my Shepherd: I have all that I need" (Ps. 23:1).
"I am the good shepherd. The good shepherd lays down His life for the sheep" (John 10:11).

A shepherd, even today, has intimacy with his sheep and know the voice.

Jesus by the Spirit will give ears to hear and make the right choice!

TODAY...4

Today, my love for the Trinity will grow.
Today, my commitment to testifying will show.
Today, my heart is open to deeper renovation.
Today, my attitude is for more Holy Spirit inspiration.
Today, I look forward to leaving all sinful ways behind.
Today, in Jesus by the Spirit, I want to be refined.
Today, I want to confess and renounce what hinders.
Today, I want to be touched by ABBA's healing fingers.
Today, I want strengthening in areas I am weak.
Today, I want to walk humble and meek.
Today, my goal is to bring ABBA, Father in Jesus glory.
Today, guided by the Holy Spirit I look to tell the Gospel story!

"This is the day that the LORD has made; we will rejoice and be glad in it" (Ps. 118:24).

"For I am not ashamed of this Good News about Christ. It is the power of God at work, saving everyone who believes—the Jew first and also the Gentile" (Rom. 1:16).

The greatest way to rejoice and be glad is to have salvation and tell.

Jesus by the Spirit will guard all His sheep protectively well!

TODAY...3

Today, I will renew my prayer closet time.
Today, with the Holy Spirit I will stay in line.
Today, I will seek the Word to meditate.
Today, I will guard my heart diligently to better relate.
Today, I will listen to others with godly intent.
Today, when convicted of wrong, I will repent.
Today, by the Holy Spirit, I will speak with grace.
Today, I will exercise keeping a humble place.
Today, the council of the ungodly, I will resist.
Today, living by faith in Jesus, I will persist.
Today, I will use words that others uplift.
Today, I will present Jesus as ABBA, Father's gift.

"My help comes from the LORD, the Maker of heaven and earth" (Ps. 121:2).
"Peter and the other apostles replied: 'We must obey God rather than human beings!'" (Acts 5:29).

Truly obeying is what motivates God to usher His best.
Jesus by the Spirit gives His faithful the needed rest!

TODAY...2

Today, I am fixed on hearing the Holy Spirit's voice.
Today, by Jesus's power, I will make the godly choice.
Today, I will maintain a heavenly attitude.
Today, I will show mercy to those abrupt and rude.
Today, my heart I will offer as a living sacrifice.
Today, I will live on Word centered advice.
Today, I will exercise a repentant mindset.
Today, I will not use words that cause regret.
Today, I will learn to go the extra mile.
Today, I will keep a Christlike smile.
Today, I will trust God for a mind of His child.
Today, I will enjoy the Trinity's presence all the while!

"You will keep *him* in perfect peace, *Whose* mind *is* stayed *on You,* Because he trusts in You" (Isa. 26:3).

"And the peace of God, which surpasses all understanding, will guard your hearts and your minds in Christ Jesus" (Phil. 4:7).

Perfect peace in salvation is all inclusive.

Jesus by the Spirit train the submitted in ways that are maturity conducive!

TODAY...1

Today, in God's promises, I will depend.
Today, in Jesus's name, my heart and knees will bend.
Today, the Holy Spirit I will follow.
Today, I will avoid all evil and talk that is shallow.
Today, I will look to the higher road.
Today, I will obey what in the Word I am told.
Today, I will overlook offense and forgive.
Today, I will new Holy Spirit insight receive.
Today, I will pray for those that abuse.
Today, I will be kind to those the Word refuse.
Today, I will enjoy abundant life living.
Today, by faith, I will in Jesus keep believing!

"But Peter and the other apostles replied, 'We must obey God rather than men'" (Acts 5:29).

"For this reason, even though I suffer as I do, I am not ashamed; for I know whom I have believed, and I am convinced that He is able to guard what I have entrusted to Him for that day" (2 Tim. 1:12).

Obeying God daily leads to a very godly lifestyle.
Jesus by the Spirit will see us through growth all the while!

PC REWARDS!

Praying in closet is ABBA, Father directed.
The prayer closet is Holy Spirit respected.
Jesus watches the prayer closet with delight.
The Trinity is in the prayer closet site.
The prayer closet advances spiritual maturity.
The prayer closet makes aware of spiritual reality.
ABBA, Father of the closet is protective.
His ears to closet prayers are receptive.
All of heaven in the closet are watching.
They see ABBA, Father answer matching.
The prayer closet is the safest place to be.
Prayer closet makes one strong you'll see!

"Then call on me when you are in trouble, and I will rescue you, and you will give me glory" (Ps. 50:15).
"But when you pray, go away by yourself, shut the door behind you, and pray to your Father in private. Then your Father, who sees everything, will reward you" (Matt. 6:6).

We are guaranteed answers to prayers done sincerely private.
Jesus by the Spirit wants that maturity of prayer all arrive it!

AM: Thank-You Note 90

Thank you, Lord Jesus, for life on the spiritual fast track.
Thank you, Lord Jesus, that sin in my life there is no going back.
Thank you, Lord Jesus, for power to love and live.
Thank you, Lord Jesus, for a new anointing to believe.
Thank you, Holy Spirit, for a Word of truth to speak.
Thank you, Holy Spirit, for helping the things of God to seek.
Thank you, Holy Spirit, for helping me to abstain evil.
Thank you, Holy Spirit, for power to be lovingly civil.
Thank you, ABBA, Father, that life is Your hands.
Thank you, ABBA, Father, for grace to follow commands.
Thank you, ABBA, Father, for joy that is pure.
Thank you, ABBA, Father, that answers to prayer are sure.

"My help comes from the Lord, the Maker of heaven and earth" (Ps. 121:2).
"Who gave Himself for our sins to rescue us from the present evil age, according to the will of our God and Father" (Gal. 1:4).

All has been done for everyone to enjoy separation from sin.
Jesus by the Spirit is were all really will begin!

A: Closet Time 180

Holy Spirit, I worship at Your feet.
Holy Spirit, my heart and spirit with You wants to meet.
Holy Spirit, come possess me totally.
Holy Spirit, I am a willing vessel loyally.
Holy Spirit, create in me a heart that is trusting.
Holy Spirit, help me that to Your voice I am adjusting.
Holy Spirit, advance a deeper love for serving.
Holy Spirit, all of my efforts You are truly deserving.
Holy Spirit, renew my heart to be of authentic devotions.
Holy Spirit, come heal my emotions.
Holy Spirit, I welcome Your intrusion.
Holy Spirit, walking in You self-denying is a worthy collusion.
Holy Spirit, come possess me in Jesus to increase.
Holy Spirit, give me a humble mindset to decrease.

"And He said, 'I will be gracious to whom I will be gracious, and will show compassion on whom I will show compassion'" (Exod. 33:19).

"But I say, walk by the Spirit, and you will not gratify the desires of the flesh" (Gal. 5:16).

Assurance of graciousness and compassion is met in salvation.
Jesus by the Spirit wants us to advance in sanctification!

PM: Thank-You Note 90

Thank you, ABBA, Father, for life in heaven forever.
Thank you, ABBA, Father, You saved me from a sinful beggar.
Thank you, ABBA, Father, for the many tangible gifts.
Thank you, ABBA, Father, for a daily Holy Spirit lift.
Thank you, Lord Jesus, for holy living beyond compare.
Thank you, Lord Jesus, that Your love with me You share.
Thank you, Lord Jesus, for my heavenly citizenship.
Thank you, Lord Jesus, that I'm firmly in Your grip.
Thank you, Holy Spirit, for helping to change my thinking.
Thank you, Holy Spirit, for a daily new linking.
Thank you, Holy Spirit, for my sins expulsion.
Thank you, Holy Spirit, for daily spiritual explosion.

"Great is the Lord, and highly to be praised, And His greatness is unsearchable" (Ps. 145:3).

"Blessed be the God and Father of our Lord Jesus Christ, the Father of mercies and God of all comfort" (1 Cor. 1:3).

Our Father uses comforting to settle us from adversity.
Jesus by the Spirit give perfect peace with certainty!

E: CLOSET TIME 180

Lord Jesus, You are the same yesterday, today, and forever.
Lord Jesus, Your power will diminish never.
Lord Jesus, those that pray in Your name are heard.
Lord Jesus, Your faithful stand on the Word.
Lord Jesus, by the Spirit, help me to meditate.
Lord Jesus, give me a mind doing Your will doesn't hesitate.
Lord Jesus, control my heart to do my spiritual best.
Lord Jesus, rebaptize me that I may continue my quest.
Lord Jesus, refill me with holy fire.
Lord Jesus, help me to meet the conditions You desire.
Lord Jesus, search me for hidden sinful ways.
Lord Jesus, anoint my tongue to be careful what I say.
Lord Jesus, by the Spirit, guide me to higher ground.
Lord Jesus, help me trusting You is how I am found.
Lord Jesus, help me retain Your mind.
Lord Jesus, infuse me with Your ways to be lovingly kind.

"But from everlasting to everlasting the loving devotion of the LORD extends to those who fear Him" (Ps. 103:17).

"God anointed Jesus…with the Holy Spirit and with power. Then Jesus went around doing good and healing all who were oppressed by the devil, for God was with Him" (Acts 10:38).

The loving devotion of our Maker is still available to the devout.

Jesus by the Spirit wants priority in the prayer closet for all to be about!

AM: THANK-YOU NOTE 91

Thank you, ABBA, Father, that us You lovingly watch.
Thank you, ABBA, Father, for hands in our stumble to catch.
Thank you, ABBA, Father, that You never change.
Thank you, ABBA, Father, for things in us You rearrange.
Thank you, Lord Jesus, for daily interceding.
Thank you, Lord Jesus, that grace to us You keep repeating.
Thank you, Lord Jesus, that in our life You are involved.
Thank you, Lord Jesus, that in the prayer closet all is resolved.
Thank you, Holy Spirit, for daily learning.
Thank you, Holy Spirit, that for Jesus I keep yearning.
Thank you, Holy Spirit, for all the spiritual enlightenment.
Thank you, Holy Spirit, for all the godly excitement.

"But as for me, I shall sing of Your strength; Yes, I shall joyfully sing of Your lovingkindness in the morning, For You have been my stronghold, And a refuge in the day of my distress" (Ps. 59:16).

"As far as the east is from the west, so far has He removed our transgressions from us" (Ps. 103:8).

Our Father is our best Protector anywhere and at all times.
Jesus by the Spirit will keep us from the enemy's mines!

TODAY...43

Today, I will not be influenced by unbelief.
Today, I will hear Holy Spirit wanting others to relief.
Today, I will take time to tell of God's intervention.
Today, I will to the Word pay more attention.
Today, I will in quiet confidence speak less.
Today, I will look how others I can bless.
Today, I will seek God's Kingdom first.
Today, I will revive meditation with hunger and thirst.
Today, I will frequent my prayer closet.
Today, I will testify of all ABBA's prayer deposit!
Today, I will ABBA in Jesus by the Spirit give all glory!
Today, I will enthusiastically tell the Gospel story!

"As far as the east is from the west, so far has He removed our transgressions from us" (Ps. 103:12).

"In everything, then, do to others as you would have them do to you. For this is the essence of the Law and the Prophets" (Matt. 7:12).

A person's salvation life can be gaged by the treatment of others. Jesus by the Spirit has power to help from the past recover!

Dear ABBA, Father 11

I come to Your presence for wisdom and attention.
I come for power in sinful prevention.
I come because what I need to succeed You provide.
I come knowing You are on my side.
I come because in Jesus I can.
I come to strengthen my holy and faithful stand.
I come to serve You in genuine repentance.
I come in Jesus by the Spirit to sense Your acceptance.
I come that from the heart's subtlety of sin to recover.
I come to present my body for a spiritual makeover.
I come for my soul and spirit's renewal.
I come for new favor, blessings, and approval.
I come to be renewed in the spirit of my mind.
I come to be enhanced in being Christlike kind.

"As a father has compassion on his children, so the LORD has compassion on those who fear Him" (Ps. 103:13).

"Come to Me, all you who are weary and burdened, and I will give you rest" (Matt. 11:28).

We are His children because He is our eternal Father.
Jesus by the Spirit will meet all our needs like no other!

A: Closet Time 204

Lord Jesus, I praise Your work of salvation.
Lord Jesus, I give You honor and exaltation.
Lord Jesus, empower me that I stay kind and humble.
Lord Jesus, help me from grace not to stumble.
Lord Jesus, make my heart tender and soft.
Lord Jesus, give me a new love for the lost.
Lord Jesus, create in me a deeper joy.
Lord Jesus, help me be aware of the enemy's ploy.
Lord Jesus, help me love ABBA, Father as priority.
Lord Jesus, make the heavenly's a greater reality.
Lord Jesus, help me enjoy my name in Your book.
Lord Jesus, grant me a new upward look!

"Gracious is the Lord, and righteous; Yes, our God is compassionate" (Ps. 116:5).
"The LORD is compassionate and gracious, slow to anger, abounding in loving devotion" (Ps. 103:8).

The unconditional love of God is forever a standing offer.
Jesus by the Spirit has myriads of gifts from a bottomless coffer!

M: Closet Time 181

Lord Jesus, I commit myself in surrender.
Lord Jesus, I come to You to be my Defender.
Lord Jesus, I come to expose my heart.
Lord Jesus, I ask for a healing touch as the day starts.
Lord Jesus, take away all that in my heart favor impedes.
Lord Jesus, purge my heart to plant Gospel seeds.
Lord Jesus, help me to appreciate Your work more.
Lord Jesus, help me of You power be reassured as before.
Lord Jesus, show me Your might.
Lord Jesus, in me put a new faith fight.
Lord Jesus, help me to humbly obey.
Lord Jesus, by the Spirit help me hear what You say.

"The Father loves the Son and has given all things into His hand" (Matt. 3:35).

"And Jesus came up and spoke to them, saying, "All authority has been given to Me in heaven and on earth" (Matt. 28:18).

The power to change a sinner is available in God's son.
Jesus by the Spirit will open eyes to show He is the One!

Always the Same 4

Jesus knew of all His testings and temptations.
Jesus full of the Holy Spirit had overcoming qualifications.
Jesus read the thoughts of the many.
Jesus fixated that saving others He didn't lose any.
Jesus associated with "sinners and tax collectors."
Jesus came primary to be an ABBA, Father reflector.
Jesus modeled a walk of daily self-denial.
Jesus intended to save the many all the while.
Jesus avoided the leadership anti-ruckus.
Jesus on "the least of these" kept His focus.
Jesus spoke much about Holy Spirit power.
Jesus moved as the Holy Spirit guided all hours.

"Bless the LORD, O my soul; all that is within me, bless His holy name" (Ps. 103:1).

"Then Jesus, full of the Holy Spirit, returned from the Jordan River. He was led by the Spirit in the wilderness" (Luke 4:1).

Every need He will provide if we fully trust.
Jesus by the Spirit will remind us of the things that are a must!

Always the Same 3

Jesus was essential in the life of all that breathe.
Jesus knew that only He could rescue from eternal death.
Jesus made many pre-earth entries.
Jesus had closely watched through the centuries.
Jesus has angels at His beck and calling.
Jesus sends help when the devout in trouble are falling.
Jesus has given power to defeat temptation.
Jesus by the Spirit expedites sanctification.
Jesus by the Spirit the road to salvation has paved.
Jesus from heaven protects those being saved.
Jesus looks for all those that keep great appreciation.
Jesus for all the faithful has a great reception.

"My eyes favor the faithful of the land, that they may dwell with Me; he who walks in the way of integrity shall minister to Me" (Ps. 101:6).

"I have told you these things so that in Me you may have peace. You will have suffering in this world. Be courageous! I have conquered the world" (John 16:33).

God keeps tabs us not to hurt, but to advance.
Jesus by the Spirit gives everyone equal chance!

ALWAYS THE SAME 2

Jesus was there when the brothers committed betrayal.
Jesus will always hate all evil portrayal.
Jesus is forgiving and merciful every day.
Jesus gives overcoming grace to all who pray.
Jesus made the axe handle to float.
Jesus is repelled when believers gloat.
Jesus never makes impossible demands.
Jesus gives power to successfully follow commands.
Jesus mourns the death of any sinner.
Jesus wants real repentance to make an eternal winner!
Jesus looks to see all come to His side.
Jesus by the Spirit wants all in Him to abide!

"I will sing of Your loving devotion and justice; to You, O LORD,
I will sing praises" (Ps. 101).

"But You are the same, And Your years will not fail" (Heb.
1:12b).

Since God created us in His image, we are His concern.
Jesus by the Spirit advances those that want to learn!

ALWAYS THE SAME 1

The Lord is always the same.
Jesus was ready to rescue what by Him came.
Through eternity, He watched in loving anticipation.
With a loving desire, He waited with expectation.
He foreknew that moment of Adam's horrible act.
He foresaw that rescuing was an eternal fact.
Empathy was the constant feeling for all creation.
Intervening for His sake was to avoid human's extermination.
In the interim, Jesus manifested through the ages.
Serious seekers of Jesus would become sages.
Jesus embraced the time of His birth.
Now humanity can see what to God they are worth.
Now in sin we will indulge never.
Now about sin we cease to be deceptively clever!

"For the LORD is good, and His loving devotion endures forever; His faithfulness continues to all generations" (Ps. 100:5).

"Jesus Christ is the same yesterday, today, and forever" (Heb. 13:8).

That His faithfulness continues is in sending a Savior.
Jesus by the Spirit concentrate on changing our behavior!

PM: THANK-YOU NOTE 91

Thank you, ABBA, Father, for the great promises to live.
Thank you, ABBA, Father, that the greatest promise is to forgive.
Thank you, ABBA, Father, filling our empty soul.
Thank you, ABBA, Father, by the Spirit, we are Christlike whole.
Thank you, Lord Jesus, for life, truth, and the way.
Thank you, Lord Jesus, that You left us all You had to say.
Thank you, Lord Jesus, for daily insight and grace.
Thank you, Lord Jesus, for keeping us in place.
Thank you, Holy Spirit, for helping us to train.
Thank you, Holy Spirit, for keeping us from the vain.
Thank you, Holy Spirit, that You know what's ahead.
Thank you, Holy Spirit, that in hardship You warn us instead.

"Know that the LORD is God. It is He who made us, and we are His; we are His people, and the sheep of His pasture" (Ps. 100:3).
"Seven times a day I praise You, Because of Your righteous ordinances" (Ps. 119:164).

Praising helps break past sinful habits that hold us back.
Jesus by the Spirit will put us on the fast-learning track!

A: Closet Time 181

ABBA, Father, my heart longs for Your anointing.
ABBA, Father, strengthen that to Jesus others I'm pointing.
ABBA, Father, help me not be weary in doing well.
ABBA, Father, of Your mercy and love others I will tell.
ABBA, Father, rekindle in me Your love that is pure.
ABBA, Father, I look to Your Word as my spiritual cure.
ABBA, Father, forgive me for sins of omission.
ABBA, Father, forgive sins of the mind I am guilty of commission.
ABBA, Father, order my steps as I'm willing.
ABBA, Father, grant me a new Holy Spirit infilling.
ABBA, Father, help me to be led as others in the past.
ABBA, Father, refill me to overflowing to last.
ABBA, Father, help quiet my soul.
ABBA, Father, by the Spirit make me whole.

"Let them praise Your great and awesome name—He is holy!"
"Exalt the Lord our God And worship at His holy hill, For holy is the Lord our God" (Ps. 99:9).

Even in awesome power, He is gentle to His sheep.
Jesus by the Spirit in God's way the faithful He will keep!

God's Intervention

ABBA, Father intervenes for the sake of sinful prevention.
The Holy Spirit intervenes to bring a sinner to salvation.
ABBA, Father intervenes to give the thirsty water.
The Trinity intervenes to stop an unnecessary slaughter!
Jesus intervenes to stop the persecution.
The Trinity intervenes to stop the sin's pollution.
Jesus intervenes to give sight to the blind.
Jesus intervenes when a legion possess He finds.
ABBA, Father intervenes to judge the proud.
The Trinity intervenes to humble the bragging loud.
The reason we can brag on God is His intervention.
Jesus by the Spirit has the greatest intention!

"I will proclaim Your name to my brothers; I will praise You in the assembly" (Ps. 22:22).
"For He has not despised or detested the torment of the afflicted. He has not hidden His face from him, but has attended to his cry for help" (Ps. 22:24).

God continues to intervene against a bully.
Jesus by the Spirit will equip us fully!

LOOKING BACK

Remember Lot's wife!
Looking back can make us want our past life.
In the wilderness, they kept living in retrospect.
For God's presence and Word, they lost respect.
Even the leadership they tried to overthrow.
The blame game begins when not in the Holy Spirit flow.
Looking into ourselves by our own leads to wrong conclusions.
Where we are deficient is by lack of Holy Spirit solutions.
Starting every day new has to be with repentance.
Genuine open-heart closet time with God has acceptance.
Avoiding ungodliness is essential.
In Jesus by the Spirit, we get overcoming credentials.

"No, dear brothers… I focus on this one thing: Forgetting the past and looking forward to what lies ahead, I press on toward the goal to win the prize for which God has called me heavenward in Christ Jesus" (Phil. 3:13–14).

The past is for the purpose of giving God glory.
Jesus by the Spirit prepare us for habitually telling the Gospel story!

Dear Abba, Father 34

I come my soul and heart to bear.
I come that in Your perfect will today I may share.
I come to be on the cutting edge of growing.
I come Your perfect will to be sowing.
I come for a spiritual checkup.
I come that with grace You would fill my cup!
I come to continue being about Your business.
I come to be a better and bold witness!
I come for my spiritual vision to be enhanced.
I come that for the things of the Spirit I am advanced.
I come to be refreshed in genuine humility.
I come that humbleness in me becomes a reality!

"The LORD is my shepherd; *a* I shall not want" (Ps. 23:1).
"Surely goodness and mercy will follow me all the days of my life, and I will dwell in the house of the LORD forever" (Ps. 23:6).

As our Shepherd, He secures an abundant living.
Jesus by the Spirit will keep us in the realm of believing!

M: CLOSET TIME 204

ABBA, Father, I give You worship and exaltation.
ABBA, Father, I come for wisdom and revelation.
ABBA, Father, rectify in me what is lacking.
ABBA, Father, by the Spirit show me how I'm slacking.
ABBA, Father, my trusting and obeying needs affirmation.
ABBA, Father, today I look to You for confirmation.
ABBA, Father, help me to love You sincerely.
ABBA, Father, give me a love for the Word that is dearly!
ABBA, Father, in Jesus increase my belief.
ABBA, Father, help me be full of the Spirit when You I leave.
ABBA, Father, give me a new hunger for souls.
ABBA, Father, by the Spirit in Jesus help me be whole!

"I will proclaim Your name to my brothers; I will praise You in the assembly" (Ps. 22:22).

"For He has not despised or detested the torment of the afflicted. He has not hidden His face from him, but has attended to his cry for help" (Ps. 22:24).

The reason we can brag on God is His intervention.
Jesus by the Spirit has the greatest intention!

AM: THANK-YOU NOTE 112

Thank you, Holy Spirit, for helping to trust You each day.
Thank you, Holy Spirit, for helping me in Jesus to stay.
Thank you, Holy Spirit, that You forever my Helper.
Thank you, Holy Spirit, that in You I will always find shelter.
Thank you, Lord Jesus, that You the enemy disarmed.
Thank you, Lord Jesus, that in You I can't be harmed.
Thank you, ABBA, Father, that You our spirit protect.
Thank you, ABBA, Father, for help in You to respect.
Thank you, ABBA, Father, that You are Friend.
Thank you, ABBA, Father, that You will be there at the end!

"He asked You for life, and You granted it length of days, forever and ever" (Ps. 21:4).

"Be exalted, O LORD, in Your strength; we will sing and praise Your power" (Ps. 21:13).

The strength and power of God is enough to richly provide.
Jesus by the Spirit aspires to never leave our side!

TODAY...65

Today, I will walk desirous of Holy Spirit guidance.
Today, I will meditate on the Word in silence.
Today, I will do all with a godly attitude.
Today, I will listen to others and not my intrude.
Today, I will for others take time to intercede.
Today, I will my faults and failures concede.
Today, I will warn others when they are at a spiritual cliff.
Today, I will by the Spirit impart to others a godly lift.
Today, I will seek to be in God's presence.
Today, I will pursue becoming part of God's Essence.
Today, I will tell the Gospel with loving boldness.
Today, I will by the Spirit ask for Christ in me fullness!

"May He give you the desires of your heart and make all your plans succeed" (Ps. 20:4).
"Some trust in chariots and others in horses, but we trust in the name of the LORD our God."

Trusting in God begins with real morning prayer.
Jesus by the Spirit will make the humble a giant slayer!

E: Closet Time 181

Holy Spirit, I welcome Your ever presence and intent.
Holy Spirit, this evening, my body to You I present.
Holy Spirit, I need Your power and instruction.
Holy Spirit, I look to You for guidance and promotion.
Holy Spirit, come search my inner being.
Holy Spirit, search for all sins in me to be freeing.
Holy Spirit, renew my desire of You to be filled.
Holy Spirit, of being led by You help to be thrilled.
Holy Spirit, anoint me to look for You with anticipation.
Holy Spirit, help me live the life of a new creation.
Holy Spirit, I ask that You take me deeper.
Holy Spirit, help me appreciate my Keeper.

"And the Spirit of the Lord shall rest upon Him, the Spirit of wisdom and understanding, the Spirit of counsel and might, the Spirit of knowledge and the fear of the Lord" (Isa. 11:2).

"But you will receive power when the Holy Spirit comes upon you" (Acts 1:8a).

"Power to live the abundant life is centered on intimacy with the Holy Spirit.

Jesus by the Spirit will make sure that the Word you will get it!

RESTORE MY HEART

ABBA, Father, in Jesus, I come for restoration.
ABBA, Father, by the Spirit, come do a heart renovation.
ABBA, Father, help me to fully submit.
ABBA, Father, to Your perfect will I commit.
ABBA, Father, grant me to stay in obedience.
ABBA, Father, deliver me from my own convenience.
ABBA, Father, You are the Potter and I am the clay.
ABBA, Father, mold me as You desire today.
ABBA, Father, help me learn real submission.
ABBA, Father, being childlike I ask permission.
ABBA, Father, I offer my body on Your altar.
ABBA, Father, search my heart and purge what falters.
ABBA, Father, make me Christlike faithful.
ABBA, Father, help me walk humble and grateful.
ABBA, Father, renew authentic trust.
ABBA, Father, flush my spirit from all impeding lust.
ABBA, Father, begin in me a spirit renewal.
ABBA, Father, by the Spirit, do a heart removal.
ABBA, Father, grant a heart quiet, confident and still.
ABBA, Father, grant me a Holy Spirit refill.

"I will give them a heart to know Me, for I am the Lord; and they will be My people, and I will be their God, for they will return to Me with their whole heart" (Jer. 24:7).

"That is why the LORD says, 'Turn to me now, while there is time. Give me your hearts'" (Joel 2:12a).

In order to enjoy heaven's best giving God our heart gets the best results.

Jesus by the Spirit will make the devoted to spiritual adults!

E: Closet Time 203

Lord Jesus, I with reverence and respect.
Lord Jesus, I come I as a blood bought elect.
Lord Jesus, I come to confess and renounce.
Lord Jesus, my sins and iniquities I soundly renounce.
Lord Jesus, work in me to abhor sinful behavior.
Lord Jesus, I look to You as my only Savior.
Lord Jesus, to You I am sold out.
Lord Jesus, anoint my spirit to dance and shout.
Lord Jesus, thank you for help to conquer strongholds.
Lord Jesus, I stand submitted to do what I am told.
Lord Jesus, I will forever give You glory.
Lord Jesus, empower me to tell the Gospel story!

"For today in the city of David there has been born for you a Savior, who is Christ the Lord" (Luke 2:12).

"Whatever you do in word or deed, do all in the name of the Lord Jesus, giving thanks through Him to God the Father" (Col. 3:17).

That Jesus is Lord has been affirmed by His resurrection.
Jesus by the Spirit will prepare the meek for great expectations!

PM: THANK-YOU NOTE 111

Thank you, ABBA, Father, for a wonderful day.

Thank you, ABBA, Father, for love that You daily convey.

Thank you, ABBA, Father, that You grant me favor.

Thank you, ABBA, Father, for blessings as I labor.

Thank you, Lord Jesus, for help with wisdom to overcome.

Thank you, Lord Jesus, that Your salvation will never be outdone!

Thank you, Lord Jesus, for my name in Your Book.

Thank you, Lord Jesus, for a heavenly outlook!

Thank you, Holy Spirit, for helping me to faithfully pray.

Thank you, Holy Spirit, for guiding the best way.

Thank you, Holy Spirit, for insight and words to speak.

Thank you, Holy Spirit, that You help me Jesus to daily seek!

"The Lord looks down from heaven on all mankind to see if there are any who understand, any who seek God" (Ps. 14:2).

"The heavens declare the glory of God; the skies proclaim the work of his hands" (Ps. 19:1).

Understanding who He is and seeking to know Him is all that is required.

Jesus by the Spirit is looking for those that ABBA, Father admire!

TODAY…44

Today, I will seek to have my heart reconstructed.
Today, I will seek to be Holy Spirit instructed.
Today, I will walk humbly before my Redeemer.
Today, I will walk as a God-fearing believer.
Today, I will pray in the Spirit and not budge.
Today, I will help others and not judge.
Today, I will render mercy as I point to grace.
Today, I will the Holy Spirit's steps trace.
Today, I will avoid all semblances of evil.
Today, I will walk quietly, lovingly and civil.
Today, I will others need for Jesus lament.
Today, I will be a vessel to help others repent.
Today, I will expose to God my shortcomings.
Today, I will recall that in Jesus I am becoming.
Today, I will testify of Jesus without shame.
Today, I will tell the lost why Jesus came!

"Now therefore thus saith the Lord of hosts; Consider your ways" (Haggai 1:5).
"But the Lord said to him, 'Go your way, for he is My chosen vessel to bear My name…'" (Acts 9:15).

The vessels for God are always getting ready for use.
Jesus by the Spirit uses vessels that commands never refuse!

Dear Abba, Father 12

I come to Your presence with much joy and praise.
I come my body a living sacrifice to You raise.
I come to gain Your daily approval.
I come to confess sins and have their roots removal.
I come to be refilled by the Holy Spirit to overflowing.
I come that Christlikeness in me will be glowing.
I come to be strengthened in my inner man.
I come to respect and follow every command.
I come to release my will to Your oversight.
I come in obedience to humbly do what is right.
I come that my works to You will be pleasing.
I come that the aroma of Jesus in me continue releasing.
I come to seek the Kingdom and Your righteousness.
I come to stay until You bless.
I come to keep the prayer closet time a priority.
I come to renew in my heart that You are my Authority!

"But He is unique and who can turn Him? And what His soul desires, that He does" (Job 23:13).

"But our God is in the heavens; He does whatever He pleases" (Ps. 115:3).

Our Father has the best gifts for those diligently faithful.
Jesus by the Spirit will teach us to be grateful!

AM: THANK-YOU NOTE 92

Thank you, Holy Spirit, for helping to advance Jesus in me.
Thank you, Holy Spirit, that all things You see.
Thank you, Holy Spirit, that my future is in Yours hands.
Thank you, Holy Spirit, for grace to follow commands.
Thank you, Holy Spirit, for daily cleansing.
Thank you, Holy Spirit, that my soul You are fixing.
Thank you, Holy Spirit, for life on a spiritual cutting edge.
Thank you, Holy Spirit, for helping to prevent from sin's ledge.
Thank you, Holy Spirit, for priority to honoring Jesus Christ.
Thank you, Holy Spirit, for expert advice.
Thank you, Holy Spirit, for helpful correction.
Thank you, Holy Spirit, helping me in sanctification.

"Cast me not forth from Thy presence, And Thy Holy Spirit take not from me" (Ps. 51:11).

"But the Helper, the Holy Spirit, whom the Father will send in My name, will teach you all things and remind you of everything that I have told you" (John 14:26).

That the Holy Spirit is Helper is clear in the Sacred Book.
Jesus by the Spirit will have an upward look!

M: Closet Time 182

Holy Spirit, take over my body for Your will.
Holy Spirit, come in power renew and fill.
Holy Spirit, help me to know and see Jesus better.
Holy Spirit, come possess me and be my Pacesetter.
Holy Spirit, give me counseling on my inner needs.
Holy Spirit, empower me to place Gospel seeds.
Holy Spirit, let not my heart go astray.
Holy Spirit, help me follow ABBA's perfect way.
Holy Spirit, help me from Your way to never deviate.
Holy Spirit, guide me that with others I can best relate.
Holy Spirit, help me to listen from others point of view.
Holy Spirit, come in power and give me a heavenly preview.

"Rather, as it is written: 'No eye has seen, no ear has heard, no heart has imagined, what God has prepared for those who love Him. But God has revealed it to us by the Spirit. The Spirit searches all things, even the deep things of God'" (1 Cor. 2:9–10).

God in Jesus has revealed by the Spirit very much.
Jesus by the Spirit will help us in prayer ABBA, Father to touch!

CHRISTLIKENESS IMPARTED

ABBA, Father, thank you for a faith that is precious.
ABBA, Father, Your salvation makes me gracious.
ABBA, Father, Your graciousness delivers from carnal strife.
ABBA, Father, Your divine power makes me godly in life.
ABBA, Father, in Jesus, You gave me His divine power.
ABBA, Father, thanks for making me like Jesus every hour.
ABBA, Father, thanks that I am able to escape corruption.
ABBA, Father, in Jesus, lust in my heart meets destruction.
ABBA, Father, thanks for a way to grow.
ABBA, Father, thanks for faith and virtue to make Jesus show.
ABBA, Father, it is alluring to be partaker of Jesus' nature.
ABBA, Father, perform Your will in me at Your pleasure!

"May grace and peace be...in the knowledge of God and of Jesus our Lord. His divine power has granted to us all things that pertain to life and godliness, through the knowledge of Him who called us to His own glory and excellence, by which He has granted to us His precious and very great promises, so that through them you may become partakers of the divine nature, having escaped from the corruption that is in the world because of sinful desire" (2 Pet. 1:2b–4).

The power of the submitted is beyond compare.
Jesus by the Spirit the power of God did come to share!

PM: Thank-You Note 92

Thank you, Lord Jesus, for Your divine nature imparted.
Thank you, Lord Jesus, the saving work in me started.
Thank you, Lord Jesus, for many promises with blessings.
Thank you, Lord Jesus, for the Spirit that impedes regressing.
Thank you, Holy Spirit, for help to know Jesus with intimacy.
Thank you, Holy Spirit, that I can know You intimately.
Thank you, Holy Spirit, for the love of Jesus to share.
Thank you, Holy Spirit, that You are with me everywhere.
Thank you, ABBA, Father, for daily affirmation.
Thank you, ABBA, Father, for holy confirmation.
Thank you, ABBA, Father, for love that is everlasting.
Thank you, ABBA, Father, that to You my cares I keep casting!

"I will praise the LORD at all times. I will constantly speak his praises" (Ps. 34:1).

"Give thanks to the Lord, for He is good; His love endures forever" (Ps. 107:1).

The reasons for thanking God are endless.
Jesus by the Spirit daily just want to give favor and bless!

E: Closet Time 182

Lord Jesus, I praise You for generosity.
Lord Jesus, thank you for fulfilling every spiritual curiosity.
Lord Jesus, I will serve You with intent.
Lord Jesus, in the Spirit it's easy to daily repent.
Lord Jesus, rebaptize me in the Holy Spirit and fire.
Lord Jesus, renew in me a heart that Your will desires.
Lord Jesus, exchange my heart for one gentle and kind.
Lord Jesus, by the Spirit help me Your perfect will to find.
Lord Jesus, I need Your touch on my soul.
Lord Jesus, anoint me that I may never grow cold.
Lord Jesus, renew a heart that is devoted.
Lord Jesus, I ask for a mindset that of the Word is loaded.
Lord Jesus, help again think on things above.
Lord Jesus, help me walk wise as serpent and gentle as a dove.
Lord Jesus, wash me in Your blood anew.
Lord Jesus, by the Spirit help me to be more like You!

"Immediately the boy's father exclaimed, 'I do believe; help me overcome my unbelief!'" (Mark 9:24).
"He must increase, but I *must* decrease" (John 3:30).

Asking and repenting goes a long way toward becoming.
Jesus by the Spirit help the process of Jesus forming!

THE OLD IS BETTER

The world moves daily ahead.
Many continue to reminisce on the past instead.
God moves forward forgiving the past.
Faithful believers that are God progressive will last.
The wilderness shows a constant disgruntled crowd.
Miracles came consistently but God was not allowed.
They bickered and moaned and God they couldn't hear.
Thinking of the past, they missed that God was daily near.
Then God in Jesus came in the mist.
The best they could do was to vehemently resist.
The old is better is a sin attitude hard to recover.
The old is better wouldn't allow a Jesus takeover!

"Forget the former things; do not dwell on the past" (Isa. 43:18).
"Then He added, 'Every teacher...who becomes a disciple in the Kingdom of Heaven...brings from his storeroom new gems of truth as well as old'" (Matt. 13:52).

Dwelling on the past clouds the future while distracting from the present.
Jesus by the Spirit ABBA's perfect will augment!

A: CLOSET TIME 203

Holy Spirit, I exalt Your awesome power.
Holy Spirit, I come to praise and worship this hour.
Holy Spirit, I come to gain Your approval.
Holy Spirit, help me make the needed heart sin removal!
Holy Spirit, possess me to be my utter delight.
Holy Spirit, anoint my heart and brighten my light.
Holy Spirit, walk me through this day.
Holy Spirit, empower my soul to be subject to Your way.
Holy Spirit, help me to discern when You clearly speak.
Holy Spirit, renew in my soul a move toward being meek.
Holy Spirit, You I really want to follow and know.
Holy Spirit, bless me that to the world Jesus I show!

"And the Holy Spirit descended on Him in bodily form, like a dove; and a voice came from heaven, 'You are My beloved Son; with You I am well pleased'" (Luke 3:22).

"Do you not know that your bodies are temples of the Holy Spirit, who is in you, whom you have received from God? You are not your own" (1 Cor. 6:19).

When Jesus becomes Savior, the Holy Spirit wants control.
Jesus by the Spirit look for the submitted in the fold!

JESUS HEARS 4

Jesus hears when we to Him voice our cares.
Jesus hears those that their burdens share.
Jesus hears the secrets of a bedroom.
Jesus hears us speaking as we push a broom.
Jesus hears the threats of the proud.
Jesus hears rebellious meetings very loud.
Jesus hears the humble plea of the widow.
Jesus hears the terminally ill weeping on the pillow.
Jesus hears the child whose father just left.
Jesus hears the wailing of the bereft.
Jesus hears an atheist mocking a believer.
Jesus hears the plans of our deceiver.
Jesus hears all earnest intercession.
Jesus hears and by the Spirit sends revelation!

"Jesus knew what they were thinking, so He asked them, 'Why do you have such evil thoughts in your hearts?'" (Matt. 9:4).

"The guards replied, 'Never [at any time] has a man talked the way this Man talks!'" (John 7:46).

Jesus spoke spiritual words that still raise the dead.
Jesus by the Spirit speak words to tell of what's ahead!

JESUS HEARS 3

Jesus hears the songs of praise from the birds below.
Jesus hears when the obedient spiritually grow.
Jesus hears the scheming of the demented.
Jesus hears the cries of the tormented.
Jesus hears the incarcerated.
Jesus hears the cry of sinners wanting to be separated.
Jesus hears the call of those that are being abused.
Jesus hears when righteous justice is being refused.
Jesus hears the earnest prayers of the oppressed.
Jesus hears when a backslider sincerely has confessed.
Jesus hears the songs of the devout.
Jesus hears of those testifying what He is about!

"We know that God does not listen to sinners, but if anyone is a worshiper of God and does His will, God listens to him" (John 9:31).

"And this is the confidence that we have toward Him, that if we ask anything according to His will He hears us" (1 John 5:14).

Worshiping and honoring His will gives in heaven great standing.

Jesus by the Spirit ABBA's best will is always reminding!

JESUS HEARS 2

Jesus hears the cry of a woman left in an emotional turmoil.
Her life had from the beginning cost her to mentally recoil.
Jesus hears her inner voice grasping for what is real.
The Holy Spirit agrees that she deserves a better deal.
Jesus hears the heart moaning for relief from mental strife.
As she settles into mid-age success flees in this life.
Jesus hears grasping for the God that she heard.
The Holy Spirit makes a date for her to meet the Living Word!
Jesus hears her in an area where it is hard to reach.
Jesus by the Spirit decide to go there and preach.
Jesus hears and sees her by a day deserted well.
Jesus by the Spirit hears that by the Living water her thirst They
will quell.
Jesus hears her to feel her out.
The woman at the well curiously wants to see what He is about.
Jesus hears her honest reaction.
Jesus by the Spirit offers Living Water as a spiritual attraction.
The woman responds desirous with affirmation.
Jesus by the Spirit send her away to spread salvation!

"Come and see the works of God; how awesome are His deeds toward mankind" (Ps. 66:5).

"Then the woman left her water jar, went back into the town, and said to the people, 'Come, see a man who told me everything I ever did. Could this be the Christ?'" (John 4:28–29).

Our Father in Jesus by the Spirit still hear the cry of the many.
Jesus by the Spirit still will quench spiritual thirst of any!

Jesus Hears 1

Lord Jesus, my request is for help to lift You higher.
Lord Jesus, come and be my temple Occupier.
Lord Jesus, for the Spirit, give me a new hunger and thirst.
Lord Jesus, rekindle in my heart to seek the Kingdom first.
Lord Jesus, refill me with the Spirit and holy fire.
Lord Jesus, by the Spirit, enhance my spiritual desire.
Lord Jesus, make me thoughtful of others speaking.
Lord Jesus, by the Spirit, help Your will to be seeking.
Lord Jesus, author new faith in me.
Lord Jesus, strengthen the faith that I have from Thee.
Lord Jesus, renew in me the joy of the Lord.
Lord Jesus, help me with the Trinity to be in accord!

"Before a word is on my tongue you, LORD, know it completely" (Ps. 139:4).

"But Jesus, knowing the thoughts of their hearts, had a little child stand beside Him" (Luke 9:47).

Our Father in Jesus wants to deliver and conform.
Jesus by the Spirit can the willing to His image transform!

RUNNING FROM GOD 3

Running from God is a foolish choice.
Running from God doesn't stop God's voice.
Running from God is a waste of time.
Running from God ends in a worldly slime.
Running from God disturbs all affections.
Running from God makes for seeking wrong directions.
Running from God comes from the pit of hell.
Running from God to the enemy our soul we sell.
Running from God brings on a psychological nightmare.
Running from God daily to hell we draw near.
Running from God makes us to be self-centered.
Running from God is the worse trap entered!

"When I refused to confess my sin, my body wasted away, and I groaned all day long. Day and night Your hand of discipline was heavy on me. My strength evaporated like water in the summer heat" (Ps. 32:3–4).

"You were running well. Who hindered you from obeying the truth?" (Gal. 5:7).

We are either running from or to God—our choice.
Jesus by the Spirit will train our ears to hear His voice!

Running from God 2

Running from God will never get too far.
Running from God is silly since He knows where you are.
Running from God is a condition of the will.
Running from God doesn't allow for the soul to be still.
Running from God is thinking of the past.
Running from God leads to a hellish life at last.
Running from God is Satan's distraction.
Running from God leads to a false attraction.
Running from God you will disregard being discreet.
Running from God will make you a spiritual cheat.
Running from God's forgiveness will be hard to get.
Running from God His ways we will forget.
Running from God rids opportunity.
Running from God leads to a false reality.

"I will run in the way of Your commandments when You enlarge my heart!" (Ps. 119:32).

"Where shall I go from Your Spirit? Or where shall I flee from Your presence?… If I take the wings of the morning and dwell in the uttermost parts of the sea, even there Your hand shall lead me, and Your right hand shall hold me" (Ps. 139:7–10).

Daily going to the Word, to God we are running.
Jesus by the Spirit in the prayer closet gives a new beginning!

RUNNING FROM GOD 1

Running from God is a malady of the heart.
Running from God is a slow walk at the start.
Running from God is Satan's ploy.
Running from God leads to false joy.
Running from God ends in a whale of a mess.
Running from God stops the presence to bless.
Running from God is a dead-end street.
Running from God with Jesus you won't meet.
Running from God makes good opportunities flea.
Running from God delays making a repentant plea.
Running from God is bad advice.
Running from God stops talking about Christ!

"But Jonah got up and went in the opposite direction to get away from the LORD… He bought a ticket…hoping to escape from the LORD…" (Jonah 1:3).

"Behold, I will bring to it health and healing, and I will heal them; and I will reveal to them an abundance of peace and truth" (Jer. 33:6).

Our Father is always waiting for our unconditional return.
Jesus by the Spirit will teach how God's voice we can discern!

AM: Thank-You Note 111

Thank you, ABBA, Father, that my prayers You hear.
Thank you, ABBA, Father, that You are always near.
Thank you, ABBA, Father, that answer every call.
Thank you, ABBA, Father, that You forgive when I fall.
Thank you, Lord Jesus, that my life is Your priority.
Thank you, Lord Jesus, that You and I are the majority.
Thank you, Lord Jesus, for mercy when You could judge.
Thank you, Lord Jesus, for help from You to not budge.
Thank you, Holy Spirit, for another being present today.
Thank you, Holy Spirit, for ears to hear what You say.
Thank you, Holy Spirit, for knowing what is ahead.
Thank you, Holy Spirit, that today by You I will the Gospel spread!

"Surely, Lord, You bless the righteous; You surround them with Your favor as with a shield" (Ps. 5:12).
"In every thing give thanks: for this is the will of God in Christ Jesus concerning you" (1 Thess. 5:18).

The directive to give thanks starts by using our will.
Jesus by the Spirit wants to daily give a baptism refill!

Dear ABBA, Father 33

I come to be a diligent seeker at Your disposal.
I come by the Holy Spirit to hear the day's proposal.
I come to be restored to worship and praise.
I come my anxiety and cares to You raise.
I come to gain a childlike mindset.
I come to live the day without being upset.
I come to ask help in becoming an intercessor.
I come with my sins to be an honest confessor.
I come to have You set my spirit free.
I come to first serve and honor Thee!
I come to deny self and pick up my cross.
I come in Jesus by the Spirit to respect You as my Boss!

"My help comes from the LORD, the Maker of heaven and earth" (Ps. 121:2).
"Give all your worries and cares to God, for He cares about you" (1 Pet. 5:7).

Talking to God in Jesus is meeting with our best Friend.
Jesus by the Spirit tells us ABBA's love He did send!

TODAY...64

Today, I will turn my prayer to the One who hears.
Today, I will stay close to the One who takes away my fears.
Today, I will repent of all that my godly walk hinders.
Today, I will look for a healing touch of ABBA's fingers.
Today, I will refuse to react from the flesh.
Today, I will from the prayer closet leave afresh.
Today, I will overlook the vilest insults.
Today, I will intercede for others godly results.
Today, I will expose to Jesus my sinful nature.
Today, I will by the Spirit bring the Trinity pleasure.
Today, I will give the Holy Spirit my will to control.
Today, I will stay in my Shepherd's fold.

"Then I acknowledged my sin to You and did not cover up my iniquity. I said, 'I will confess my transgressions to the Lord.' And You forgave the guilt of my sin" (Ps. 32:5).

"For the eyes of the Lord are on the righteous, and his ears are open to their prayer. But the face of the Lord is against those who do evil" (1 Pet. 3:12).

It is essential to recall daily that He listens for those who call.
Jesus by the Spirit helps on our prayer knees to fall!

M: Closet Time 203

ABBA, Father, I come to lay my sacrifice on the altar.
ABBA, Father, I come offering my body that mine ways You alter.
ABBA, Father, search me for sins of omission.
ABBA, Father, I seek forgiveness and favorable permission!
ABBA, Father, deliver me from the enemy's wiles.
ABBA, Father, in Jesus, grant a saintly smile!
ABBA, Father, I ask for favor on my upcoming deeds.
ABBA, Father, strengthen my quest to plant Gospel seeds.
ABBA, Father, anoint my spirit to be gentle and kind.
ABBA, Father, by the Spirit, help me Your perfect will to find.
ABBA, Father, rekindle a love for Word learning.
ABBA, Father, for things above help me to be yearning!

"For we are taking pains to do what is right, not only in the eyes of the Lord but also in the eyes of man" (2 Cor. 8:21).

"Do not lie to each other, since you have taken off your old self with its practices" (Col. 3:9).

Although God is always first, considering others is honorable with Him too.
Jesus by the Spirit will empower all needed to do!

E: CLOSET TIME 202

Holy Spirit, I come to praise You!
Holy Spirit, I come to exalt Your presence too.
Holy Spirit, I come to rejoice that for me You came.
Holy Spirit, thank you that Your faithfulness is still the same!
Holy Spirit, I want to know You personally.
Holy Spirit, I want to know You intimately.
Holy Spirit, search the depths of my soul.
Holy Spirit, empower me that for Jesus I am gracefully bold.
Holy Spirit, control my heart to better think.
Holy Spirit, give me a hatred for evil so at sin I never wink.
Holy Spirit, help me to speak and live without pretenses.
Holy Spirit, help me see sin with spiritual lenses!
Holy Spirit, possess me that to ABBA, Father I draw near.
Holy Spirit, open my eyes to see Jesus clear!

"Uncover my eyes so that I may see the miraculous things in Your teachings" (Ps. 119:18).

"And with that He breathed on them and said, 'Receive the Holy Spirit'" (John 20:22).

In order to crave the Word receiving the Holy Spirit is essential. Jesus by the Spirit will equip us with all the spiritual credentials!

PM: THANK-YOU NOTE 110

Thank you, ABBA, Father, for mercy in my failings.
Thank you, ABBA, Father, for the years of Word trainings.
Thank you, ABBA, Father, for trials the make me stronger.
Thank you, ABBA, Father, that I'm in Your presence longer!
Thank you, Lord Jesus, that You forgive when I confess.
Thank you, Lord Jesus, that in You ABBA, continues to bless.
Thank you, Lord Jesus, for abundant living.
Thank you, Lord Jesus, that Your grace I keep receiving.
Thank you, Holy Spirit, for guiding me to know the Word.
Thank you, Holy Spirit, for help to retain what I have heard.
Thank you, Holy Spirit, for wisdom that makes me smart.
Thank you, Holy Spirit, that daily in Your presence I start!

"Your word is a lamp to guide my feet and a light for my path"
(Ps. 119:105).
"Work hard so you can present yourself to God and receive His
approval. Be a good worker, one who does not need to be ashamed
and who correctly explains the word of truth" (2 Tim. 2:15).

The Word of God is perfect and will perfect the imperfect!
Jesus by the Spirit uses the Word to bring favorable affect!

TODAY...45A

Today, I will enjoy those around me.
Today, I will in Jesus by the Spirit ABBA, Father see.
Today, I will count my every blessing.
Today, I will with sinful ways stop messing.
Today, I will relearn to repent sincerely and quick.
Today, I will walk humbly and meek.
Today, I will prioritize ABBA, Father to please.
Today, I will look for ABBA, Father rewards to release.
Today, I will meditate on the Word and God's deeds.
Today, I will spread Gospel seeds.
Today, I will water seeds that are planted.
Today, I will avoid when the Word is slanted.
Today, I will bury opinions in the cemetery.
Today, I will my own perspective on the Word not carry.
Today, I will lift up the Lord for others to know.
Today, I will let the Holy Spirit in me, His power to show!

"Don't be impressed with your own wisdom. Instead, fear the Lord and turn away from evil" (Prov. 3:7).

"But He giveth more grace; therefore He saith, 'God resisteth the proud, but giveth grace unto the humble'" (James 4:6).

When genuine humbleness is shown, there is lots of grace.
Jesus by the Spirit will keep our heart in the right place!

DEAR ABBA, FATHER 32

I come my soul and heart to bear.
I come to seek Your presence because You care.
I come with You to get reacquainted.
I come for Your power that acting on sin is prevented.
I come to give You honor and glory in my day.
I come to hear You along the way.
I come to the prayer closet for daily security.
I come to live out Your promises, for rewarding surety.
I come to learn from the Holy Spirit something new.
I come to know more of my Lord too.
I come to submit my body for Kingdom use.
I come to be strong in sinful situations to refuse.
I come from my setbacks to recover.
I come to request by the Spirit a spiritual makeover!

"To do righteousness and justice is more acceptable to the Lord than sacrifice" (Prov. 21:3).

"Like newborn babies, long for the pure milk of the word, so that by it you may grow in respect to salvation" (1 Pet. 2:2).

Sacrifices often is the carnal nature trying to appease.
Jesus by the Spirit will show how ABBA, Father we can please!

DEAR ABBA, FATHER 13

I come to walk in the abundant living.
I come for greater grace from Jesus receiving.
I come to cast down any remaining stronghold.
I come to gain confidence in being gracefully bold.
I come to rekindle trusting You all day long.
I come to walk in the Spirit and in the Lord be strong.
I come to learn to become all things to all.
I come to prepare for rescuing those that in sin fall.
I come in Your presence to "consider my ways."
I come to receive what of me You have to say.
I come by the Holy Spirit to alter my thinking.
I come to Your perfect will to be linking!

"But when Jesus saw this, He was indignant and said to them, 'Permit the children to come to Me; do not hinder them; for the kingdom of God belongs to such as these'" (Mark 10:14).

"So you have not received a spirit that makes you fearful slaves. Instead, you received God's Spirit when He adopted you as His own children. Now we call Him, 'Abba, Father'" (Rom. 8:15).

For eternity we will embrace His eternal Fatherhood.

Jesus by the Spirit exposes the Fatherhood to those that act like they should!

AM: THANK-YOU NOTE 93

Thank you, ABBA, Father, for a day to be fruitful.
Thank you, ABBA, Father, to enjoy all that is beautiful.
Thank you, ABBA, Father, for lines that I will not cross.
Thank you, ABBA, Father, that You are my Spiritual Boss!
Thank you, Lord Jesus, for the shedding of Your blood.
Thank you, Lord Jesus, that Your love is a torrent flood.
Thank you, Lord Jesus, for daily intervention.
Thank you, Lord Jesus, that I have Your attention.
Thank you, Holy Spirit, that You make promises come through.
Thank you, Holy Spirit, that nothing fools You.
Thank you, Holy Spirit, for helping me ABBA, Father to respect.
Thank you, Holy Spirit, for recall that I'm of God elect!

"Sacrifice thank offerings to God, fulfill your vows to the Most High, and call on Me in the day of trouble; I will deliver You, and You will honor Me" (Ps. 50:15).

"When he calls out to Me, I will answer him; I will be with him in trouble. I will deliver him and honor him" (Ps. 91:15).

When we maintain a priority prayer closet, Him, we are calling.
Jesus by the Spirit will keep us from falling!

A: Closet Time 202

Lord Jesus, by the Spirit come work in me deeper.
Lord Jesus, bring greater clarity to You being my Keeper.
Lord Jesus, anoint me to appreciate of ABBA, Father.
Lord Jesus, help me to love God like no other.
Lord Jesus, by the Spirit help me be more willing.
Lord Jesus, strengthen my ways to hate sinning.
Lord Jesus, help me partake of Your agape love.
Lord Jesus, help me keep my mind on things above.
Lord Jesus, renew in me Your will to yearn.
Lord Jesus, give a childlike heart to continue to learn.
Lord Jesus, make me desirous of revival.
Lord Jesus, anoint my resolve for spiritual survival!

"Whoever then humbles himself as this child, he is the greatest in the kingdom of heaven" (Matt. 18:4).

"Truly I say to you, whoever does not receive the kingdom of God like a child will not enter it at all" (Luke 18:17).

Childlikeness exudes a genuine trust level worthy of all heavenly attention.

Jesus by the Spirit takes childlike followers to the fast track of redemption!

M: CLOSET TIME 183

Lord Jesus, I come for wisdom to accomplish this task.
Lord Jesus, I come because in Your name I can ask.
Lord Jesus, I seek Your input and Your might is my reliance.
Lord Jesus, by the Spirit, I commit to compliance.
Lord Jesus, I come to seek Your will on the influential approval.
Lord Jesus, I open my heart for flushing all needing removal.
Lord Jesus, I come to submit my will.
Lord Jesus, grant grace to be quiet, confident and still.
Lord Jesus, I come with the Spirit to be clothed.
Lord Jesus, may my heart and mind to You be transposed.
Lord Jesus, I give You my inner man.
Lord Jesus, make me the best vessel You can.

"The One forming light and creating darkness, Causing well-being and creating calamity; I am the Lord who does all these" (Isa. 45:7).

"And Jesus came and spake unto them, saying, All power is given unto me in heaven and in earth" (Matt. 28:18).

Every person who calls Jesus their Savior heaven writes it down.
Jesus by the Spirit will heal all that by sin bound!

A: Closet Time 183

Holy Spirit, I come to be fully guided.
Holy Spirit, I come to know how in the Word I am abiding.
Holy Spirit, I ask for You to show me how to pray.
Holy Spirit, take my heart and guide along God's way.
Holy Spirit, come perfect in me something new.
Holy Spirit, anoint my mind to better sense You.
Holy Spirit, possess my will to be best led.
Holy Spirit, control my tongue and will to shed.
Holy Spirit, come live in this temple today.
Holy Spirit, come make Your home in me to stay.
Holy Spirit, help me to submit my body a living sacrifice.
Holy Spirit, help me present selfishness as the ultimate price.
Holy Spirit, purge from my will what is self-inclined.
Holy Spirit, direct me that in Your perfect will I'm aligned.
Holy Spirit, possess me as You help heal my emotions.
Holy Spirit, flush my heart from all past commotions.
Holy Spirit, anoint my spirit to best carry my sword.
Holy Spirit, create in me a mindset of my Lord.

"At that same time Jesus was filled with the joy of the Holy Spirit, and He said, 'O Father, Lord of heaven and earth, thank you for hiding these things from those who think themselves wise and clever, and for revealing them to the childlike. Yes, Father, it pleased you to do it this way'" (Luke 10:21).

"So in Christ Jesus you are all children of God through faith" (Gal. 3:26).

God in Jesus by the Spirit reclaims His children in the act of salvation.

Jesus by the Spirit starts the process by making us a new creation!

PM: Thank-You Note 93

Thank you, ABBA, Father, for watching me with Your eyes.
Thank you, ABBA, Father, that my life in Jesus is actualize.
Thank you, ABBA, Father, for the promise of eternal bliss.
Thank you, ABBA, Father, for promises filled that I reminisce.
Thank you, Lord Jesus, for sending the Spirit to lead.
Thank you, Lord Jesus, for Your eternal deed.
Thank you, Lord Jesus, for being at the prayer closet.
Thank you, Lord Jesus, for Your timely deposit.
Thank you, Holy Spirit, for Your daily indwelling.
Thank you, Holy Spirit, that my heart for You keeps swelling.
Thank you, Holy Spirit, for the work in me.
Thank you, Holy Spirit, for the things in the Word I see.
Thank you, Holy Spirit, that You will never leave.
Thank you, Holy Spirit, for helping me know when You I grieve!

"Whoever believes and is baptized will be saved, but whoever does not believe will be condemned" (Mark 16:16).

"May the grace of the Lord Jesus Christ, and the love of God, and the fellowship of the Holy Spirit be with you all" (2 Cor. 13:14).

Salvation is consummated when water baptism follows.
Jesus by the Spirit will keep the believer from the shallow!

E: Closet Time 183

ABBA, Father, thank you for another eventful night.
ABBA, Father, I'm grateful that You help me do right.
ABBA, Father, I praise and exalt who You are.
ABBA, Father, it is comforting to know that You watch from afar.
ABBA, Father, heal my sinful deficiencies.
ABBA, Father, thanks for nullifying my hostilities.
ABBA, Father, create in me a heart that's pure.
ABBA, Father, by the Spirit, help me walk secure.
ABBA, Father, help me to trust in You for all.
ABBA, Father, enhance in me to spontaneously call.
ABBA, Father, by the Spirit, draw me closer to Thee.
ABBA, Father, help through Your eyes the world to see!

"For as many of you as were baptized into Christ have put on Christ" (Gal. 3:27).
"Because you are His sons, God sent the Spirit of His Son into our hearts, the Spirit who calls out, '*Abba, Father*'" (Gal. 4:6).

Salvation ushers in new life and a new way of thinking.
Jesus by the Spirit will facilitate our heavenly linking!

TODAY…45B

Today, I will take a spiritual inventory.
Today, I will repent of all that I am sincerely sorry.
Today, I will with any offended try to make amends.
Today, I will hear and obey were the Holy Spirit sends.
Today, I will in God's mirror look at my attitude.
Today, I will by the Spirit regain the gift of servitude.
Today, I will search my heart for selfish impulses.
Today, I will castoff all that the Trinity repulses.
Today, I will relinquish any personal right.
Today, I will continue to be in the center of ABBA's sight.
Today, I will walk in the Spirit and not fulfill the flesh.
Today, I will by ABBA, Father in Jesus look to be afresh!

"Create in me a clean heart, O God. Renew a loyal spirit within me" (Ps. 51:10).

"And my God will meet all your needs according to the riches of his glory in Christ Jesus" (Phil. 4:19).

To have is to want if we ask for daily needs.
Jesus by the Spirit never forget those that plant seeds!

DEAR ABBA, FATHER 30

I come my heart and soul to bare.
I come knowing that You even count my hair.
I come because You are the perfect Father.
I come because truly You are like no other.
I come my burdens to unstrap and to You release.
I come by the Spirit that what I do You I may please.
I come to ever draw closer to Your presence.
I come to ask for a portion of Your Essence.
I come to continue being a diligent seeker.
I come that only by the Holy Spirit I become a speaker.
I come that You can make me more like the only Begotten.
I come that testifying of Jesus is never forgotten!

"He is like a tree planted by streams of water, yielding its fruit in season, whose leaf does not wither, and who prospers in all he does" (Ps. 1:3).
"He was...full of the Holy Spirit and faith, and a great number of people were brought to the Lord" (Acts 11:24).

God has definitely set out many spiritual perks.
Jesus by the Spirit will guide to what are real heavenly works!

M: Closet Time 202

Lord Jesus, to Your presence, I come to explore.
Lord Jesus, I come to know You better and more.
Lord Jesus, I come to You exposing my heart of flesh.
Lord Jesus, search and purge as my spirit You refresh.
Lord Jesus, renew what is frail.
Lord Jesus, empower me over the flesh to prevail.
Lord Jesus, come extract from me what is carnally vain.
Lord Jesus, help me in Holy Spirit to faithfully remain!
Lord Jesus, rebaptize me in the Spirit and holy fire.
Lord Jesus, help that Your anointing in me never expire!
Lord Jesus, come in my temple to do a new work of grace.
Lord Jesus, anoint me that with Your perfect will I keep pace!

"Then He said, 'I tell you the truth, unless you turn from your sins and become like little children, you will never get into the Kingdom of Heaven'" (Matt. 18:3).

"You can pray for anything, and if you have faith, you will receive it" (Matt. 21:22).

Becoming a child is real for the many who meet ABBA, Father.

Jesus by the Spirit will make sure that all know He is like no other!

AM: THANK-YOU NOTE 110

Thank you, ABBA, Father, for words in prayer to write.
Thank you, ABBA, Father, for help the enemy's wiles to fight.
Thank you, ABBA, Father, for love that is pure.
Thank you, ABBA, Father, that I have a place in heaven for sure.
Thank you, Lord Jesus, for life abundantly.
Thank you, Lord Jesus, for the many in salvation accompany.
Thank you, Lord Jesus, for being my eternal substitute.
Thank you, Lord Jesus, that my salvation is absolute!
Thank you, Holy Spirit, for helping me of the Trinity to learn.
Thank you, Holy Spirit, that Jesus You help me to yearn.
Thank you, Holy Spirit, for what You will teach today.
Thank you, Holy Spirit, for help in the straight and narrow to stay!

"God blesses those people who refuse evil advice and won't follow sinners or join in sneering at God" (Ps. 1:1).
"Because strait is the gate, and narrow is the way, which leadeth unto life, and few there be that find it" (Matt. 7:14).

Real believers avoid situations that are ungodly.
Jesus by the Spirit wants to teach abundant living gladly!

TODAY...63

Today, I will be a vessel of the Holy Spirit's use.
Today, I will for Jesus's sake nothing refuse.
Today, I will look to God's mirror for needed adjustment.
Today, I will avoid sinful ways that lead to judgement.
Today, I will show that ABBA, Father I honor and revere.
Today, I will for Jesus by the Spirit show respectful fear.
Today, I will love the Lord with all my heart, soul and might.
Today, I will do what ABBA, Father says is right!
Today, I will walk in the Spirit to be more productive.
Today, I will take from the Holy Spirit what is instructive.
Today, I will reawaken a desire to be a witness.
Today, I will by the Spirit be about ABBA, Father's business!

"Seek the Kingdom of God above all else, and live righteously, and He will give you everything you need" (Matt. 6:33).
"So don't worry about tomorrow, for tomorrow will bring its own worries. Today's trouble is enough for today" (Matt. 6:34).

Learning to seek God first will relieve all of the day's worry.
Jesus by the Spirit will all Your burdens carry!

Dear ABBA, Father 14

I come to submit my will and heart.
I come for mercy, grace, and a brand-new start.
I come to be made new in ways needing attention.
I come for a meditative mindset retention.
I come to ask, seek, and knock for change that is lasting.
I come for all my anxieties and cares to You I am casting.
I come to request Your direct intervention.
I come for the Holy Spirit's direction.
I come to regain the faith of a child.
I come so that today I enjoy an eternal smile.
I come to relearn perfect submission.
I come to learn asking and following permission.
I come for an infusion of being lowly of heart and meek.
I come to give priority when in the Word You speak.
I come ABBA, Father to seek Your perfect advice.
I come Holy Spirit to be guided to Christ!

"And if it seem evil unto you to serve the LORD, choose you this day whom you will serve; whether the gods which your fathers served...but as for me and my house, we will serve the LORD" (Josh. 24:15).

"Chosen according to the foreknowledge of God the Father, through the sanctifying work of the Spirit, to be obedient to Jesus Christ and sprinkled with his blood: Grace and peace be yours in abundance" (1 Pet. 1:2).

Choosing for God is the greatest act of bravery.
Jesus by the Spirit release believers from sinful slavery!

AM: THANK-YOU NOTE 94

Thank you, ABBA, Father, for hearing my prayer request.
Thank you, ABBA, Father, for always answering the best.
Thank you, ABBA, Father, for always caring.
Thank you, ABBA, Father, for help on You to be sharing.
Thank you, Lord Jesus, for dying on the cross.
Thank you, Lord Jesus, that You love the ones still loss.
Thank you, Lord Jesus, for modeling a servant's walk.
Thank you, Lord Jesus, that daily with You I can talk.
Thank you, Holy Spirit, for being my Quality Control.
Thank you, Holy Spirit, for strength to do what I'm told.
Thank you, Holy Spirit, for helping to making whole my pieces.
Thank you, Holy Spirit, that You show me Jesus!

"Now therefore fear the LORD, and serve Him in sincerity and in truth: and put away" (Josh. 24:14a).

"Therefore, brethren, select from among you seven men of good reputation, full of the Spirit and of wisdom, whom we may put in charge of this task" (Acts 6:3).

Serving the Trinity with sincerity and truth is a must.
Jesus by the Spirit in salvation makes all righteous and just!

A: Closet Time 201

ABBA, Father, strengthen my hate for sin.
ABBA, Father, others in Jesus help me assist as they begin.
ABBA, Father, help me to meditate on Your deeds.
ABBA, Father, help me be guided as the Holy Spirit leads.
ABBA, Father, take me deeper into Your will.
ABBA, Father, I ask for a new Holy Spirit refill.
ABBA, Father, help me to trust.
ABBA, Father, help me repent when I must.
ABBA, Father, give me a heart of gold.
ABBA, Father, by the Spirit, help me do what I'm told.
ABBA, Father, for Your sake keep me from sins that are colossal.
ABBA, Father, in Jesus, make me docile!

"And the Holy Spirit descended on Him in bodily form like a dove. And a voice came from heaven: 'You are My Son, whom I love; with You I am well pleased.'"

"Jesus, full of the Holy Spirit, returned from the Jordan and was led around by the Spirit in the wilderness" (Luke 4:11).

The Holy Spirit still wants to lead in the wilderness of life.
Jesus by the Spirit will teach us how to live above strife!

E: Closet Time 201

Holy Spirit, I persist in reaching out to know You.
Holy Spirit, daily I want You to fill my temple too.
Holy Spirit, I am grateful for all conviction.
Holy Spirit, search my heart purge and make sins eviction.
Holy Spirit, flush past residue of any hint is sin.
Holy Spirit, into a deeper journey do help me begin.
Holy Spirit, possess my spirit to better obey.
Holy Spirit, anoint my ears to hear what You say.
Holy Spirit, renew in me the Word to ponder.
Holy Spirit, in Jesus may I enjoy Your miraculous wonder.
Holy Spirit, I ask for a greater desire to intercede.
Holy Spirit, help me in Your perfect will to proceed.
Holy Spirit, restore in me more resolved consecration.
Holy Spirit, advance me in my sanctification.
Holy Spirit, increase my initiative to be holy.
Holy Spirit, as my Guide help me to trust You only!

"On the other hand, I am filled with power—With the Spirit of the Lord…" (Mic. 3:8a).

"Now to Him who is able to do so much more than all we ask or imagine, according to His power that is at work within us" (Ephesians 3:20).

The power of the Holy Spirit is available "to the least of these."
Jesus by the Spirit will take us so that serving we will Him please!

PM: Thank-You Note 109

Thank you, ABBA, Father, for a day of victory and insight.
Thank you, ABBA, Father, that diligence brings You delight.
Thank you, ABBA, Father, for daily affirmation.
Thank you, ABBA, Father, for love to enhance inspiration.
Thank you, Lord Jesus, for life that is just beginning.
Thank you, Lord Jesus, that in eternity there is no ending.
Thank you, Lord Jesus, for paying my sins price.
Thank you, Lord Jesus, for help out of sin and vice.
Thank you, Holy Spirit, for helping to enjoy my day.
Thank you, Holy Spirit, for ears to hear what You say.
Thank you, Holy Spirit, for holy conviction.
Thank you, Holy Spirit, for help to overcome all addiction!

"When He comes, He will prove the world to be in the wrong about sin and righteousness and judgment" (John 16:8).

When the Holy Spirit convicts it is only to correct.
Jesus by the Spirit gives grace to who His will respect!

"Because you are His sons, God sent the Spirit of His Son into our hearts, the Spirit who calls out, 'ABBA, Father'" (Gal. 4:6).

M: Closet Time 184

ABBA, Father, my heart is in need of repair.
ABBA, Father, I seek Your wisdom in all my affairs.
ABBA, Father, I come to the Throne in surrender.
ABBA, Father, I come for Your touch to make me tender.
ABBA, Father, I come boldly for essential grace.
ABBA, Father, in my decision making, I seek Your face.
ABBA, Father, in Jesus, to You I release my cares.
ABBA, Father, by the Spirit, anoint and strengthen my prayers.
ABBA, Father, help me to walk in agape love.
ABBA, Father, by the Spirit, help keep my mind on above.
ABBA, Father, help me rejoice that my name is in Your book.
ABBA, Father, help throughout this day to Your will be hooked.

"Then I will go to the altar of God, To God my exceeding joy; And upon the lyre I shall praise You, O God, my God" (Ps. 43:4).

"Let us then with confidence draw near to the throne of grace, that we may receive mercy and find grace to help in time of need" (Heb. 4:16).

Frequenting the prayer closet will change exude joy at the altar. Jesus by the Spirit will undergird and cover us when we falter!

A: Closet Time 184

Lord Jesus, I come to request Your intervention.
Lord Jesus, help me move in Your direction.
Lord Jesus, make me a vessel of gold.
Lord Jesus, by the Spirit, help me be lovingly bold.
Lord Jesus, heal my feelings and emotions.
Lord Jesus, strengthen in me to give You full devotion.
Lord Jesus, help me to better hear when You speak.
Lord Jesus, erase from my heart things that my attention seek.
Lord Jesus, possess my heart and make me holy.
Lord Jesus, purge in me what is impeding to serve You only.
Lord Jesus, renew my impetus to serve.
Lord Jesus, strengthen my faith that my heart for You I preserve.

"Ask Me, and I will make the nations your inheritance, the ends of the earth your possession" (Ps. 2:8).

"And I will do whatever you ask in My name, so that the Father may be glorified in the Son" (John 14:13).

Asking for what most delights God is a sure way to get.
Jesus by the Spirit looks upon the faithful and never forget!

PM: Thank-You Note 94

Thank you, ABBA, Father, for using me today.
Thank you, ABBA, Father, that I was a blessing in some way.
Thank you, ABBA, Father, for years of not backsliding.
Thank you, ABBA, Father, for all You continue providing.
Thank you, Lord Jesus, that You speak of me in heaven.
Thank you, Lord Jesus, for help to keep me from sinful leaven.
Thank you, Lord Jesus, for a life of faith and grace.
Thank you, Lord Jesus, for help to stay in my spiritual place.
Thank you, Holy Spirit, that You never are tire of me.
Thank you, Holy Spirit, that by Your blood You set me free.
Thank you, Holy Spirit, for always being there.
Thank you, Holy Spirit, that You go with me everywhere!

"Offer to God a sacrifice of thanksgiving, And pay your vows to the Most High" (Ps. 50:14).

"The grace of the Lord Jesus Christ and the love of God and the fellowship of the Holy Spirit be with you all" (2 Cor. 13:14).

Thanksgiving is a sacrifice until Spirit revelation.
Jesus by the Spirit give grace to form thankful appreciation!

E: Closet Time 184

Holy Spirit, I exalt You as my Friend.
Holy Spirit, I praise that You are with me till the end.
Holy Spirit, help me to know You firsthand.
Holy Spirit, help me follow when You give a command.
Holy Spirit, possess my spirit to faithfully obey.
Holy Spirit, open my heart and mind to better pray.
Holy Spirit, renew my meditation.
Holy Spirit, grant me new wisdom and revelation.
Holy Spirit, infuse in me the power to be humble.
Holy Spirit, help my reactive defenses to crumble.
Holy Spirit, help me to be slow to speak and fast to hear.
Holy Spirit, make my will in things more clear.
Holy Spirit, flush my heart from all that hinders.
Holy Spirit, touch me where it is deficient with Your fingers.
Holy Spirit, I release all hint of sin from my inner soul.
Holy Spirit, I confess and reject sin to be whole.
Holy Spirit, expose any secret in my heart.
Holy Spirit, reconstruct all my broken parts.

"My mouth is filled with Your praise, And with Your glory all day long" (Ps. 71:8).

"God of our Lord Jesus Christ, the Father of glory, may give you the Spirit of wisdom and of revelation in the knowledge of Him" (Eph. 1:17).

Habitual sincere praising of God expedites the spiritual walk.
Jesus by the Spirit awaits at the prayer closet to talk!

A Trinity's Intimacy

Intimacy with the Holy Spirit is for the childlike curious.
In Jesus by the Spirit, our resolve must be intensely serious!
Childlikeness is ABBA, Father advanced.
Childlikeness is willingly following a command.
Intimacy gets greater in honest obedience.
We can't improvise out of convenience!
Intimacy desires the other more than self.
Intimacy puts feelings on a shelf.
Intimacy is a long-term commitment.
Intimacy is done with God's equipment.
Intimacy isn't there when daily we ask not.
Intimacy with the Spirit you know you got!

"But He will baptize you with the Holy Spirit" (Mark 1:8b).
"And whether you turn to the right or to the left, your ears will hear this command behind you: 'This is the way. Walk in it'" (Isa. 30:21).

All intimacies will take effort if it is genuinely sincere.
Jesus by the Spirit wait in the prayer closet for us to draw near!

AM: Thank-You Note 95

Thank you, ABBA, Father, that You put things in order.
Thank you, ABBA, Father, for making me a Word hoarder.
Thank you, ABBA, Father, healing all disorders.
Thank you, ABBA, Father, that our life in Jesus is on recorders.
Thank you, Lord Jesus, for help to succeed.
Thank you, Lord Jesus, that Your power meets every need.
Thank you, Lord Jesus, for accountability.
Thank you, Lord Jesus, that by the Spirit I have credibility.
Thank you, Holy Spirit, for help in correcting wrong.
Thank you, Holy Spirit, that You don't let me stay in sin long.
Thank you, Holy Spirit, that You are gentle.
Thank you, Holy Spirit, for healing issues that are mental!

"So I will bless You as long as I live; I will lift up my hands in Your name" (Ps. 63:4).

"So then we pursue the things which make for peace and the building up of one another" (Rom. 14:19).

Christianity is about building up one another.
Jesus by the Spirit is there when betrayed to recover!

M: Closet Time 185

Lord Jesus, I come to the closet for renewal.
Lord Jesus, I come for refill and spiritual refuel.
Lord Jesus, my heart needs repair.
Lord Jesus, anoint my spirit that I can show genuine care.
Lord Jesus, restore my faith to better witness.
Lord Jesus, help me be about my ABBA's business.
Lord Jesus, possess my soul and renew my mind.
Lord Jesus, help me focus on Your will to find.
Lord Jesus, to You this day I recommit.
Lord Jesus, bless my efforts to submit.
Lord Jesus, I ask for commitment to stay faithful.
Lord Jesus, strengthen me to stay graceful.
Lord Jesus, I ask that You in and with the Spirit rebaptize.
Lord Jesus, help me ABBA's will to realize.
Lord Jesus, anoint my tongue to speak.
Lord Jesus, help me be lowly of heart and meek.

"The Lord opens the eyes of the blind; The Lord raises up those who are bowed down; The Lord loves the righteous" (Ps. 146:8).
"Blessed are the peacemakers, for they shall be called sons of God" (Matt. 5:9).

That God loves the righteous is sure by the provided gifts.
Jesus by the Spirit gives the righteous daily lifts!

BACKSLIDING...

Backsliding is a spiritual decease.
Backsliding happens as, ABBA, we no longer please!
Backsliding is hard to self-detect.
Backsliding true prophets will reject!
Backsliding is Satan's slow motion ploy.
Backsliding loses spontaneous joy!
Backsliding is a heart malady, needing repair.
Backsliding makes excuses with care.
Backsliding purports to be very spiritual.
Backsliding, blaming others, is habitual.
Backsliding will the condition justify.
Backsliding doesn't allow for Jesus sin to verify!

"If we confess our sins, He is faithful and just to forgive us our sins and to cleanse us from all unrighteousness" (1 John 1:9)

"But since you are like lukewarm water, neither hot nor cold, I will spit you out of My mouth" (Rev. 3:16)!

Forgiveness from the Lord is always free.
Jesus by the Spirit will the repentant see!

TODAY...46

Today, I will pray more and worry less.
Today, I will walk in the Spirit that others I bless.
Today, I will take time to focus on sharing.
Today, I will with others not be comparing.
Today, I will keep my mind stay on You.
Today, I will increase my faith by showing I trust too.
Today, I will go the extra mile when mistreated.
Today, I will return good for evil when the ill is repeated.
Today, I will present my body a living sacrifice.
Today, I will train to be a vessel of gold no matter the price.
Today, I will to the Word pay more attention.
Today, I will look and think in heaven's direction!

"But they delight in the law of the LORD, meditating on it day and night" (Ps. 1:2).

"My help comes from the LORD, who made heaven and earth!" (Ps. 121:2).

A godly resolution a day will keep us focused on what we say.
Jesus by the Spirit strengthens all that we pray!

Dear Abba, Father 15

I come to worship You as the God of all creation.
I come to exalt You as the Sovereign of salvation.
I come to show my reverence and respect.
I come praise and honor You without regret.
I come to have my heart set properly.
I come to present myself to You bodily.
I come to be a vessel of honor and glory.
I come to be reminded that this life is merely transitory.
I come my feelings and selfish ways to surrender.
I come to exalt You as my only Defender.
I come to confess and renounce my failures and faults.
I come to seek favorable results.
I come to be healed from old ways of thinking.
I come with the Holy Spirit to be linking.
I come to learn to love You with a perfect heart.
I come to daily from Your presence never to part!

"The LORD is my light and my salvation—whom shall I fear? The LORD is the stronghold of my life—whom shall I dread?" (Ps. 27:1).

"Where can I go from Your Spirit? Or where can I flee from Your presence? If I ascend into heaven, You *are* there; If I make my bed in hell, behold, You *are there*" (Ps. 139:7–8).

In ABBA's presence, we must bare all.
Jesus by the Spirit will heal from that sinful fall!

SPEAKING TO GOD

Spiritual language is God's direct connection.
ABBA, Father opened it for joyous affirmation.
Speaking your spiritual language will advance how you mature.
ABBA, Father will not allow any interruption for sure.
The enemy will try to destroy or distract.
As you pray in tongues the enemy will retract.
Spiritual prayer language is in private only.
Watch your heart thinking you're so holy!
Spiritual prayer language will to ABBA, Father draw you closer.
You learn to empathetically overlook the negative poser.
Speaking in private with God is very rewarding.
Speaking in tongues is God the diligent seeker awarding!

"For he who speaks in a tongue does not speak to men, but to God. Indeed, no one understands him; he utters mysteries in the Spirit" (1 Cor. 14:2).
"So...do not forbid the speaking with tongues" (1 Cor. 14:39).

Speaking to God direct is a rewarding affirmation.
Jesus by the Spirit has made a direct prayer connection!

DEAR ABBA, FATHER 29

I come my heart and soul to bare.
I come my inner turmoil to detail and share.
I come to be strong in the Lord.
I come with the Trinity to stay in one accord.
I come to confess and renounce all stunts spiritually growing.
I come that by the Spirit in Jesus I am flowing.
I come to refocus on telling the Gospel story.
I come to seek God first and expand my spiritual auditory.
I come to restore my mind on things above.
I come to be renewed with agape love.
I come to continue to know my Lord infinitely.
I come by the Spirit to know Jesus with intimacy.

"Then Jesus said, 'Come to Me, all of you who are weary and carry heavy burdens, and I will give you rest'" (Matt. 11:28).
"Everyone the Father gives Me will come to Me, and the one who comes to Me I will never drive away" (John 6:37).

It is comforting that the Lord will never a repentant person reject.
Jesus by the Spirit is forever ready to all accept!

TODAY...62

Today, I will seek the Lord with priority.
Today, I will avoid all appearance of sin and frivolity.
Today, I will seek to know the Holy Spirit more.
Today, I will move forward when in Jesus I am sure.
Today, I will walk in the Spirit and talk less.
Today, I will look to ABBA, Father for Him to bless.
Today, I will respect the Trinity in my endeavors.
Today, I will reject anything that doing God's will severs.
Today, I will expose myself to ABBA, for scrutiny.
Today, I will order my ways to be faithful and be fruitfully.
Today, I will submit my body for Holy Spirit possession.
Today, I will trust Jesus with my candid confession!

"Trust in the LORD with all your heart; do not depend on your own understanding" (Prov. 3:5).

"If we confess our sins, He is faithful and just to forgive us our sins and to cleanse us from all unrighteousness" (1 John 1:9).

Trusting God is an acquired habit by an act of the will.
Jesus by the Spirit daily wants all to come for a refill!

AM: Thank-You Note 109

Thank you, ABBA, Father, that You I can fully trust.
Thank you, ABBA, Father, that gifts in Jesus are a must.
Thank you, ABBA, Father, for perfect peace.
Thank you, ABBA, Father, for answering my original fleece.
Thank you, Lord Jesus, in sending the Holy Spirit to bless.
Thank you, Lord Jesus, that in knowing You I obsess.
Thank you, Lord Jesus, that this faith walk is real.
Thank you, Lord Jesus, that You are the only deal!
Thank you, Holy Spirit, for opening my eyes to see Jesus.
Thank you, Holy Spirit, in recovering my broken pieces.
Thank you, Holy Spirit, that You are guiding.
Thank you, Holy Spirit, for help in Jesus to continue abiding.

"The thief's purpose is to steal and kill and destroy. My purpose is to give them a rich and satisfying life" (John 10:10).
"Now you are My friends, since I have told you everything the Father told Me" (John 15:15b).

Being grateful recalls God's past experienced deeds.
In Jesus by the Holy Spirit we gladly plant seeds!

M: Closet Time 201

Lord Jesus, I will forever give You praise.
Lord Jesus, I come my body as a sacrifice to You raise.
Lord Jesus, I come to experience Your Lordship.
Lord Jesus, from Your hands, I will never slip.
Lord Jesus, I'm resolved to serve You only.
Lord Jesus, I ask that by the Spirit I am made holy!
Lord Jesus, I come my sinful heart to expose.
Lord Jesus, humility and humbleness is what I chose.
Lord Jesus, search for what in my heart needs purging.
Lord Jesus, help me see that holiness is emerging.
Lord Jesus, give me the courage to confess.
Lord Jesus, flush out all that by the Spirit You bless!

"Restore us to You, O Lord, that we may be restored; Renew our days…" (Lam. 5:21).

"Your former manner of life, you lay aside the old self…and that you be renewed in the spirit of your mind, and put on the new self, which in the likeness of God has been created in righteousness and holiness of the truth" (Eph. 4:22–24).

Asking, seeking, and knocking for daily restoration is preventive.
Renewal and restoration prayers the Trinity are very attentive!

E: Closet Time 200

Holy Spirit, I praise You for making me succeed.
Holy Spirit, I honor You for the wisdom to proceed.
Holy Spirit, I worship You for the way You inspire.
Holy Spirit, I exalt that Your power has me with inner fire.
Holy Spirit, I am grateful that You my spirit possess.
Holy Spirit, thank you that You keep me from sin and regress.
Holy Spirit, I ask for power to be daily guided.
Holy Spirit, help me use the insight provided.
Holy Spirit, increase in proficiency with the Word.
Holy Spirit, bring back to my memory what I've heard.
Holy Spirit, help me renew my prayer closet.
Holy Spirit, possess me and continue the spiritual deposit.
Holy Spirit, help me feel ABBA's righteous right hand.
Holy Spirit, anoint my spirit to dutifully obey Your command!

"And I will ask the Father, and He will give you another Helper, to be with you forever" (John 14:16).
"Now the Lord is the Spirit, and where the Spirit of the Lord is, there is freedom" (2 Cor. 3:17).

The Person of the Holy Spirit came to set everyone free.
The Holy Spirit even gets sinners to come to Jesus and see!

FEAR NOT

ABBA, Father, thank you I don't need to fear.
ABBA, Father, thank you that You are near.
ABBA, Father, to know You are with me is spiritually helpful.
ABBA, Father, by the Spirit, I can prevent being fretful.
ABBA, Father, that You protect is well documented.
ABBA, Father, disasters of others Your power prevented.
ABBA, Father, Your power has not diminished.
ABBA, Father, only You can say when something is finished!
ABBA, Father, I will continue to seek by You to be strengthen.
ABBA, Father, I am grateful that in Jesus my life is lengthen.
ABBA, Father, Your help has been my lifeline.
ABBA, Father, in trouble Your promises are my goldmine.
ABBA, Father, You uphold me by a righteous right hand.
ABBA, Father, in Jesus, I will follow Your every command!

"Do not fear, for I am with you; Do not anxiously look about you, for I am your God. I will strengthen you, surely I will help you, Surely I will uphold you with My righteous right hand" (Isa. 41:10).
"For God gave us a spirit not of fear but of power and love and self-control" (2 Tim. 1:7).

Knowing what is between the Bible equips for success.
Knowing Jesus by the Spirit makes God daily bless!

PM: THANK-YOU NOTE 108

Thank you, Holy Spirit, for never making me look bad.
Thank you, Holy Spirit, for comfort when I become sad.
Thank you, Holy Spirit, for wisdom and revelation.
Thank you, Holy Spirit, for securing my spiritual walk.
Thank you, Holy Spirit, that I hear You better when You talk.
Thank you, Lord Jesus, for being my Substitute.
Thank you, Lord Jesus, for help to live with life of rectitude.
Thank you, Lord Jesus, for making me wiser.
Thank you, Lord Jesus, for the Holy Spirit as my Adviser.
Thank you, ABBA, Father, that Your faithfulness always new.
Thank you, ABBA, Father, for feelings to love You!
Thank you, ABBA, Father, for a place in eternity.
Thank you, ABBA, Father, for saving a vile sinner like me!

"I sought the Lord, and He answered me and delivered me from all my fears" (Ps. 34:4).

"For you did not receive the spirit of slavery to fall back into fear, but you have received the Spirit of adoption as sons, by whom we cry, 'Abba! Father!'" (Rom. 8:15).

The faithfulness of the Trinity is chronicled in Jesus's resurrection. Overcoming all anxieties and phobias starts with salvation!

A: Closet Time 185

ABBA, Father, I come to thank you for a life of peace.
ABBA, Father, I'm grateful that Your love in me will increase.
ABBA, Father, thank you for saving me from sinful living.
ABBA, Father, corrective insight I love receiving.
ABBA, Father, help me fulfill my earthly mission.
ABBA, Father, by the Spirit, expand my vision.
ABBA, Father, in Jesus, sent me revival.
ABBA, Father, strengthen me to help a new arrival.
ABBA, Father, grant me empathy for a backslider.
ABBA, Father, grant discernment to avoid a backbiter.
ABBA, Father, heal my propensity to think with cynicism.
ABBA, Father, deliver me from catering to criticism.

"I will bless the Lord at all times; His praise shall continually be in my mouth" (Ps. 34:1).
"Every day I will bless You, And I will praise Your name forever and ever" (Ps. 145:2).

The eyes of God look for the diligently devoted.
Jesus by the Spirit know how to get anyone promoted!

PM: Thank-You Note 95

Thank you, ABBA, Father, that You made me like Jesus.
Thank you, ABBA, Father, You salvaged my soul in pieces.
Thank you, ABBA, Father, for rescuing me from hell.
Thank you, ABBA, Father, by the Spirit unto Jesus I will jell.
Thank you, Lord Jesus, that You shield from enemy's attack.
Thank you, Lord Jesus, that soon You will be coming back.
Thank you, Lord Jesus, that believers You will resurrect.
Thank you, Lord Jesus, showing me to give ABBA respect!
Thank you, Holy Spirit, for help to know the enemy's ploy.
Thank you, Holy Spirit, for gifts to enjoy.
Thank you, Holy Spirit, for helping the will of God not to forsake.
Thank you, Holy Spirit, for all the efforts in our behalf You make!

"Thy way, O God, is holy. What god is great like our God?" (Ps. 77:13).

"Great is the Lord, and highly to be praised, And His greatness is unsearchable" (Ps. 145:3).

Thanksgiving is the fastest way to get God's ear.
Jesus by the Spirit will quickly come near!

E: Closet Time 185

Holy Spirit, I rejoice at knowing You are here.
Holy Spirit, I praise You just to sense You near.
Holy Spirit, come in this temple and make repairs.
Holy Spirit, come search within me everywhere.
Holy Spirit, please expose when I need repenting.
Holy Spirit, deliver me from selfish venting.
Holy Spirit, anoint my spirit mind.
Holy Spirit, help me Your will to hear and find.
Holy Spirit, warn me when You I am grieving.
Holy Spirit, strengthen my heart in the Trinity believing.
Holy Spirit, make me aware when You I quench.
Holy Spirit, help me in Your daily will to entrench.
Holy Spirit, come take me deeper.
Holy Spirit, come be this temple's Keeper.
Holy Spirit, help me model the life of Jesus in my walk.
Holy Spirit, anoint my speech that like Jesus I talk!

"But I tell you the truth, it is for your benefit that I am going away. Unless I go away, the Advocate will not come to you; but if I go, I will send Him to you" (John 16:7).

"In the same way, the Spirit helps us in our weakness. For we do not know how we ought to pray, but the Spirit Himself intercedes for us with groans too deep for words" (Rom. 8:26).

The Holy Spirit will help in many capacities.
Asking in Jesus's name makes the Holy Spirit work realities!

A VESSEL OF GOLD 10

Refilled and Refined
A vessel of gold works with any government staff.
Vessels of gold live only on God's behalf.
A vessel of gold will avoid the world's dietary ways.
Vessels of gold with the mundane are not fazed.
A vessel of gold will help the needy.
Vessels of gold aren't hoarders or greedy.
A vessel of gold is prepared to advance the devout.
Vessels of gold helping the faithful they use clout.
A vessel of gold is humble, meek, lowly of heart, and fair.
Vessels of gold avoid partaking in any worldly affair.
A vessel of gold becomes wise by testifying.
Vessels of gold know that God their efforts is verifying.

"If we are thrown into the blazing furnace, the God whom we serve is able to save us. He will rescue us from your power, Your Majesty" (Dan. 3:17).

"Then the king promoted Shadrach, Meshach, and Abednego to even higher positions in the province of Babylon" (Dan. 3:30).

Vessels of gold will not cower from dire circumstances.
God in Jesus by the Spirit will promote and make advances!

A Vessel of Gold 9

Refilled and Refined
A vessel of gold cultivates a repentant mindset.
Vessels of gold want a clear conscience without regret.
A vessel of goal will warn of coming disaster.
Vessels of gold sharing truth trust the Master.
A vessel of gold to God for others will intercede.
Vessels of gold with God first always proceed.
A vessel of gold looks only to God for affirmation.
Vessels of gold trust the Spirit for enhancing sanctification.
A vessel of gold habitually uses the prayer closet.
Vessels of gold linger in prayer for a Holy Spirit deposit.
A vessel of gold wants to bring God honor and glory.
Vessels of gold creatively tell the Gospel story.

"But they who wait upon the Lord will get new strength. They will rise up with wings like eagles. They will run and not get tired. They will walk and not become weak" (Isa. 40:31).

"How beautiful…are the feet of those who bring good news, who proclaim peace, who bring good tidings, who proclaim salvation, who say…, 'Your God reigns!'" (Isa. 52:7).

Vessels of God listen for time of rest.
Jesus by the Spirit prepares vessels to enjoy the best!

A VESSEL OF GOLD 8

Refilled and Refined
A vessel of gold goes on a self-rigid training.
Vessels of gold know with God they are reigning.
A vessel of gold enjoys Kingdom membership now.
Vessels of gold know they will be resurrected somehow.
A vessel of gold aspires daily to seek God and go deeper.
Vessels of God are comfortable with Jesus as their Keeper.
A vessel of gold loves not life unto death.
Vessels of gold will speak truth in love till their last breath.
A vessel of gold doesn't criticize and falsely accuse.
Vessels of gold will the sight of evil refuse.
A vessel of gold meditates day and night.
Vessels of gold diligently seek to ABBA, Father's delight!

"And [in reverent fear and obedience] Enoch walked with God; and he was not [found among men], because God took him [away to be home with Him]" (Gen. 5:24).

"Therefore, 'Come out from among them and be separate, says the Lord. Do not touch what is unclean, and I will receive you'" (2 Cor. 6:17).

Choices are always done with eternity in mind.
In Jesus by the Spirit the perfect will anyone can find!

A Vessel of Gold 7

Refilled and Refined
A vessel of gold doesn't go around finding fault.
Vessels of gold encourage a God-driven result.
A vessel of gold treats everyone with honor and respect.
Vessels of gold when delivering the Word are direct.
A vessel of gold is not involved in doubtful disputation.
Vessels of gold stirs listeners from real temptation.
A vessel of gold objectively precludes from taking sides.
Vessels of gold exemplify how in God to abide.
A vessel of gold works for God until the next task.
Vessels of gold are accustomed in God to trust and ask.
A vessel of gold keeps their godly integrity intact.
Vessels of gold function only with Word-fact!

"The apostles left the high council rejoicing that God had counted them worthy to suffer disgrace for the name of Jesus" (Acts 5:41).

"Let love be your highest goal! But you should also desire the special abilities the Spirit gives—especially the ability to prophesy" (1 Cor. 14:1).

Vessels of goal see persecution through spiritual lenses.
Being a sacrifice for God means He refines the senses!

A VESSEL OF GOLD 6

Refilled and Refined
A vessel of gold will only take direct orders.
Vessels of gold aren't impressed with religious hoarders.
A vessel of gold becomes a giant slayer.
Vessels of gold are quick to frequent prayer.
A vessel of gold knows how to get God's attention.
Vessels of gold are certain of Jesus's ascension.
A vessel of gold is not bothered when wrongly reproved.
Vessels of gold study to show themselves approved.
A vessel of gold when attacked will not retaliate.
Vessels of gold demonstrating for God don't hesitate.
A vessel of gold has no regrets.
Vessels of gold honoring God first never forgets!

"Respect and obey the LORD! This is the beginning of wisdom. To have understanding, you must know the Holy God" (Prov. 9:10).

"The fruit of the righteous is a tree of life, and whoever captures souls is wise" (Prov. 11:30).

Respect and obedience is prerequisite for vessels of gold.
Respect and obedience is followed by doing what you are told!

A VESSEL OF GOLD 5

Refilled and Refined
A vessel of gold is prepared for the battle.
Vessels of gold against opposition never rattle.
A vessel of gold never vacillates with indecision.
Vessels of gold execute God's commands with precision.
A vessel of gold has no personal opinion.
Vessels of gold are fixated in Kingdom dominion.
A vessel of gold is not worldly concern.
Vessels of gold only for God's power and wisdom yearn.
A vessel of gold is not beholden to the religious crowd.
Vessels of gold are cognizant they are heaven bound.
A vessel of gold settles for what seems less.
Vessels of gold daily look to how God in Christ will bless.

"Though He slay me, yet will I trust in Him: but I will maintain mine own ways before Him" (Job 13:15).

"But I know that my Redeemer lives, and in the end He will stand upon the earth" (Job 19:25).

Becoming a vessel is a matter of preference and choice.
Truly submitted believers learn to hear God's voice!

A VESSEL OF GOLD 4

Refilled and Refined
Vessels of gold has to learn self-denial.
A vessel of gold will be alone for a long while.
Vessels of gold never initiate harm.
A vessel of gold with sinful strife are highly alarm.
Vessels of gold a personally by ABBA, Father set apart.
A vessel of gold knows the end from the start.
Vessels of gold despise religious pretenders.
A vessel of gold at the prayer closet daily surrenders.
Vessels of gold in doing evil are always dissuaded.
A vessel of gold sharing the Gospel are daily persuaded.
Vessels of gold don't worry about the outcome.
A vessel of gold knows that they are not alone!

"May the LORD our God be with us as he was with our ancestors; may he never leave us nor forsake us" (1 Kings 8:57).

"And Daniel purposed in his heart that he would not pollute himself and he requested…that he might not have to pollute himself" (Dan. 1:8).

Salvation is free to all: going deeper is the Holy Spirit's call.
Jesus will undergird vessels of gold from a drastic fall!

A VESSEL OF GOLD 3

Refilled and Refined
A vessel of gold has to be put in the process.
Vessels of gold cannot afford to regress.
A vessel of gold will be tried and tested.
Vessels of gold is safe when in the Master's hand rested.
A vessel of gold automatically exudes light.
Vessels of gold trains and practice what is eternally right.
A vessel of gold never settles for second best.
Vessels of gold are honoring of God as a priority quest.
A vessel of gold is aware to keep a Christlike shine.
Vessels of gold run from sinful slime.
Vessels of gold enjoy benefits of spiritual behavior.
Vessels of gold aspire for the faith of their Savior!

"Those who are wise will shine as bright as the sky, and those who lead many to righteousness will shine like the stars forever" (Dan. 12:3).

"But God's firm foundation stands, bearing this seal: 'The Lord knows those who are His,' and, 'Let everyone who names the name of the Lord depart from iniquity'" (2 Tim. 2:19).

The best vessels are always departing ill behavior.
Vessels of gold daily look to honor their Savior!

A VESSEL OF GOLD 2

Refilled and Refined
In God's house, there are vessels for daily use.
Vessels can be of many types that God will not refuse.
There are vessels of wood, metal, and earth.
ABBA, Father in Jesus uses all vessels giving them worth.
Vessels of silver and gold are the Trinity's for special occasions.
ABBA, Father has training for those with aspirations.
The Holy Spirit will be the abundant life Coach.
He works with those that make easy His approach.
In Jesus, the aspirants know the Spirit becomes Quality Control.
In the process, He earmarks those willing to be told.
The humble, submitted, and meek He will perfectly guide.
Vessels of gold must rid excessive baggage inside.

"But in a great house there are not only vessels of gold and of silver, but also of wood and of earth; and some to honour, and some to dishonour. If a man therefore purge himself from these, he shall be a vessel unto honour, sanctified, and meet for the Master's use, and prepared unto every good work" (2 Tim. 2:20–21).

Self-purging of ill behaviors is the first step toward fulfillment.
Jesus by the Spirit gives grace to complete any commitment!

A VESSEL OF GOLD 1

Refilled to be Refined
Anyone can be a vessel of gold.
The best vessel only does what they told.
In order to always do, one must come near.
Prayer closet time has to be very dear.
Jesus awaken by the Spirit at crack of dawn.
Early to a solitary place, He was gone.
Vessels of gold as habitually persistent.
Vessels of gold avoid excuses consistent.
Vessels of gold put up with much disrespect.
Vessels of gold in the closet the best expect.
Vessels of gold listen to Holy Spirit advice!
Vessels of gold fixate on being like Christ!

"Do not be afraid, little flock, for your Father is pleased to give you the kingdom" (Luke 12:32).

"Looking to Jesus, the founder and perfecter of our faith, who for the joy that was set before Him endured the cross, despising the shame, and is seated at the right hand of the throne of God" (Heb. 12:2).

In creating all, Our Father has great expectation.
The earlier we gravitate to His intent, the faster the realization!

GOD'S GOLD VESSEL

Living for God confidently, there is never guessing.
The enemy's best initiative is with our mind messing.
The confident believer is always one step ahead.
Rather than the enemy, he listens to the Holy Spirit instead.
Confidence is built one day at a time praying.
Confident believers in the prayer closet hear what God is saying.
Confident believers follow a Holy Spirit command.
Confident believers see the Lord's will as a demand.
Confident disciplines know that Jesus is Lord of all.
Confident believers will answer His call.
Confident believers will know when a real angel is speaking.
Confident believers help others Jesus to be seeking!

"But as for me, I am filled with power—with the Spirit of the LORD. I am filled with justice and strength to boldly declare…sin and rebellion" (Mic. 3:8).

"Now an angel of the Lord said to Philip, 'Get up and go south to the desert road that goes down from Jerusalem to Gaza'" (Acts 8:26).

Anyone can become confident in the Lord and His power.
Meditating on the Word day and night is still prerequisite…at all hours!

WORK COMPLETED

Lord, I look to You until the work is completed.
Holy Spirit, I will my ways adjust until the sin has been deleted.
ABBA, Father, strengthen me to diligently obey.
Lord Jesus, help me heed all that You have to say.
Holy Spirit, complete the work of restoration.
Lord Jesus, complete the work of sin nature causation.
ABBA, Father, work in me to complete humility.
Lord Jesus, complete the work in me of docility.
Holy Spirit, complete the work of turning the other cheek.
ABBA, Father, complete the work that daily You I seek.
Lord Jesus, work humbleness in me until completion.
Holy Spirit, complete the work of transformation!

"So our faces are not covered. They show the bright glory of the Lord, as the Lord's Spirit makes us more and more like our glorious Lord" (2 Cor. 3:18).

"I want to know Christ—yes, to know the power of His resurrection and participation in His sufferings, becoming like Him in His death" (Phil. 3:10).

Changing into the image of Jesus is a matter of submission.
Jesus by the Spirit does need our complete permission!

PRAY FOR ME

Pray for a deeper sensibility to others' needs.
Pray that in listening I plant greater empathetic seeds.
Pray that humbleness shows as others I assist.
Pray that loving one another I genuinely persist.
Pray that humility my every word and action pervades.
Pray that in speech Holy Spirit words in me cascades.
Pray for breaking all strongholds of cynicism.
Pray that I remove myself from all criticism.
Pray that I become Christlike in understanding.
Pray that I continue becoming less demanding.
Pray that Jesus in me is clearly manifest.
Pray that in the Holy Spirit power I live and rest!

"And the LORD turned the captivity...when he prayed for his friends: also the LORD gave...twice as much as he had before" (Job 42:10).

"Confess [your] faults one to another, and pray one for another, that you may be healed. The effectual fervent prayer of a righteous man avails much" (James 5:16).

Praying for others helps selfish ways to be removed.
By the Trinity's prayer respond we can see prayers approved!

Dear ABBA, Father 28a

I come to confess and renounce my hidden faults.
I come that in my soul I gain healing results.
I come to be released from sins that obstruct.
I come that by the Spirit my heart You may reconstruct.
I come to live in the fullness of a new creation.
I come to appreciate again my salvation.
I come to be made new in my thinking.
I come for Your perfect will to be linking.
I come to learn hating sin as You do.
I come by the Holy Spirit that I can mimic Jesus, too!
I come that my horizons for Jesus be expanded.
I come for an anointing to follow all You have commanded!

"You saw me before I was born. Every day of my life was recorded in Your book. Every moment was laid out before a single day had passed" (Ps. 139:16).

"Why, you do not even know what will happen tomorrow. What is your life? You are a mist that appears for a little while and then vanishes" (James 4:14).

Tomorrow is promised to those that do right by God today.
Jesus has many titles: to reach the Father He is the only Way!

TODAY...61

Today, I will in a Christlike way show my optimism.
Today, I will curtail being part of any criticism.
Today, I will seek listening and not talk.
Today, I will encourage all towards a Christlike walk.
Today, I will my burdens to the Lord carry.
Today, I will in the prayer closet release all worry.
Today, I will look to the Holy Spirit for Christ directed advise.
Today, I will follow the Word to become wise.
Today, I will give more and take less.
Today, I will look to see how others I can bless.
Today, I will seek for firsthand Holy Spirit leading.
Today, I will make sure that Jesus in me is interceding!

"Everyone who acknowledges Me publicly here on earth, I will also acknowledge before My Father in heaven" (Matt. 10:32).
"I tell you the truth, everyone who acknowledges Me publicly here on earth, the Son of Man will also acknowledge in the presence of God's angels."

Actually, Jesus knows who He is and always will.
He wants us to talk about Him that by the Spirit we stay fill!

AM: THANK-YOU NOTE 108

Thank you, Holy Spirit, for work to be quiet, confident and still.
Thank you, Holy Spirit, that daily my temple You refill.
Thank you, Holy Spirit, that You will never leave.
Thank you, Holy Spirit, for the new understanding I receive.
Thank you, Lord Jesus, for being my Savior.
Thank you, Lord Jesus, for grace Your Word to savor.
Thank you, Lord Jesus, for help to wrong attitudes to correct.
Thank you, Lord Jesus, that daily my heart You inspect.
Thank you, ABBA, Father, for love that is pure.
Thank you, ABBA, Father, that in You I feel secure.
Thank you, ABBA, Father, for help to carry my cross.
Thank you, ABBA, Father, for being my Eternal Boss!

"I will give You thanks in the great assembly; among the throngs I will praise You" (Ps. 35:18).

"I will praise God's name in song and glorify Him with thanksgiving" (Ps. 69:30).

Thanksgiving is a daily habit that transforms.
Jesus modeled thanksgiving as in ABBA's will He did conform!

M: Closet Time 200

Lord Jesus, my praises for You will be clearer.
Lord Jesus, I exalt and worship so that I come nearer.
Lord Jesus, by the Spirit, help me stay in Your world.
Lord Jesus, may ABBA's love in my spirit unfurl.
Lord Jesus, make me a vessel useable in Your hand.
Lord Jesus, anoint me anew to follow every command.
Lord Jesus, prepare my heart for what is ahead.
Lord Jesus, empower me to diligently the Gospel spread.
Lord Jesus, purge what in my heart others offend.
Lord Jesus, help me by the Spirit of Your grace to depend.
Lord Jesus, help me this day doing Your will not to fail.
Lord Jesus, possess my spirit that You increasing prevails.

"If you abide in Me, and My words abide in you, you shall ask what you will, and it shall be done unto you" (John 15:7).

"And I will do whatever you ask in My name, so that the Father may be glorified in the Son" (John 14:13).

Getting real with God about our shortcomings is expected.
Asking Jesus sincerely honest questions is highly respected!

PRAISING HIM!

Praising Him acknowledges His Deity!
Praising Him keeps us aware of Kingdom reality!
Praising Him allows us in His perfect will to grow stronger.
Praising Him in self-denial to continue longer.
Praising Him can help dissipate all worldly ruckus.
Praising Him enhances hope on a heavenly focus.
Praising Him advances exuding daily humility.
Praising Him nurtures exaltation and worship in spontaneity.
Praising Him will make a lame spirit to talk.
Praising Him will motivate weak feet to walk.
Praising Him is the fastest way the enemy to overcome.
Praising Him will show the Trinity never leaves a sheep alone!

A Holy Spirit Invite

Holy Spirit, help me not take You for granted.

Holy Spirit, help me know that grieving You makes my view slanted.

Holy Spirit, help me realize that quenching You stunts power.

Holy Spirit, help me let You speak to me at all hours.

Holy Spirit, help me know that sin makes You recoil.

Holy Spirit, help the enemy's will in me to foil.

Holy Spirit, help me develop our communication.

Holy Spirit, help me prioritize my sanctification.

Holy Spirit, help me retain a heart that is submitted.

Holy Spirit, help not grieving and quenching to be committed.

Holy Spirit, help me realize minus You I am powerless.

Holy Spirit, help me realize that when You control You bless.

"Whether you turn to the right or to the left, your ears will hear a voice behind you, saying, 'This is the way; walk in it'" (Isa. 30:21).

"But you will receive power when the Holy Spirit comes upon you. And you will be my witnesses, telling people about me everywhere…" (Acts 1:8a).

The Holy Spirit speaks clearer when He is permitted control. Jesus is looking for devoted humble sheep from the fold!

M: Closet Time 186

Holy Spirit, I come to praise and exalt.
Holy Spirit, I come for intimacy with You as my end result.
Holy Spirit, I ask that You make Yourself known.
Holy Spirit, in Jesus, manifest what He to You has shown.
Holy Spirit, help me love ABBA, Father with respect.
Holy Spirit, come today and my heart inspect.
Holy Spirit, help break the habit with You not speaking.
Holy Spirit, come possess me that Your will I'm seeking.
Holy Spirit, come reveal Jesus for my greater appreciation.
Holy Spirit, help me give the Word much meditation.
Holy Spirit, help me stop making excuses for what I'm doing.
Holy Spirit, come direct me where I am going.
Holy Spirit, help me to hear Your distinct voice.
Holy Spirit, possess me to make the eternal choice.
Holy Spirit, come fill me to overflowing.
Holy Spirit, come make Jesus in me glowing!

"And I will ask the Father, and He will give you another Advocate, who will never leave you" (John 14:16).

"I will not leave you as orphans; I will come to You" (John 14:18).

The Advocate desires to help with overcoming.
Jesus overcame much by the Spirit directing His going!

TODAY...47

Today, I will seek to know the Holy Spirit with intimacy.
Today, I will nurture hearing the Holy Spirit intimately.
Today, I will request of God in Jesus a godly child's mind.
Today, I will hope that when speaking others Jesus find.
Today, I will forgive those that their ways try to impose.
Today, I will any hint of sin confess and expose.
Today, I will sit at the feet of Jesus like Mary.
Today, I will to ABBA, Father my cares carry.
Today, I will let go of what in my heart hinders.
Today, I will ask ABBA, Father to heal with His fingers.
Today, I will speak less and hear more.
Today, I will answer when I am Holy Spirit sure.

"The LORD will guide you always; He will satisfy your needs in a sun-scorched land and will strengthen your frame. You will be like a well-watered garden, like a spring whose waters never fail" (Isa. 58:11).

"And my God will supply every need of yours according to His riches in glory in Christ Jesus" (Phil. 4:19).

God in Jesus will provide as needed, when needed.
Jesus modeled a live that to ABBA by the Spirit He conceded!

ABBA, FATHER

With pure loving kindness, You called a vile sinner.
Your call was for any to share as a spiritual beginner.
You looked past our sins and sought an inkling of being sorry.
You readily made available all Your excellent glory.
You collaborated with the Holy Spirit to exude real repentance.
The stage by the Spirit in Jesus was set for eternal acceptance!
The Holy Spirit worked to open eyes for Christ to see.
Now in Jesus we can partake of His eternity.
Yes, in the world momentarily, we will be tried.
Jesus by the Spirit on promises of deliverance we can rely.
Those Spirit led will be restored, coached, and strengthened.
Now by the firm foundation of Jesus in the Spirit, life is lengthened!

"O give thanks unto the LORD, for [He is] good: for His mercy [endureth] for ever" (Ps. 107:1).

"In His kindness God called you to share in His eternal glory by means of Christ Jesus. So after you have suffered a little while, He will restore, support, and strengthen you, and He will place you on a firm foundation" (1 Pet. 5:10).

God in Jesus always has kindness toward us extended.
Jesus by the Spirit works best when our will and His grace are blended!

PM: THANK-YOU NOTE 107

Thank you, Lord Jesus, for a fruitful day.
Thank you, Lord Jesus, that You are the only Way!
Thank you, Lord Jesus, for help to stay faithful.
Thank you, Lord Jesus, for keeping me grateful.
Thank you, Holy Spirit, that You never willingly leave.
Thank you, Holy Spirit, for the blessings from You I receive!
Thank you, Holy Spirit, that You help me avoid sin.
Thank you, Holy Spirit, that You and I will be together till the end.
Thank you, ABBA, Father, for holiness to match.
Thank you, ABBA, Father, in Jesus to You I am attached.
Thank you, ABBA, Father, for help to avoid worldly leaven.
Thank you, ABBA, Father, for a place in heaven!

"Now therefore, our God, we thank Thee and praise Thy glorious name" (1 Chron. 29:13).
"Giving thanks always for all things unto God and the Father in the name of our Lord Jesus Christ" (Eph. 5:20).

Praising God in Jesus by the Spirit is habit forming.
Daily in our prayer closet to Jesus we are conforming!

E: Closet Time 199

ABBA, Father, I come to Your throne.
ABBA, Father, I come to You in Jesus name alone.
ABBA, Father, I come to gain and seek Your favor.
ABBA, Father, I am committed for You to labor.
ABBA, Father, help me a diligent seeker to continue.
ABBA, Father, to keep testifying please find me a new venue.
ABBA, Father, let not my heart grow cold.
ABBA, Father, keep me faithfully in Your fold.
ABBA, Father, search me for what in my heart hinders.
ABBA, Father, I ask for a healing touch of Your fingers!
ABBA, Father, deliver me from all that is forbidden.
ABBA, Father, look in the crevices of my heart for sin hidden.
ABBA, Father, by the Spirit, in Your power I will rest.
ABBA, Father, in Jesus daily I look for Your best!

"God gives wisdom, knowledge, and joy to those who please Him…" (Eccles. 2:26a).

"And without faith it is impossible to please God, because anyone who approaches Him must believe that He exists and that He rewards those who earnestly seek Him" (Heb. 11:6).

Trusting God is supplemented by the Holy Spirit with best results.

Jesus will never turn anyone away with faults!

GREATEST GIFT 4

The greatest gift is to taste and see that the Lord is good.
The greatest gift is in training our spirit as much as we could.
The greatest gift is to share in His divine nature.
The greatest gift is to peacefully live for His pleasure.
The greatest gift is to taste what heaven will be like on earth.
The greatest gift is ABBA, Father showing us eternal worth.
The greatest gift is keeping the spiritual mind of a child.
The greatest gift is being Holy Spirit led all the while.
The greatest gift is maintaining a Christlike attitude.
The greatest gift is walking in spiritual rectitude.
The greatest gift is honoring Jesus twenty-four seven.
The greatest gift is the certainty of being bound for heaven!

"Rather, as it is written: 'No eye has seen, no ear has heard, no heart has imagined, what God has prepared for those who love Him.' But God has revealed it to us by the Spirit. The Spirit searches all things, even the deep things of God" (1 Cor. 2:9–10).

God in Jesus wants believers that will study His Word.
Jesus sent the Holy Spirit to tell what He has heard!

GREATEST GIFT 3

The greatest gift is being honest and full of grace.
The greatest gift is continuing the faith race.
The greatest gift is facing evil with resolve.
The greatest gift is when in soul winning, we are involved.
The greatest gift is on God's Word meditating.
The greatest gift is with God personally relating.
The greatest gift is putting your feelings on hold.
The greatest gift is to hear and obey what is being told.
The greatest gift is never judging.
The greatest gift is telling the truth without budging.
The greatest gift is submissively suffering for Christ.
The greatest gift is clearly listening to Holy Spirit advice!

"For the gifts and the calling of God are irrevocable" (Rom. 11:29).

"As each one has received a special gift, employ it in serving one another as good stewards of the manifold grace of God" (1 Pet. 4:10).

Gifts are for the provider with God in Jesus to stay align.
Jesus uses gifts to make the servants light shine!

GREATEST GIFT 2

The greatest gift is knowing the Trinity firsthand.
The greatest gift is following every command.
The greatest gift is learning how to never offend.
The greatest gift is when on the Holy Spirit we depend.
The greatest gift is making God's choice.
The greatest gift is hearing the Holy Spirit's voice.
The greatest gift is having the Holy Spirit as Coach.
The greatest gift is when in confidence God we approach.
The greatest gift is a clear conscience with God and man.
The greatest gift is with the Trinity doing all we can.
The greatest gift is willingly of Jesus to talk.
The greatest gift is in Jesus by the Spirit we daily walk!

"So if you sinful people know how to give good gifts to your children, how much more will your heavenly Father give the Holy Spirit to those who ask Him" (Luke 11:13).

"All...empowered by one and the same Spirit, who apportions to each one individually as He wills" (1 Cor. 12:11).

The gifts that God in Jesus gives are irrevocable.
Jesus knows those that their commitment is reputable!

GREATEST GIFT 1

ABBA's greatest gift is eternal living.
The greatest gift is the ability in the Trinity believing.
The greatest gift is knowing we are protected.
The greatest gift is in God's presence accepted.
The greatest gift is knowing our name is written in God's Book.
The greatest gift is constantly having an upward look.
The greatest gift is power over sin.
The greatest gift is a prayer closet for our day to begin.
The greatest gift is knowing that we are never forgotten.
The greatest gift is ABBA, Father sending His only Begotten!
The greatest gift is the baptism with the Holy Spirit and fire!
The greatest gift is when others for Jesus we inspire!

"And when he had called unto *him* his twelve disciples, he gave them power *against* unclean spirits, to cast them out, and to heal all manner of sickness and all manner of disease" (Matt. 10:1).

"But God has revealed it to us by the Spirit. The Spirit searches all things, even the deep things of God" (1 Cor. 2:10).

The Trinity collaborates to maximize winning souls.
Jesus takes lowly of heart willing to do what they are told!

DEAR ABBA, FATHER 16A

I come to draw closer and come nearer.
I come Your perfect will to see it clearer.
I come to relinquish unresolved sin.
I come my heart to bear and expose within.
I come to maintain a clear path to the throne room.
I come to be strengthened for the enemy's doom and gloom.
I come to walk in righteousness and love.
I come to honor Your will above.
I come to seek a humble and lowly heart.
I come to be used by the Spirit to win those set apart.
I come to be wiser in You and Your mighty power.
I come to gain a new measure of Your love this prayer hour.
I come to renew my commitment to obey.
I come to be redirected in Your perfect way.

"My heart is confident in You, O God; my heart is confident.
No wonder I can sing Your praises!" (Ps. 57:7).
"Seven times a day I praise You, Because of Your righteous ordinances" (Ps. 119:164).

Genuine believers learn to be confident in Christ.
Faith in Jesus is enhanced with Holy Spirit advice!

A: Closet Time 186

Holy Spirit, I praise Your work among the lost.
Holy Spirit, I exalt You for helping me in training to pay the cost.
Holy Spirit, thank you for increase of learning.
Holy Spirit, possess me to advance my spiritual yearning.
Holy Spirit, help me walk humbly before my Maker.
Holy Spirit, help me to be a giver and not a taker.
Holy Spirit, create in me a heart that is tender.
Holy Spirit, refill me and be my Defender.
Holy Spirit, help me get up if I should stumble.
Holy Spirit, increase in me being meek, merciful and humble.
Holy Spirit, rekindle a new fire for the prayer closet.
Holy Spirit, clothe me with power as You make a new deposit!

"I will extol You, my God, O King, And I will bless Your name forever and ever" (Ps. 145:1).
"But the Helper, the Holy Spirit, whom the Father will send in my name, he will teach you all things and bring to your remembrance all that I have said to you" (John 14:26).

Speaking with the Holy Spirit can expedite change.
Jesus needs for the devout to stay in His spiritual range!

PM: THANK-YOU NOTE 96

Thank you, Lord Jesus, for Your full attention.
Thank you, Holy Spirit, that You are my first line of prevention.
Thank you, ABBA, Father, for wanting my success.
Thank you, Lord Jesus, that You came all to bless.
Thank you, Holy Spirit, for being my eternal Friend.
Thank you, ABBA, Father, that You are with me till the end.
Thank you, Lord Jesus, for grace upon grace.
Thank you, Holy Spirit, for helping win souls You know the place.
Thank you, ABBA, Father, for angels that protect.
Thank you, Lord Jesus, for wisdom the Trinity to respect.
Thank you, Holy Spirit, for helping me from God's will not deviate.
Thank you, ABBA, Father, in Jesus to the Kingdom I relate!

"Let them give glory to the Lord And declare His praise in the coastlands" (Isa. 42:12).
"Work willingly at whatever you do, as though you were working for the Lord rather than for people" (Col. 3:23).

ABBA, Father in Jesus has job openings everywhere.
Jesus by the Spirit will equip and send out with power to spare!

E: CLOSET TIME 186

ABBA, Father, help me to not be weary in doing well.
ABBA, Father, by the Spirit, may my love for righteousness swell.
ABBA, Father, renew in my heart a desire to testify.
ABBA, Father, by the Spirit, my work do verify.
ABBA, Father, search me for sin still lodged in my soul.
ABBA, Father, let not my heart grow cold.
ABBA, Father, come reconstruct my thinking.
ABBA, Father, help me to heaven's registry to be linking.
ABBA, Father, resurrect in me truth and humility.
ABBA, Father, may Your love flow in me with mercy and gentility.

"The Lord, the Lord God, merciful and gracious, longsuffering, and abounding in goodness and truth" (Exod. 34:6).

"And you must love the LORD your God with all your heart, all your soul, and all your strength" (Deut. 6:5).

The mercies and compassion of God are always free.
In Jesus crucifixion, God's love all can see!

TODAY...48

Today, I will be thankful for being in God's plan.
Today, I will follow the "love one another" command.
Today, I will ask the Holy Spirit for direction.
Today, I will be forgiving with no exception.
Today, I will in the prayer closet do a heart check.
Today, I will not allow sin in my heart to peck.
Today, I will reject from becoming lukewarm.
Today, I will heed any Holy Spirit alarm.
Today, I will meditate on God, the Word, and His deeds.
Today, I will seek Holy Spirit help in planting seeds.
Today, I will pick up the cross and follow the Christ way.
Today, I will deny myself in what I do and say.
Today, I will others not offend.
Today, I will guidance from the Holy Spirit depend.

"You will keep in perfect *and* constant peace *the one* whose mind is steadfast [that is, committed and focused on You—in both inclination and character], Because he trusts *and* takes refuge in You [with hope and confident expectation]" (Isa. 26:3 AMP).

"Come to Me, all you who are weary and burdened and I will give you rest" (Matt. 11:28).

Perfect peace is available to those that diligently obey.
Jesus will keep focused on those that see Him as the only Way!

Dear Abba, Father 16b

I come with gratefulness and adoration.
I come with joy and great expectation.
I come to confess and renounce any hint of sin.
I come to ask for a refill of the Holy Spirit within.
I come to avoid heart deceptive presumption.
I come to be healed from sinful assumption.
I come to pursue a heart of integrity.
I come to learn to think and speak with loving clarity.
I come to bear my soul open for Your perusal.
I come because I trust You not to give me a refusal.
I come because I will get what I pray.
I come my cares and concerns at Your feet to lay.
I come because You heal all hurts and pain.
I come because in Jesus by the Spirit I have so much to gain.

"I take joy in doing Your will, my God, for Your instructions are written on my heart."
"Here I am, I have come to do your will" (Heb. 10:9a).

Willingness to honor Jesus is always declared.
Jesus by the Spirit will His disciples send fully prepared!

A: Closet Time 199

Holy Spirit, come in this vessel to best control.
Holy Spirit, grant me power to be faithfully bold.
Holy Spirit, help me to meditate day and night.
Holy Spirit, help me to shine my image of Jesus bright.
Holy Spirit, possess me to be best guided.
Holy Spirit, renew my heart to keep from being divided.
Holy Spirit, purge whatever hinders my walk.
Holy Spirit, control my tongue to better talk.
Holy Spirit, increase in me the God trust.
Holy Spirit, flush my heart from any sinful lust.
Holy Spirit, grant be an anointed revival.
Holy Spirit, fill me to overflowing as I wait on Your arrival!

"And the Spirit of God moved upon the face of the waters" (Gen. 1:2b).

"God's Spirit moved throughout the earth, causing the flood waters to subside" (Gen. 8:1).

The Holy Spirit is always looking for those God willing.
The Lord Jesus will genuinely give the Holy Spirit infilling!

TODAY...34

Today, I will look to release what in my heart progress impedes.
Today, I will look to creatively drop Gospel seeds.
Today, I will allow the Holy Spirit more control.
Today, I will withstand the testing and trials and not fold.
Today, I will care for those around me by paying attention.
Today, I will show others godly affection.
Today, I will take nothing for granted.
Today, I will look for the will of God to have planted.
Today, I will with grace curb my emotions.
Today, I will look to God in Jesus for my promotion.
Today, I will to the Holy Spirit expose my broken pieces.
Today, I will diligently seek to honor my Lord Jesus!

"Give thanks to the Lord, for He is good; His love endures forever" (Ps. 118:1).

"Blessed are the pure in heart, for they shall see God" (Matt. 5:8).

We seek purity because seeing God is a goal.
Becoming starts when doing what in the Word we're told!

A: Closet Time 172

Lord Jesus, I want to serve with all my spirit and soul.
Lord Jesus, I am willing to do as told.
Lord Jesus, heal in me what needs healing.
Lord Jesus, I don't want to do Your will on feelings.
Lord Jesus, refill me with the Holy Spirit and holy fire.
Lord Jesus, by the Spirit, help me that others I may inspire.
Lord Jesus, take me to the Holies of Holies.
Lord Jesus, in the Spirit, give me a heart humble and lowly.
Lord Jesus, help me to know You better.
Lord Jesus, I ask that my life to others be a Christlike letter.
Lord Jesus, empower me to be faithful to the end.
Lord Jesus, anoint my spirit to tell others ABBA, You did send!

"The only letter of recommendation we need is you yourselves. Your lives are a letter written in our hearts; everyone can read it and recognize our good work among you" (2 Cor. 3:2).
"Devote yourselves to prayer being watchful and thankful" (Col. 4:2).

The world is looking for authentic God pleaser.
ABBA, Father is wanting those that are Christlike releaser!

AM: THANK-YOU NOTE 105

Thank you, ABBA, Father, for this new day.
Thank you, ABBA, Father, that my mind on You will stay.
Thank you, ABBA, Father, for love that is secure.
Thank you, ABBA, Father, that my eternity is sure.
Thank you, Lord Jesus, for help to see my need for You.
Thank you, Lord Jesus, that You saved me too.
Thank you, Lord Jesus, seeing me through my trials.
Thank you, Lord Jesus, for my name in heaven's Book.
Thank you, Lord Jesus, for always being present for me look.
Thank you, Holy Spirit, for helping me to diligently obey.
Thank you, Holy Spirit, for guiding me this day.
Thank you, Holy Spirit, for blessing my all that I do.
Thank you, Holy Spirit, for daily grace to honor You!

"O taste and see that the LORD *is* good: blessed *is* the man *that* trusteth in Him" (Ps. 34:8).
"I will give thanks to you, LORD, with all my heart; I will tell of all you're wonderful deeds" (Ps. 9:1).

Thankfulness to God is more than something we say.
Thankfulness is how we respect God in Jesus along the way.

AM: THANK-YOU NOTE 97

Thank you, ABBA, Father, for faith in You to trust.
Thank you, ABBA, Father, that in Jesus, answering is a must.
Thank you, ABBA, Father, for the seal of approval.
Thank you, ABBA, Father, that by the Spirit I have sin's removal.
Thank you, Lord Jesus, for daily revelation.
Thank you, Lord Jesus, for eternal salvation.
Thank you, Lord Jesus, that by Your stripes I am healed.
Thank you, Lord Jesus, that by Your blood I am shielded.
Thank you, Holy Spirit, for helping to heal my attitude.
Thank you, Holy Spirit, for helping me practice gratitude.
Thank you, Holy Spirit, for helping my heart to heal.
Thank you, Holy Spirit, for helping me in repentance to kneel.

"I will give thanks to You, Lord, with all my heart; I will tell of all Your wonderful deeds" (Ps. 9:1).
"Give thanks to the God of heaven, for his steadfast love endures forever" (Ps. 136:26).

A thankful attitude toward God is manifest as of Him we speak.
God continues to reward those that diligently seek!

M: Closet Time 187

ABBA, Father, I come because all is in Your sight.
ABBA, Father, I come to make my heart right.
ABBA, Father, I come this day to continue healing.
ABBA, Father, I come to not live on what I'm feeling.
ABBA, Father, by the Spirit, search for the unwarranted.
ABBA, Father, I ask that Your anointing on me be granted.
ABBA, Father, recover for me what the enemy has stolen.
ABBA, Father, help me in doing Your will to be embolden.
ABBA, Father, put back my heart's broken pieces.
ABBA, Father, by the Spirit, make me more like Jesus.
ABBA, Father, renew my resolve to be faithful.
ABBA, Father, deliver me from being cold and hateful.
ABBA, Father, create in me a Christlike demeanor.
ABBA, Father, make a me diligent Word gleaner.

"Create in me a clean heart, O God. Renew a loyal spirit within me" (Ps. 51:10).

"To You, O God of my fathers, I give thanks and praise, For You have given me wisdom and power; Even now You have made known to me what we requested of You, For You have made known to us…" (Dan. 2:23).

The essentials of a clean heart only God in Jesus can provide.

Through praise and thanks, His prayer answers He will not hide!

Choices Reap 2

Adam chose to disregard and disobey.
His choice put all humanity in disarray!
Choices reap without hesitating to think.
Choices reap while putting many at hell's brink!
Cain chose to get upset with his brother's act.
Consequences of his choice reaped a murderous fact.
Choices reap when judgement was a torment.
Consequences of his choice reaped complaining in lament.
Choices reap habits that are future destroyers.
Choices reap as in anguish they become our employers.
Choices reap as we sow to the wind reaping the world wind.
Choices reap as in "maturity" we are steeped in carnal sin!

"And Cain said unto the LORD, My punishment *is* greater than I can bear" (Gen. 4:13).

"Adam disobeyed God and caused many others to be sinners. But Jesus obeyed Him and will make many people acceptable to God" (Rom. 5:19).

Sowing and reaping is a way of life.
Salvation in Jesus can save for perpetual strife!

CHOICES REAP 1

Be careful the company that we keep.
Different agendas will detour from the deep!
We are always sowing and reaping.
In salvation, sow godly and reap safekeeping!
Sowing and reaping is habit forming.
To someone we are conforming.
"Bad company corrupts good character."
Careful company choice is always a factor.
Walking with the Spirit is a best reaping deed.
Jesus was accompanied by the Spirit in all He did!

"Do not deceive yourselves; no one makes a fool of God. You will reap exactly what you plant" (Gal. 6:7).
"But those who live to please the Spirit will harvest everlasting life from the Spirit" (Gal. 6:8b).

The Holy Spirit is the best company to keep for life.
In Jesus by the Spirit, we can overcome all strife!

TODAY...60

Today, I will avoid anything that is for God in Jesus distracting.
Today, I will by the Holy Spirit to Jesus continue advancing.
Today, I will forgive the vilest insults.
Today, I will look to the Holy Spirit for Christlike results.
Today, I will keep "looking unto Jesus."
Today, I will ask the Spirit to heal my soul's inner pieces.
Today, I will on the Word reflect.
Today, I will the promises of God in my life expect.
Today, I will sow godliness for Jesus's sake.
Today, I will seek a Holy Spirit remake.
Today, I will listen to hear the Holy Spirit speak.
Today, I will be more like Jesus seek!

"Thanks be to God for His indescribable gift" (2 Cor. 5:17).

"I want to know Christ and the power of His resurrection and the fellowship of His sufferings, being conformed to Him in His death" (Phil. 3:10).

God's indestructible gift is wrapped in Jesus.
God by the Holy Spirit came to heal heart's broken pieces!

Dear ABBA, Father 28b

I come seeking to be strengthened and transformed.
I come Your perfect will to conform.
I come to present my body a living sacrifice.
I come in You presence of Your will to be appraised.
I come for a heart renovation.
I come for extractions needed to gain revival inspiration.
I come to put on God's provided armor.
I come that evil towards any I don't harbor.
I come continuing the journey to be a vessel of gold.
I come to obediently follow what in the Word I am told.
I come to ask for a new repentant mindset.
I come by Spirit to do what ABBA, Father expect!

When you sacrifice a sacrifice of thanksgiving to the Lord, you shall sacrifice it so that you may be accepted" (Lev. 22:29).
"Offer to God a sacrifice of thanksgiving; And pay your vows to the Most High" (Ps. 50:14).

Oftentimes, being thankful becomes a battle with the flesh.
Thanksgiving to God often will soul make afresh!

AM: THANK-YOU NOTE 107

Thank you, ABBA, Father, for using me to motivate.
Thank you, ABBA, Father, for grace with others to relate.
Thank you, ABBA, Father, for the Holy Spirit who is my Coach.
Thank you, ABBA, Father, that You I can always approach.
Thank you, Lord Jesus, that You always forgive.
Thank you, Lord Jesus, for faith to daily believe.
Thank you, Lord Jesus, that in heaven You intercede.
Thank you, Lord Jesus, that Your power the enemy can't impede.
Thank you, Holy Spirit, for waking me today.
Thank you, Holy Spirit, that You always have new things to say.
Thank you, Holy Spirit, that Your protection is around the clock.
Thank you, Holy Spirit, for helping me to stay in Jesus's flock!

"Then Jesus lifted His eyes upward and said, 'Father, I thank You that You have heard Me'" (John 11:41).

"But thanks be to God that, though you once were slaves to sin, you wholeheartedly obeyed the form of teaching to which you were committed" (Rom. 6:17).

Jesus modeled giving thanks for the sake of others.
Embracing genuine thankfulness our spirit and soul recovers!

M: Closet Time 199

Lord Jesus, I call out to You for assurance.
Lord Jesus, my heart is Yours for spiritual endurance.
Lord Jesus, help me maintain a mind that is humble.
Lord Jesus, anoint me do the will of God without grumble.
Lord Jesus, cleanse my heart of sin's residue.
Lord Jesus, help me to retain a learning attitude.
Lord Jesus, I confess and renounce all in my heart hidden.
Lord Jesus, empower me to run from what is forbidden.
Lord Jesus, forgive and deliver me from all heart cynicism.
Lord Jesus, deliver me from the un-forgiveness prison.
Lord Jesus, help me of others to not be critical.
Lord Jesus, deliver me from catering to the physical.
Lord Jesus, I ask for a baptism renewal and new fire.
Lord Jesus, make me the vessel that You desire!

"If you keep yourself pure, you will be a special utensil for honorable use. Your life will be clean, and you will be ready for the Master to use you for every good work" (2 Tim. 2:21).

"So flee youthful passions and pursue righteousness, faith, love, and peace, along with those who call on the Lord from a pure heart" (2 Tim. 2:22).

Purity of heart is a life pursuit.
Purity of heart will daily make the believer spiritually astute!

GOD IS NOT MOCKED

The Sovereign Creator has all under His sight.
His decrees will ultimately be manifest right.
In Jesus, humanity is attempted to be persuaded.
ABBA, Father's decisions will never be blockaded.
God is not mocked as He was disregarded prior the deluge.
All perished as mockery kept them from the Ark refuge.
Mockery of God was in the Tower of Babel being erected.
The Trinity collaborated as the mockery was not accepted.
All the effort in building was suddenly destroyed.
Those that mock God, their plans become null and void!
God is not mocked is truth that forgetting we can't afford.
They mocked Jesus throughout as He became Lord!

"Do not deceive yourselves; no one makes a fool of God. You will reap exactly what you plant" (Gal. 6:7).

"Those who live only to satisfy their own sinful nature will harvest decay and death from that sinful nature. But those who live to please the Spirit will harvest everlasting life from the Spirit" (Gal. 6:8).

Throughout life we are always sowing and reaping.
In salvation, we can sow godly and reap safekeeping!

AWESOME: GOD ALONE

God is Awesome in all of His ways.
The Trinity is so Awesome wanting all to come and stay.
ABBA, created an Awesome avenue to recover the lost.
In our unworthiness, He decided to pay the Awesome cost.
He is so Awesome He sent salvation free to all.
All we have to do is upon Jesus name call.
Awesome, the Holy Spirit is present to convict and correct.
It is Awesome, with consent, in us Christ He will perfect.
Awesomely, He is willing to forgive all our past.
Calling was Jesus our Savior for eternity we will last!!
God alone is Awesome in all of creation.
The Awesome gift of Jesus was wrapped in salvation!

"For God did not send His Son into the world to condemn the world, but to save the world through Him" (John 3:17).

"No temptation has overtaken you except what is common to mankind. And God is faithful; he will not let you be tempted beyond what you can bear. But when you are tempted, he will also provide a way out so that you can endure it" (1 Cor. 10:13).

Salvation for everyone is God's mandate.
Calling upon Jesus for salvation is never too late!

GOD'S TWILIGHT ZONE

Adam found himself in a perfect world.
He was mesmerized at all that God had unfurl.
All was done with the utmost sense of perfection.
Daily they enjoyed a God guided conversation.
Angels looked in wonder and mystified.
That humanity was God worthy and qualified.
Daily parents of humans visited in this perfect land.
Remaining residents only required to follow a command.
All expected was doable as they found perfect rest.
ABBA, Father in Jesus providing the ultimate best.
Adam for God had priority honor and highest respect.
The Creator-creation conversation was perfect.

"He who has an ear, let him hear what the Spirit says to the churches. To the one who conquers I will grant to eat of the tree of life, which is in the paradise of God" (Rev. 2:7).

"And I heard a loud voice from the throne saying, 'Look! God's dwelling place is now among the people, and He will dwell with them. They will be His people, and God Himself will be with them and be their God'" (Rev 21:3).

Upon Jesus arrival to heaven, all was now complete.
Jesus has prepared believers eternal suite!

SALVATION PRAYER!

I realize that I have not given You my life!
I no longer want to live in anxiety and strife.
I believe that You are the Savior of the world.
I believe that You came from heaven with love to unfurl.
I believe in my heart that You rose from the dead.
I believe that You came to give me life eternal instead.
I ask forgiveness for my sinful past.
In Your name, Lord Jesus, I receive forgiveness that will last!
I invite You, Lord Jesus, into my heart.
I thank you that by faith, I have You and a new start.
Thank you for making me a new creation!
Thank you, Lord Jesus, for eternal SALVATION!

"If you openly declare that Jesus is Lord and believe in your heart that God raised him from the dead, you will be saved. For it is by believing in your heart that you are made right with God, and it is by openly declaring your faith that you are saved" (Rom. 10:9–10).

JESUS, FILL ME WITH THE HOLY SPIRIT!

Lord Jesus, I praise You for love and faithfulness.
Lord Jesus, daily I look at You with gratefulness!
Lord Jesus, You I will fully obey.
Lord Jesus, I want to live by all You say.
Lord Jesus, all that You have to give I am willing!
Lord Jesus, use my body for the Holy Spirit infilling.
Lord Jesus, I want to be more like You every hour!
Lord Jesus, to be like You I need the Holy Spirit with power.
Lord, help, me show Your grace, love and gifts to others.
Lord Jesus, use me that many may recover!
Lord Jesus, fill me with the Holy Spirit to overflowing!
Lord Jesus, thank you for the power and ability for growing.
Lord Jesus, with a childlike faith I now receive.
Lord Jesus, thanks for the baptism in the Holy Spirit and fire.
Lord Jesus, I praise You that this baptism will never expire!

"I baptize you with water for repentance, but after me will come One more powerful than I, whose sandals I am not worthy to carry. He will baptize you with the Holy Spirit and with fire" (Matt. 3:11).

"But you will receive power when the Holy Spirit comes upon you, and you will be My witnesses in Jerusalem, and in all Judea and Samaria, and to the ends of the earth" (Acts 1:8).

ABOUT THE AUTHOR

Carlos R. Correa Sr. life was dramatically changed at his late twenties while on the run for two heinous crimes. His life was deep in drugs; as a youth, he frequented jails with many stints in the penitentiary.

Upon his dramatic salvation, God intervened to change his life forever.

While pursuing higher education, he worked with the homeless, prisoners, battered females, and senior citizens. As God provided, he completed two master's degrees and became a school.

He and his wife Maria were blessed of God with Monica, Carlos Junior, Paul, and Melissa. There are many grand and great-grandchildren!

As a family, they know that "as for me and my house, we will worship the Lord."

CPSIA information can be obtained
at www.ICGtesting.com
Printed in the USA
BVHW031213141221
623918BV00017B/67